Number Thirteen: The Centennial Series of
The Association of Former Students
Texas A&M University

SUL ROSS

Lawrence Sullivan Ross in later years. *Courtesy of Dr. and Mrs. Neville P. Clarke, private collection.*

SUL ROSS

Soldier, Statesman, Educator

By

JUDITH ANN BENNER , 1942-

TEXAS A&M UNIVERSITY PRESS

College Station

Library of Congress Cataloging in Publication Data

Benner, Judith Ann, 1942–
    Sul Ross, soldier, statesman, educator

    (The Centennial Series of the Association of Former
Students, Texas A&M University; no. 13)
        Bibliography: p.
        Includes index.
            1. Ross, Lawrence Sullivan, 1838–98.   2. Texas—
History—1846–1950.   3. Texas—Governors—Biography.
4. Texas A&M University—Presidents—Biography.
I. Title.   II. Series.
F391.R84B46   1983   976.4′061′0924 [B]   82-45891
ISBN 0-89096-142-5

Manufactured in the United States of America

FIRST EDITION

62,790

To Neville P. and Marselaine Clarke

Contents

Illustrations

Acknowledgments

MANY persons have made completion of this study possible. First, I want to express my sincere gratitude to the members of my dissertation committee and to Dr. William C. Nunn, Dr. Donald E. Worcester, and Dr. Frank T. Reuter of the History Department and Dr. Fred Erisman of the English Department of Texas Christian University for their able counsel, guidance, and assistance during that stage of my scholarship. Also, I am grateful to members of the Ross family who assisted me in my search for primary materials. These are the late Elizabeth Ross Clarke, granddaughter of Lawrence Sullivan Ross, formerly of Waco and Bryan, Texas; Elizabeth Williams Estes, grandniece of Lawrence Sullivan Ross, Lorena, Texas; Mrs. Paul Mason, great-granddaughter of Lawrence Sullivan Ross, College Station, Texas; the late Laura Clarke Mittell, great-granddaughter of Lawrence Sullivan Ross, Houston, Texas; and Dr. and Mrs. Neville P. Clarke, of Bryan, Texas. Dr. Clarke is a great-grandson of Sul Ross, and his wife, Marselaine Clarke, is interested in family history and has done considerable research. Nevertheless, this study could not have been successfully completed had it not been for a grant provided by the Association of Former Students of Texas A&M University. To the members of the association and their former executive director, Mr. Richard Weirus, I extend my sincerest gratitude.

At the same time I wish to express my appreciation to Dr. and Mrs. Malcolm D. McLean, Arlington, Texas; Dr. Homer Kerr, Arlington, Texas; Mrs. Walter J. Williams, Waco, Texas; the late Mrs. Thomas O'Connor, Sr., Victoria, Texas; Dr. Henry C. Dethloff, College Station, Texas; and Colonel Harold B. Simpson, Hillsboro, Texas, for making available otherwise unobtainable source materials. I am grateful for the aid extended by the staffs of the Library of Congress and the National Archives, the Texas Christian University Library, the

San Antonio and the Fort Worth public libraries, the Texas Collection of Baylor University, the Alamo Library, the Barker Texas History Center, the Texas State Library, the Amon Carter Museum, the Confederate Research Center, and the libraries of Yale, Trinity, Saint Mary's, and Texas A&M universities. Also exceedingly helpful were the members of the administrative staff, Texas A&M University, and Dr. Charles Schultz and the staff of the Texas A&M University Archives.

Finally, I would like to thank my parents, employers, and friends who uncomplainingly made sacrifices of time, effort, and finance so that I could complete my study. To these and many others I give my deepest and sincerest appreciation.

SUL ROSS

The Lone Star Beckons

RUFUS C. BURLESON, that stern Baptist divine and president of Baylor University, may have looked upon himself as an anointed vessel of the Lord, but it is doubtful that he ever imagined himself filling the office of a prophet. Nevertheless, Burleson uttered something akin to prophecy that evening in 1856 when he looked into the grave eyes of teenage Lawrence Sullivan Ross and told him, "You will be governor of Texas some day, and I will vote for you."[1]

Ross did indeed become governor of Texas, and Dr. Burleson did cast a vote in his behalf, but what the unwitting prophet did not know was that before taking the governor's chair, Sul Ross would also gain fame as a Texas Ranger. Neither did he foresee the conspicuous Confederate military career awaiting the young man, who would emerge from the coming war as the ninth youngest general officer to wear the gray.[2] Equally hidden in the obscurity of the future were Ross's terms as sheriff and state senator. Finally, Burleson's second sight did not enable him to look past the statehouse to the position so similar to his own that Ross would hold at his death—the presidency of Texas A&M College.[3]

The future general and governor was born September 27, 1838, at Bentonsport, Iowa Territory, in what is now Van Buren County. The second son and fourth child of Shapley Prince Ross and Catherine Fulkerson Ross, he was named in honor of a paternal grandfather and brother, both Lawrence Ross, and a paternal uncle, Giles O. Sullivan. Apparently it was to distinguish him from the latter that Ross was first

---

[1] Georgia J. Burleson, *The Life and Writings of Rufus C. Burleson, D.D., LL.D.,* p. 591.

[2] Author's own computation, based on data from Ezra J. Warner, *Generals in Gray: Lives of the Confederate Commanders.*

[3] *Dictionary of American Biography,* s.v. "Ross, Lawrence Sullivan."

known in the family as "Little Sul" and then finally as "Sul," the given
name he preferred and used throughout his life.[4]

Indeed, Sul's was a heritage of which any individual—or family—
could be proud. His father's paternal ancestors traced their descent
from the followers of the ancient clan chiefs of Ross in Scotland, while
his father's maternal forebears were wealthy English farmers who settled in Williamsburg, Virginia. The maternal side of the family tree
combined, among other strains, German and Irish elements in a blend
of frontier and plantation, soldiers and statesmen. There was, in addition, a fair sprinkling of particularly illustrious or interesting ancestors
from both the maternal and paternal lines.

Sul's great-grandfather Lawrence had been captured at the age of
six by Indians who raided the Virginia frontier school he was attending,
and he lived with the Cherokees until he was twenty-three years old.
It was with great difficulty that relatives persuaded him to return to
the white world. One of Sul's great-uncles, William Prince, was instrumental in the settlement of Indiana. His mother's side included his
grandfather Isaac Fulkerson—planter, sheriff, and member of the Missouri legislature—and an uncle, William N. Fulkerson, also a sheriff
and state legislator. Other forebears were military men, and Sul was
related by the marriages of two paternal uncles to the family of Zachary
Taylor.[5]

Sul's own parents were equally notable. They deserve mention
here because of the influence of their varying backgrounds on the formation of Sul's character. His father was born near Louisville, Kentucky, in 1811. Six years later the family moved to Missouri, settling in
Lincoln County, where Shapley grew up. A typical son of the frontier,
Shapley Ross endured formal schooling only six months. A year spent
on an older brother's farm failed to quench his restless spirit; at sixteen
he traded his share of the harvest for a horse and rifle and joined the
fortune seekers at the Galena lead mines. From mining he turned to
the livestock trade, specializing in blooded horses, which he raced successfully. Eventually he saved enough of his winnings to purchase a
farm near those of his relatives.

[4]"Captain Shapley P. Ross, Waco, Texas," Ross Family Papers, Texas Collection,
Baylor University, Waco, Texas (hereafter cited as Ross Family Papers, Baylor), pp. 1–3,
7.

[5]Ibid.; John Henry Brown, *Indian Wars and Pioneers of Texas*, p. 315; L. Sage
Jones to Ross Kinsman, undated, in Ross Family Scrapbook, Mrs. Paul Mason Collection, College Station, Texas; "Shapley Ross," Ross Family Papers, Baylor, p. 1.

In November, 1830, Shapley Ross married Catherine Fulkerson, daughter of a wealthy German planter who had moved to neighboring Saint Charles County, Missouri, from Virginia. Convent educated and raised in a slaveholding family well staffed with household servants, Catherine had never dressed herself or even put on her own shoes until her marriage.[6] As Mrs. Ross, the life of the planter's daughter changed drastically. Although comfortably situated financially, Shapley was never a large-scale slaveowner and did most of his farm work himself, assisted at first by his wife and later by one male slave and his own sons.[7]

The couple remained on their farm for one year, when Ross's restlessness again precipitated a move, first to Troy, Missouri, and then, in 1834, to the Sauk and Fox Indian Reservation along the Des Moines River. When the Indian lands were absorbed by the federal government preparatory to the formation of Iowa Territory, Shapley Ross obtained four lots in the new town of Bentonsport in return for building and maintaining a hotel. Hotelkeeping occupied him from 1835 to the fall of 1838, during which time his family increased by two sons, Peter Fulkerson and Lawrence Sullivan. It was shortly after the birth of the latter that Shapley sold his Iowa holdings and took his family back to Missouri. Although a large man of great strength and endurance, Ross found that the cold of the northern climate had begun to undermine his robust health.[8]

One day early in 1839, a traveler newly arrived from the young Republic of Texas stopped at the Ross home. In the course of the night's entertainment the stranger told of rich opportunities to be found under the Lone Star. This traveler's tale struck a responsive chord in the soul of Shapley Ross, for he had long been intrigued by the favorable reports filtering in to the old states from the sister republic.

After the stranger's departure, Shapley and Catherine discussed

[6]"Shapley Ross," Ross Family Papers, Baylor, pp. 1–3, 5–7; *Waco Tribune-Herald*, October 30, 1949. This centennial edition was thoroughly researched by Waco historians and contains much of interest to students of the era.

[7]In 1850 Shapley was worth $5,000 and owned one male slave. By 1860 he owned real property worth $10,526 and personal property worth $10,250. Included in the total were seven slaves—three adults and four children (U.S. Bureau of the Census, unpublished returns, "Seventh Census of the United States, 1850: Population Schedules, Milam County, Texas"; Census Bureau, unpublished returns, "Eighth Census, 1860: Free Inhabitants and Slave Population Schedules, McLennan County, Texas").

[8]"Shapley Ross," Ross Family Papers, Baylor, p. 3; Brown, *Indian Wars*, p. 316.

moving to Texas. She agreed to the scheme, but the couple's Missouri relatives tried to dissuade them from taking such a step. The arguments of these well-meaning relatives against the new land only hardened Ross's resolve to go there. At last the dissenting family members despaired of reshaping his thinking and dismissed him with the prediction that in a few years he would be glad to return his wife and children to the safety and schoolhouses of Missouri.[9]

Sul was too young to remember any of the long and hazardous journey to the land of his father's choice, but according to his children's accounts he heard Shapley in later years recall the beauty and wonder of that first trip to Texas. It was prophetic of the future of the Ross family that on the way to the settlements on the lower Brazos the party camped one night at Waco Springs. But the establishment of a white settlement at Waco was still ten years off. At the time of the journey Shapley was interested in reaching the centers of population in Milam County. On his arrival at Nashville, he took the oath of allegiance to the Republic of Texas, which entitled him to a headright of 640 acres. He chose land where the town of Cameron now stands, but Indian depredations soon forced the Ross party to join other settlers on the Little River.[10]

From the first, the position of the settlers was precarious. Even in the best of times, diet, lodging, and clothing were spartan. To make life more difficult, Indian raiders prowled about seeking horses and scalps. Shapley Ross often took part in citizen reprisals against the raiders; it is likely that Sul's earliest memories of his tall, handsome father centered around Shapley as an Indian fighter, because Sul's earliest ambition was to emulate him.[11]

With Shapley Ross's growing reputation as an Indian fighter, it was not surprising that Sul's first brush with hostile red men came in company with his father. One evening when Sul was not much more than a toddler, Shapley took the boy with him when he walked over to visit a neighbor. The moon had risen before father and son started home. As they hiked across the prairie toward the Ross cabin, Shapley

[9] Elizabeth Ross Clarke, "Life of Sul Ross," Ross Family Papers, Baylor, pp. 3–4.

[10] Ibid., pp. 4–8; *Waco Tribune-Herald*, October 30, 1949; Clarke, "Life of Sul Ross," Ross Family Papers, Baylor, p. 9; "Shapley Ross," Ross Family Papers, Baylor, pp. 3–4.

[11] Clarke, "Life of Sul Ross," Ross Family Papers, Baylor, p. 12; *San Antonio Daily Express*, November 22, 1908; Victor M. Rose, *Ross' Texas Brigade: Being a Narrative of Events Connected with Its Service in the Late War Between the States*, p. 158.

became uneasy, some intuition warning him of danger. Halting, he bent over Sul and told the child he feared Indians were nearby. If he had to throw Sul onto his back and run for the cabin, could the boy hold on until they reached safety?

Sul answered satisfactorily, and Shapley and his son walked on. They were almost to their goal when fifteen mounted Comanche warriors charged. Shapley tossed Sul onto his back and with the child clinging tightly to his shoulders bounded swiftly toward the cabin. Amid a shower of arrows Ross leaped the dooryard fence, set Sul down, and told him to go inside. But, he cautioned, there was no need to tell his mother about the incident since they were not hurt. However, the experience proved to be too much for Sul's reticence. When his father followed him into the cabin, the boy excitedly asked, "Whew, Papa, didn't we fairly fly?" thus unintentionally revealing what Shapley had wished to conceal. But all of this was part of growing up on the frontier, where children did not remain babies long. Every hand, no matter how small, was needed to assist the family efforts in winning food, shelter, and clothing from the wilderness. As soon as possible, offspring were assigned tasks proportionate to their strength and skill.[12]

Play was likewise practical, teaching skills needed later in life as well as how to face danger, should it threaten. Since the Ross family was in almost constant danger from Indian forays, Shapley counseled his little brood on what to do if an attack should occur while they were outside the house. And if they should happen to be captured, the children were warned not to show fear or pain to their captors lest such emotions provoke some act of savagery. The Ross sons and daughters were well drilled, and "the Indians are coming" soon became a favorite game. At a warning cry, the children would run to hide in the brush as if from a real enemy.

Thanks to Shapley's training and Sul's coolness in the face of danger, tragedy was averted when thirty Comanche warriors surrounded the Ross cabin not long after Shapley had killed Bigfoot, one of their chiefs.[13] On that day Sul and several of the other children had been

[12] Rose, *Ross' Texas Brigade*, p. 158; Clarke, "Life of Sul Ross," Ross Family Papers, Baylor, pp. 13–14; Everett Dick, *The Dixie Frontier: A Social History of the Southern Frontier from the First Transmontane Beginnings to the Civil War*, pp. 82, 99, 283.

[13] Clarke, "Life of Sul Ross," Ross Family Papers, Baylor, p. 13; James T. De-Shields, *Cynthia Ann Parker: The Story of Her Capture*, p. 47; *Waco Tribune-Herald*, October 30, 1949.

playing their favorite game of hiding from the Indians. Sul had tired of the game and had stretched out to rest on a quilt spread under a tree. When the warning came, he ignored it and pretended instead to be asleep. The other children scattered like quail, but Sul remained on the quilt. Presently he heard footsteps. When he opened his eyes he found himself ringed by warriors, who grabbed him and dragged him along to the cabin. Remembering what his father had taught him, the youngster was careful not to cry or show fear.

Meanwhile, Peter, the eldest boy, had raced to warn his parents. Mrs. Ross joined her husband, who was lying ill on the porch, just as the Comanches and their little captive arrived. Instead of ordering his braves to fall upon the frontiersman and his family in immediate massacre, the elderly chief began to converse with Shapley in sign language, saying that he and his followers wished to make a treaty. In the meantime, the chief indicated, he and his companions were hungry.

Hoping to allow his wife and children time to escape, Shapley told the Comanches that he had corn and melons in plenty but that the Indians would have to get the produce themselves, since he was ill and could not rise. The Indians indicated that they wished Sul to lead them to the fields. Ross agreed to this demand reluctantly, knowing that he might never see his son again. Then he told Sul that he must lead the braves to the fields and give them everything they desired. As the little fellow trotted bravely off, the Comanches swarmed around him, some of them pinching his bare legs, others whipping them with the shafts of their arrows. He did not flinch as he and his captors disappeared from his parents' view.[14]

After a seemingly endless wait the party returned, Sul still refusing to show any fear or pain although his legs were bleeding in numerous places. The Comanches were greatly pleased by his courage and speedily concluded the treaty. In later years Sul modestly attributed his family's escape to the Comanches' ignorance of the fact that Shapley had killed Bigfoot, but at least in the minds of his parents he was the hero of the hour.[15]

[14] During the early days on the frontier, boys "wore nothing but a single garment, a 'wamus' or shirt that reached down nearly to the ankles" (Dick, *The Dixie Frontier*, p. 297).

[15] There are at least four versions of the incident from which this composite sketch was written, all agreeing in substance if not in detail: (1) an undated four-page manuscript version, probably by Elizabeth Ross Clarke, found in "Notes," Ross Family Papers, Baylor; (2) the version given in Clarke, "Life of Sul Ross," Ross Family Papers,

Danger, as well as deprivation and hard work, was all a part of growing up on the Texas frontier. As Sul grew older he was able to assist more with the work around the homestead. He and Pete were especially helpful to Mrs. Ross since Shapley was often absent from home, first with a ranger company and later in an abortive attempt to free the Mier Expedition prisoners.[16]

In 1845 Shapley made a decision that affected the lives of his children. According to the account of a family friend, Shapley came to the doleful conclusion that his four eldest children were growing up in the deepest ignorance because of the failure of the only school in the neighborhood. Lest the dire prophecies of his Missouri relatives come to pass, he decided to move to Austin and enter his children in school. Mrs. Ross was not surprised by his sudden statement of intention, merely remarking that he had been a long time in reaching that decision. Shapley traded 290 acres for a wagon and a yoke of oxen, loaded his family and possessions into the vehicle, and set off for Austin, much to the relief of Armstead, the family's only slave, who feared Ross planned to move deeper into the Indian frontier.[17]

Austin at that time was a straggle of log cabins scattered along the banks of the Colorado, housing citizens, places of business, and the government, but it was already the hub of Texan life. It was also to be the scene of Sul's early demonstration of his fighting abilities. Upon their arrival, Shapley and Mrs. Ross met many friends and acquaintances. Sul's welcome, however, was of another kind. Although a sturdy seven-year-old, he was still dressed in the long shirt of the frontier. A group of older boys, already breeched, began to make fun of Sul and his costume. When the youngster realized that he was the object of their ridicule, he singled out the largest of his tormentors and waded into him, fists flailing and shirttail flying. Not in the least hampered by his long shirt, Sul soon had his opponent rolling on the ground and

Baylor, pp. 14–17; (3) that by Myrtle Whiteside, "The Life of Lawrence Sullivan Ross" (M.A. thesis, University of Texas, 1938), pp. 4–5, based on interviews with Sul's son, Harvey; and (4) the version in the *Waco Tribune-Herald*, October 30, 1949, carefully researched and written from accounts of other Ross relatives.

[16] John Sleeper and J. C. Hutchins, comps., *Waco and McLennan County, Texas: Containing a City Directory of Waco, Historical Sketches of the City and County; Biographical Sketches and Notices of a Few Prominent Citizens*, p. 86; "Shapley Ross," Ross Family Papers, Baylor, p. 4.

[17] John S. Ford, *Rip Ford's Texas*, pp. 442–43; Clarke, "Life of Sul Ross," Ross Family Papers, Baylor, pp. 29–30.

glad to own himself vanquished. As Sul's battered opponent made his way home, it was hard to say who was prouder of the exploit, Sul himself or his father, who had watched his son prove his mettle.[18]

Shapley obtained suitable clothing for his family and entered the four eldest children in school. It is not known whether the Ross children attended an academy or a mere one-room school, but they soon made excellent progress. Although Shapley soon became restless and raised a ranger company that under his captaincy served during the Mexican War, he left his wife and children in Austin to benefit from civilized society.[19]

Early in 1849 Captain Ross received an offer from Jacob de Cordova, one of the owners of a large tract of land west of the Brazos and surrounding Waco Springs. If the frontiersman would move with his family to the new settlement, he would receive four free city lots of his choice, the sole right of operating a ferry across the Brazos, and the privilege of buying up to eighty acres of farmland at one dollar an acre. Such inducements proved irresistible. In March of that same year the Ross family again moved in search of the frontier farmer's dream— rich, inexpensive bottomland. It was to be the last such family exodus. Thereafter, the names *Ross* and *Waco* were inseparably linked.[20]

Captain Ross arrived with his family two months before the first lots officially went on sale and selected his town lots, on the bluff above the springs, and his eighty farming acres. He also purchased an additional two hundred acres in what later became the south of town. As other would-be Waco settlers began to gather, the captain set about the construction of a double log house for his family. There would be much for the active Sul to put his hand to as the family settled into its new homestead. Captain Ross was eager to break ground on his farming acres and get a crop in before planting time had passed. Sul and Peter were expected to work in the fields with their father and Arm-

[18] Rutherford B. Hayes, *Diary and Letters of Rutherford B. Hayes, Nineteenth President of the United States*, I, 259–60; Melinda Rankin, *Texas in 1850*, p. 155; Clarke, "Life of Sul Ross," Ross Family Papers, Baylor, pp. 30–31.

[19] Ford, *Rip Ford's Texas*, p. 243; "Shapley Ross," Ross Family Papers, Baylor, p. 4; Clarke, "Life of Sul Ross," Ross Family Papers, Baylor, p. 31. Civilized to Texans, of course. Melinda Rankin, a New England missionary, saw little good in the Texas capital, commenting, "Austin is not remarkable for its religious character, nor for its superabundance of refined society" (*Texas in 1850*, p. 155).

[20] "Shapley Ross," Ross Family Papers, Baylor, p. 5; Clarke, "Life of Sul Ross," Ross Family Papers, Baylor, p. 35.

stead, for theirs was not a social class that looked down on a white owner for laboring shoulder-to-shoulder with his slave.[21]

Later, when Shapley Ross expanded his activities to keeping a hotel, operating a ferry, running the city waterworks, and trailing cattle to Missouri, there would be even more chores to keep a capable preteenager busy, but the captain knew the value of creative recreation.[22] As soon as his sons were old enough to sit a horse and hold a firearm, Shapley taught them to ride and shoot, instilling in them not only his love for fast horses but also his marksman's skill with rifle and revolver. They would also be expected to run, wrestle, and hold their own in any fistfight.[23]

There also were opportunities to fish or hunt in the river bottoms for deer and small game. Grown-up amusements such as quilting, husking, and cotton-picking bees and the accompanying dances might not have had much appeal for a boy like Sul just entering his teens, but he could enjoy food, fun, and fellowship with other youngsters his own age. Holidays brought additional celebrations, and political campaigns and weddings furnished still more occasions for recreation. These and many other events offered opportunities for the proud owners of fleet horseflesh to test their steeds against those of their neighbors. Captain Ross devoted a good part of his time to attending racing meets. Sul became such an expert horseman that his father regularly scheduled him to ride the family's entries in the match races held either at Waco or at one of the nearby settlements.[24]

His inherited love of action and good horses was to involve Sul in

[21]"Shapley Ross," Ross Family Papers, Baylor, p. 4; Dick, *The Dixie Frontier*, p. 82; Raymond L. Dillard, "A History of the Ross Family, Including Its Most Distinguished Member, Lawrence Sullivan Ross" (M.A. thesis, Baylor University, 1931), pp. 29–30.

[22]There were compensations, even for work done around the hotel. In the early 1850s Richard Coke, later governor of Texas and supporter of the state's Agricultural and Mechanical College, stayed at the Ross hotel. The story is told that Sul liked to sit on the arm of Coke's chair and listen as he told tales of Virginia (George Sessions Perry, *The Story of Texas A. and M.*, p. 57).

[23]Dillard, "History of the Ross Family," pp. 29–30.

[24]Dick, *The Dixie Frontier*, pp. 130–31, 139; William Ransom Hogan, *The Texas Republic: A Social and Economic History*, p. 114; *Waco Tribune-Herald*, October 30, 1949. Sul rode for his father a number of years. One old settler recalled riding against Sul, a "little boy," at Cameron when he himself was ten years old (F. M. Cross, *A Short Sketch-History from Personal Reminiscences of Early Days in Central Texas*, 2d ed. [Brownwood, Tex.: Greenwood Printing Co., 1910], pp. 9–10).

his first Indian fight while still a boy. One night, hostile tribesmen raided the settlement and drove off many horses; several animals belonging to the Ross family were stolen, among them Sul's favorite racer. Captain Ross, with the other men, soon began organizing a posse to pursue the raiders. Sul determined to go along, so carrying his rifle and accompanied by Armstead he unobtrusively joined the pursuit. The problem was that the only mount he and Armstead could find was a recalcitrant mule. On this animal, young master and slave brought up the rear of the party.

All went well until the posse caught up with the horse thieves. A running gun battle broke out between the settlers and the Indians— just the kind of excitement for an adventurous boy who longed to be an Indian fighter. Sul urged his long-eared mount to the front so he too could fire at the fleeing red men, but the mule could not be forced within fighting range of the Indians. Sul was disgusted by his failure to win his spurs in this encounter. What was worse, his father took him to task for joining the posse without permission. Secretly, however, Captain Ross was proud of the courage and spirit exhibited by his son.[25]

But Sul Ross was soon to decide that horse racing and Indian fighting were not everything in life. As he approached young manhood, he faced an ethical and moral crisis of the greatest importance. It was much to his credit and to that of his parents that he chose a course of self-sacrifice and public service.[26]

[25] Clarke, "Life of Sul Ross," Ross Family Papers, Baylor, p. 25.

[26] Sul's mother had immeasurable influence on her children. "Among the remarkable women who have helped to lay the foundations of Texas, none have rendered more enduring service, or bequeathed to it a sturdier race of sons and daughters than Mrs. Shapley P. Ross" (Elizabeth Brooks, *Prominent Women of Texas*, p. 67).

☆ **2** ☆

The Making of a Soldier

GIVEN the frontier environment, lack of educational opportunities, and his own fearless, pugnacious character, Lawrence Sullivan Ross could easily have developed into one of the profane, tobacco-chewing, whiskey-drinking, cardsharping young ruffians encountered by Frederick Law Olmsted on his trip to Texas in the mid-1850s.[1] Sul's escape from just such a limited existence was perhaps closer than he knew, for he had inherited his father's love of fast horses, passion for adventure, and restlessness of spirit. With these traits, in addition to his almost reckless courage and a willingness to resort to violence (like many of his contemporaries), he could have easily gone "bad."

A friend of Sul's told a story of how young Ross, at age eleven, was hit on the head by a stone thrown by an older boy. Sul determined on revenge, waylaid the fourteen-year-old en route to school, and gave him a thorough thrashing. He administered a similar drubbing to the older lad every morning for over a week. Finally, the teenager obtained from his father a black servant as an escort. Sul was not daunted by this strategy. The next school-day morning he appeared at the same ambuscade. This time he cowed the slave before reapplying the same "rigorous discipline of his enemy" while the servant helplessly stood by. Further application of the same revenge was prevented only by the father giving the older boy a horse and sending him on a detour route to school.[2]

The friend cited this episode as an example of Sul's boyhood pluck, but it may be used just as well to show the streak of lawlessness and violence present in his character before he learned to discipline himself. This self-discipline came from a number of sources, including

[1] Frederick Law Olmsted, *A Journey Through Texas: Or a Saddle-Trip on the Southwestern Frontier*, pp. 121–22, 369, 383.

[2] *San Antonio Daily Express*, November 22, 1908.

the family, but particularly from education and religion. The university and in a lesser measure the church greatly influenced the later character development of Sul Ross.

Someone, perhaps his cultured mother, a Waco schoolmistress, or even his self-educated father, planted in Sul's mind a desire for knowledge.[3] Despite his ambition to emulate the heroic deeds of his father, young Ross realized the need for a higher education. Accordingly, having exhausted the educational opportunities available to him in Waco, he decided in 1856 to enter the Preparatory Department of Baylor University, then located at Independence, Texas. When the new school term began in March, Sul Ross took his first step toward obtaining a college degree.[4]

Baylor University had been chartered in 1845. The institution opened the next year in a dilapidated building with one teacher and twenty-four students. Within a decade the number of students had increased tenfold, and the faculty had expanded to nine members, while the physical plant had grown into a multibuilding campus of many acres, extolled for its health as well as for its great beauty.[5]

As stipulated in the university catalog, Sul waited on the president, Rufus C. Burleson, to present his testimonials of good moral character. Burleson, a man of forceful character and dedication, demanded from his students academic excellence and the strictest attention to discipline. Stern and uncompromising, he nevertheless showed great courtesy and concern for the young men in his charge. Indeed, Burleson's sense of responsibility to his students might well have

[3] Clement Eaton points out that at this time in the Old South, "sending a son to college was a sign of success and prosperity" (*The Growth of Southern Civilization, 1790–1860,* p. 119). Prestige aside, Shapley Ross desired quality educations for all his children. Mary Rebecca and Margaret Virginia were educated at the Female Academy of Baylor University; Peter Fulkerson, Mt. Vernon Military Academy; Lawrence Sullivan, Baylor University and Florence Wesleyan; and Ann, Maddin's school in Waco ("Captain Shapley P. Ross, Waco, Texas," Ross Family Papers, Texas Collection, Baylor University, Waco, Texas [hereafter cited as Ross Family Papers, Baylor], pp. 7–8). Robert Shapley attended Baylor and St. Mary's universities (Dayton Kelley, ed., *The Handbook of Waco and McLennan County,* p. 233). The two youngest children, Kate and William, also received an education in Waco ("Shapley Ross," Ross Family Papers, Baylor, p. 8).

[4] *Fourth Annual Catalogue of the Trustees, Professors and Students of Baylor University,* pp. 8, 20.

[5] *Fifth Annual Catalogue of the Trustees, Professors and Students of Baylor University,* pp. 19, 21; *Fourth Annual Catalogue,* pp. 17, 20. The Baylor campus boasted discreetly concealed privies (Michael A. White, *The History of Baylor University, 1845–1861,* p. 59).

caused him to hesitate before introducing a possible firebrand into their midst. After all, Sul was seventeen—two years past the age recommended by Burleson for entrance into the college course. A man in all but name, he was requesting admission into the Preparatory Department, where he would be associated with students not yet in their teens.[6]

Moreover, there was Sul's family background to consider. Although of blameless life, Mrs. Ross belonged to the Church of Rome. Since she had been responsible for the spiritual training of her offspring, it was therefore likely that Sul's religious background was "tainted." Also indicative of what could prove to be future trouble for the Baptists of Baylor, Sul's father had little interest in religion and was known to possess a violent temper. As far as Burleson knew, this hotheadedness had been passed on to the son. Furthermore, in accepting the position of agent on the Brazos Indian Reserve in 1855, Shapley had made many enemies among those Texans favoring extermination, rather than assimilation, of the state's Indian population.[7]

Despite these considerations, Burleson evidently greeted Sul cordially. Before glancing over the references presented by the young man, he probably turned his questioning gaze on Sul, making, as was his habit, his own estimation of the youth's character. He would have seen a moderately tall young man nearing his mature height of about six feet, with a slender frame, tanned complexion, and modest demeanor. Collar-length black hair fell back in waves from a high, wide forehead, denoting more than average intelligence. A straight, well-chiseled nose and solemn blue eyes highlighted the upper part of an expressive oval face, while a smile hinting at good nature lurked at the corners of his full, firm lips.[8]

---

[6] *Fourth Annual Catalogue*, p. 15; White, *Baylor University*, pp. 24–25. One classmate, Sam Houston, Jr., was born in 1843. Felix H. Robertson, a sophomore in the Scientific Course and soon to become a fellow Confederate general, was a year younger than Sul (*Fourth Annual Catalogue*, pp. 6–7; Marcus J. Wright, *Texas in the War, 1861–1865*, pp. 89, 135).

[7] "Shapley Ross," Ross Family Papers, Baylor, p. 5; *Waco Tribune-Herald*, October 30, 1949; Elizabeth Ross Clarke, "Life of Sul Ross," Ross Family Papers, Baylor, pp. 31–32; Kenneth F. Neighbours, *Indian Exodus: Texan Indian Affairs, 1835–1859*, p. 107.

[8] The word portrait above is a composite from several photographs and three printed sources. The written accounts are *Galveston Daily News*, August 12, 1885; *New York Herald*, May 25, 1890; and Personne [pseud.], *Marginalia: Or, Gleanings from an Army Note-Book*, p. 169. An ambrotype portrait taken about the time Sul entered Baylor

Satisfied with both the written testimonials and the actual appearance of the young man, Burleson declared him admitted to study. Sul departed to sell his horse and equipment, needing the money to help defray the expenses of tuition, fees, and room and board.[9]

Since students were accepted into the Preparatory Department at "any age or stage of advancement," it is unlikely that Sul had to undergo the ordeal of facing an examining board, as did students wishing to enter as freshmen. Nevertheless, before he could be fully matriculated, he had to read the laws of the university and sign a declaration of his deliberate intention to obey them as long as he remained a student at Baylor.[10]

Sul's willingness to submit himself to a discipline that would have seemed restrictive to a much younger boy in order to obtain an education no doubt increased Burleson's admiration. Under the direction of James L. Smith, principal of the Preparatory Department, Ross began a course of study designed to ready him for entrance into a collegiate program.[11] According to Burleson, Sul proved to be an excellent student, noted for "modesty, firmness, good nature, a clear, well balanced mind and devotion to duty." Being more mature than other preparatory boys, he was able to complete his studies without a single demerit. Ross determined to stand high in all his classes, despite the distraction of roommates who were not as dedicated.

The president was strolling one evening on his usual inspection tour of the campus and neighboring boardinghouses when he heard loud sounds of fighting, which led him to the room shared by Sul Ross

---

proved valuable. This portrait is in the George Barnard Papers, Texas Collection, Baylor University, Waco, Texas.

[9] Henry Trantham, *1845–1920 the Diamond Jubilee: A Record of the Seventy-fifth Anniversary of the Founding of Baylor University*, p. 13. Board, including fuel and washing, was $10 to $12 per month. Annual expenses included $20 for elementary English; $26 for English grammar, geography, arithmetic, and composition; and $40 for ancient languages, mathematics, and natural sciences. There was a $1 incidental expense fee, and of the total, one-third was payable in advance (*Fourth Annual Catalogue*, pp. 17, 21).

[10] *Fourth Annual Catalogue*, pp. 15, 16.

[11] Baylor regulations included attendance of morning and evening chapel, daily student recitation with faculty evaluation, and demerits for such misdemeanors as absence from one's rooms after dark (ibid., pp. 14–15). Intoxication and profanity were, of course, forbidden (White, *Baylor University*, pp. 66–67). Freshman studies included algebra, Sallust, Latin grammar, Xenophon, Greek Testament and grammar, plane geometry, Cicero's *Orations*, Roman and Greek antiquities, and the *Iliad* (*Fourth Annual Catalogue*, p. 9).

and two other students. Opening the door, Burleson found the other two boys fighting like Kilkenny cats while Sul sat at the lamp table, studying intently. Burleson rushed into the room, separated the tussling pair, and turned with wrathful majesty to Sul, demanding to be told why he was allowing a big boy to thrash a smaller companion. With great dignity, young Ross rose and asked the president to excuse him from such interference. He had come to Baylor to study, he said, and he wanted to stand at the head of all his classes. His roommates were always quarreling; if he attempted to act as referee, he would not have any time left for study. Burleson beamed at this scholarly devotion, and it was at this time he predicted Sul's accession to the governorship.[12]

Concerned as Burleson was with the academic progress of his students, he was careful not to neglect their spiritual growth. Mandatory chapel services were held morning and evening. However, although Baylor officials strongly stressed the importance of regular church attendance, in addition to chapel, in the development of the whole man, church attendance was voluntary. Believing that daily chapel and weekly church services offered insufficient spiritual opportunities to his charges, Burleson stressed the efficacy of frequent revival meetings to bring the unrighteous to repentance.[13]

Such was the case in 1856 when, during the school year, Burleson and the pastor of the Independence Baptist Church sponsored a revival. As usual, attendance by Baylor students was encouraged but not required. In the congregation was Sul Ross. Night after night he returned, deeply concerned about spiritual matters but hesitant to make a commitment. At last the gospel pierced his hesitancy and struck a responsive chord in the spiritual depths of his nature. Before the series of meetings ended, young Ross, in the words of Dr. Burleson, "saw and joyfully embraced the plan of salvation."[14] Although Sul would not formally join a church until two years later, his conversion while a student at Baylor had a powerful and lasting influence on his life. The faith and inner strength drawn from his early religious experience would be invaluable in facing the challenges and vicissitudes of life.

As Christmas approached and the Baylor school year ended, Sul

[12] Georgia J. Burleson, *The Life and Writings of Rufus C. Burleson, D.D., LL.D.*, pp. 589–91.

[13] White, *Baylor University*, pp. 65–66.

[14] Burleson, *Rufus C. Burleson*, p. 589.

Ross faced a decision. In the year just past, he had completed the two-year program of study preparing him for entrance into college-level courses. The question was, Should he remain at Baylor for the rest of his college career or seek a degree elsewhere? For reasons now uncertain, Ross chose to transfer to the Wesleyan University in Florence, Alabama.[15]

Founded in 1855, by the next year Florence Wesleyan University was a flourishing institution, boasting a student population of 180 young men.[16] An outgrowth of and successor to La Grange College, Alabama's oldest institution of higher learning, the university drew students from above the Mason-Dixon line and from as far away as Nicaragua, as well as from the southern states. At that time Florence was considered one of the best college locations in the South. With its broad streets, white-pillared buildings, and beautiful gardens, the community had openly welcomed the school upon its removal there. The university was provided with an "elegant and ample" structure, towered and battlemented in the Gothic style and set "among broad groves and pretty hills."[17]

Relations between town and gown were extremely good—city ordinances prohibiting the sale of liquor and the playing of billiards, ball, or ninepins. The students themselves were quiet and gentlemanly. Indeed, it was one of the selling points of the school that students would have the opportunity to learn manners and refinement by living with respectable families instead of being herded together in dormitories.[18]

Because of the paucity of extant records pertaining to Florence Wesleyan, it is not known when in 1857 Sul Ross entered that institution.[19] What is known is that when he entered the crenelated walls of

[15] White, *Baylor University*, p. 61.

[16] *Nashville Christian Advocate*, July 31, 1856. At the same time, the University of Georgia had only seventy-nine students (Ellis M. Coulter, *College Life in the Old South*, pp. 250–56).

[17] Marion Elias Lazenby, *History of Methodism in Alabama and West Florida: Being an Account of the Amazing March of Methodism through Alabama and West Florida*, pp. 1022–23; *Nashville Christian Advocate*, February 2, 1855, August 7, 1856; *Birmingham News-Age Herald*, December 29, 1940. One Yankee youth attending school at Florence was Daniel McCook of Ohio, then the roommate of Davis R. Gurley of Waco, fated to die leading his Union brigade against the Confederate lines at Kennesaw Mountain, Georgia (John Milton Hubbard, *Notes of a Private*, p. 80).

[18] *Nashville Christian Advocate*, October 8, 1857, July 24, 1856.

[19] An extensive search has uncovered few helpful documents relating to Florence Wesleyan University during this period. Even the school's successor, Florence State University, lacks documents regarding the antebellum past (C. M. Arehart, registrar,

Wesleyan Hall about a month after leaving home, Ross suffered a rebuff that would have soured many other young men on higher education. Appearing before an examining board of the president and faculty, Sul proved to be so deficient in mathematics that the professors refused to admit him. He would have to spend at least a year in the Preparatory Department, the examiners told him. Greatly disappointed by this news, Ross replied that if he were not permitted to enter college after traveling such a great distance, he would return to Texas to complete his studies. The examining board could look for him at the same time next year.

Just as Sul was turning to go, Septimus P. Rice, professor of mathematics and principal of the Preparatory Department, called him back. The meaning of the young man's long journey was not lost on Rice, who had a proposal to make. If Ross would board at his house, where Rice could tutor him in mathematics at night, the instructor promised he would see to it that the young Texan kept up with his classmates. But, he cautioned, it would mean especially hard work. Sul assured the professor that he was not afraid of hard work and would be glad to accept his kind offer. His admission approved, Ross sold his mule, saddle, and bridle and settled into the life of a college student.[20]

Sul's first year at Florence was necessarily a busy one. By day he attended lectures and recited in his courses, which were heavily weighted, like most of those at Southern universities then, toward the classics and mathematics.[21] By night he worked closely with Professor Rice on mathematics. Although Sul's scholastic ability lay more in perseverance and energy than in brilliance, he nevertheless proved to be so apt a pupil that despite his initial deficiency in mathematics, he soon excelled in that subject. He also proved his scholastic ability in other subjects and was able at the end of that first session to pass examinations admitting him to studies one year ahead of his classmates.[22]

But Sul's life at the Wesleyan University was more than just hard

Florence State University, December 9, 1968, personal communication; Robert M. Guillot, president, Florence State University, August 15, 1973, personal communication).

[20] *San Antonio Daily Express*, November 22, 1908; *Nashville Christian Advocate*, July 31, 1856. Tuition and board ran from $150 to $175 per ten-month session (*Nashville Christian Advocate*, July 23, 1857).

[21] Courses were taught in moral philosophy and literature, mathematics (pure and mixed), ancient and modern languages, and natural history (*Nashville Christian Advocate*, July 23, 1857; *Memphis Commercial Appeal*, September 4, 1934).

[22] *Nashville Christian Advocate*, August 12, 1858; *San Antonio Daily Express*, No-

study and scholastic achievement. It was also a time for him to enjoy
the hospitality of the refined old families in Florence as well as mingle
in the company of young men his own age. Ross made many friends
among the townspeople and the students, forming relationships that
would be renewed under the cloud of war. Unfortunately, little is
known about the details of Sul's social life in Alabama. It is probable
that his association with refined society and gentlemen's sons during
this period taught him the gentlemanly address and knightly courtesy
for which he was later noted. It is true that someone, perhaps his aris-
tocratic mother, had put a rough polish on his manners, but until his
years among the gracious antebellum society of Florence, Sul Ross was
primarily a frontiersman. Thereafter, his nature took on a duality of
character in which the chivalric and romantic ideals of the plantation
blended with and sometimes vied with the ruthless and realistic training of the frontier. But it must be noted that after his years in Florence,
the plantation gentleman was usually in the ascendant.[23]

These years in Alabama were also critical to the formation of Sul's
convictions. As far as it is known, Sul Ross was only a nominal supporter of the peculiar institution; his father owned seven slaves in 1860,
and Sul owned none. Nevertheless, his association with the student
radicals on the Florence campus, concurrent with the almost daily in-
tensification of sectional battles in Congress and in Kansas, influenced
the young Texan's views of statesmanship and nationalism. If he was
like most southern youths of that period, Sul Ross loved the South and
fervently supported states' rights.[24] Although not a fire-eater, his modesty and natural reserve restraining him from extremism on the subject, Sul was a Southerner by "association, training and convictions."
At the same time his religious convictions were jelling, for it was during his years at Florence that Sul chose to join the Methodist Church.[25]

-----

vember 22, 1908; L. E. Daniell, comp., *Personnel of the Texas State Government With
Sketches of Distinguished Texans . . .* , p. 8.

[23] A classmate recalled that Sul was courteous, manly, and socially agreeable
(C. S. W. Price to Melburn Glass, February 1, 1930, in Myrtle Whiteside, "The Life of
Lawrence Sullivan Ross" [M.A. thesis, Barker Texas History Center, University of Texas
at Austin, 1938], p. 10).

[24] U.S. Bureau of the Census, unpublished returns, "Eighth Census, 1860: Free
Inhabitants and Slave Population Schedules, McLennan County, Texas." Alabama col-
lege students were ready to go and fight in Kansas in April, 1858 (Minnie Clare Boyd,
Alabama in the Fifties: A Social Study, p. 155).

[25] Daniell, comp., *Personnel of the Texas State Government*, pp. 8–9. Sul joined

Maturity of convictions—political, social, and religious—brought with it maturity of action. Ross developed a coolness of judgment that set him apart from his more hotheaded classmates.[26] Indeed, he was in many ways a different youth from the boy who had lost his temper in Austin or the teenager who had planned and carried out such exquisite revenge for a tossed rock only a few years before. In one way, however, he was the same—he still desired to prove his manhood by defending Texas from hostile red men.

When the university session ended on July 7, 1858, and Sul prepared to return to Texas, he faced a further testing of his newfound maturity, this time in the responsibility of command.[27] Before returning to complete his senior year, Sul Ross had taken the first step toward becoming a soldier.

---

the Methodist Episcopal Church South in late summer or fall, 1858. It is not known whether he moved for membership before or after the Indian battle that almost cost him his life. Church records are no longer extant (*McLennan County, Texas, Marriage Records, 1850–1870*, app. B, p. 11).

[26] *Waco Tribune*, January 15, 1898.

[27] *Nashville Christian Advocate*, June 24, 1858.

☆ 3 ☆

The Fight at Wichita Village

In the summer of 1858, Sul Ross was especially anxious to return to Texas.[1] Much of his eagerness to return no doubt stemmed from reports of increasing aggression by Texans against the Comanches, for the war with the fierce plains tribe was no longer merely a defensive one. Texas forces, including Shapley Ross and a number of Brazos Reservation Indians, had carried the war successfully into the Comanche homeland that year, especially at Antelope Hills in Indian Territory.

Despite this temporary setback, Comanche forays into Texas continued. An especially pernicious band, led by the notorious war chief Buffalo Hump, specialized in stripping ranches and settlements of their horses and Texans of their scalps. Even the agency Indians were not immune from such attack. Stung by repeated raids, civil and military authorities planned to follow up the victory at Antelope Hills.[2]

Upon his arrival in Waco, Sul found his indefatigable mother expertly directing the construction of a spacious two-story house on the family farm south of town. More important, however, was news that another offensive against the Comanches in their Canadian River homeland was planned—this time by army regulars who felt they were being slighted by Texas authorities. Shapley Ross and the agency Indians were again to fight as auxiliaries. This opportunity to take part in a

---

[1] Sul has been portrayed as hurrying home from college each summer and making his way to the Texas frontier where his father was agent so he could fight the Comanches. Although he did spend time on the agency before beginning his university career, he apparently quit after he entered college (Carrie Johnson Crouch, *A History of Young County, Texas*, p. 20). The summer of 1856 Sul was in school in Independence; he evidently spent that of 1857 in Alabama, returning from Florence only in midsummer of 1858 (see deposition of Lawrence S. Ross for defendant, January 3, 1893, Greer County case, *Record, Supreme Court, United States, United States* v. *Texas in Equity*, p. 957).

[2] These depredations continued throughout the summer (L. S. Ross to George Barnard, September 12, 1858, in *Dallas Herald*, September 29, 1858).

military campaign against the Comanches appears to have been just what Sul had gambled on in coming back to Texas that summer. Disregarding the imminence of the new university term, Sul left Waco and made his way hurriedly to Young County and the Brazos Indian Reserve.[3]

Four years before, the situation of what Neighbours calls the "remnant tribes" of semicivilized Indians in Texas had become intolerable. Year after year white settlers pressed upon dwindling numbers of Wacos, Caddos, Wichitas, Tonkawas, Keechies, Tehuacanas, Ionies, Anadarkos, Delawares, and Shawnees. Once formidable, these tribes had been so decimated by aggression and disease that by the mid-1850s all the tribes combined totaled only about twenty-five hundred. Although friendly to whites, these Indians had been robbed many times of their fields and farming tools and had been forced to move west of the line of American settlement.[4]

To preserve peace and a semblance of friendship with these tribes, the state legislature in 1854 authorized the federal government to organize two reservations. Accordingly, four leagues of land, nearly thirty-seven thousand acres, were set aside for the remnant tribes on the Brazos River just below the junction of the Clear and Salt forks. This was the Brazos Indian Reservation. The Penateka or Southern Comanches were settled on the Upper Reserve some forty-five miles farther west on the Clear Fork of the Brazos.[5]

In 1855, when it was necessary to replace the agent on the Brazos Reserve, the Indians themselves requested and secured the appointment of Shapley Ross.[6] In his three years as agent, Shapley had won the loyalty as well as the respect of his charges. This loyalty, combined with the Indians' concern for the agent's well-being, was to win Sul command of the agency force.

When young Ross arrived on the reserve, he found things in an uproar; the Indian chiefs, who feared for Shapley's safety, insisted that

---

[3] *Waco Tribune-Herald*, October 30, 1949; John S. Ford, *Rip Ford's Texas*, p. 243; *San Antonio Daily Express*, November 22, 1908. The university session did not end until July 7, 1858. The new semester began on September 8, 1858 (*Nashville Christian Advocate*, June 24 and July 29, 1858).

[4] Kenneth F. Neighbours, *Indian Exodus: Texan Indian Affairs, 1835–1859*, p. 98; Ford, *Rip Ford's Texas*, p. 451; Crouch, *History of Young County*, p. 21; Randolph B. Marcy, *Thirty Years of Army Life on the Border*, p. 171.

[5] Ford, *Rip Ford's Texas*, p. 219; Crouch, *History of Young County*, p. 19.

[6] Ford, *Rip Ford's Texas*, p. 452.

the agent remain behind. In spite of the opposition of the chiefs, however, Captain Ross intended to take command of the detachment of Indians to cooperate with the U.S. troops. Just as the argument was at its height, Sul rode in from Waco. The chiefs saw his timely arrival as a chance to have their own way. First they proclaimed the nineteen-year-old Sul their war leader. Then they went to Shapley Ross and told him they now had a young captain who would lead them into battle. In poor health himself, confident of Sul's judgment and courage, and trusting the devotion of the agency Indians, Shapley at last agreed. He decided, nevertheless, to make the warriors swear allegiance to their young war leader. Unhesitatingly the Indians did so and in the following weeks served their young chieftain faithfully.[7]

Even then, Shapley probably had mixed feelings about allowing his son to accompany this group of semicivilized warriors northward. After all, the boy was not yet twenty—Sul would celebrate that birthday on the march—and the hostility of the regular troops had to be considered. Texas citizens regarded the regulars with less than enthusiasm, and the army returned the dislike.[8] Could a youngster like Sul win and hold the respect of both the Indians and the regular officers and troops? Shapley could only hope so.

As for Sul, he was anxious to do more than just prove his courage in battle. The day before his departure, a party of reserve Indians returned from pursuing some Comanche horse thieves. While on the Canadian River, the agency party had met Buffalo Hump and fifty braves. More important, however, they learned that the Comanches were joining the Kickapoos, the Keechies, and other tribes for a concerted raid on the Texas frontier. As Sul wrote his brother-in-law, George Barnard, in Waco that evening, "These . . . tribes . . . are going to cause much trouble, unless this expedition produces some effect upon them." It was his determination that it should.[9]

The rendezvous point for the civilian and military units of the ex-

[7]Ibid., pp. 243, 453; Myrtle Whiteside, "The Life of Lawrence Sullivan Ross" (M.A. thesis, Barker Texas History Center, University of Texas at Austin, 1938), p. 13; Ford, Rip Ford's Texas, p. 453. The Indian chiefs included Jim Pockmark and José Casa María of the Caddos and the Anadarkos, Placido and O'Quinn of the Tonkawas, Shot Arm of the Wacos, Jim Linney of the Shawnees and Delawares, and Nidewats of the Tehuacanas (Ford, Rip Ford's Texas, pp. 231–32).

[8]Ford, Rip Ford's Texas, p. 243. John H. Reagan praised Rip Ford, Shapley Ross, and their commands, who "have done more actual good in a brief campaign, than the whole of 3000 regulars, who live in comfortable quarters and are only serviceable in keeping up 'the pomp and circumstance of War'" (Dallas Herald, August 21, 1858).

[9]Dallas Herald, September 29, 1858.

pedition was Fort Belknap, a military post on the Brazos some fifteen miles northwest of the agency. There on September 13, Sul and his 135 Indian auxiliaries joined the regular contingent of the expeditionary force. Chosen for this task of raiding the Comanche homeland were four troops from the veteran Second Cavalry and one company of the Fifth Infantry. Brevet Major Earl Van Dorn, a dapper, sandy-haired, egotistical Mississippian, was officer in charge.[10]

It was the fifteenth of September before the expedition was ready to depart. At last the command, including troops, Indians, wagons, a medical officer and ambulance, and a sutler, headed for the Canadian River, where Buffalo Hump had last been seen. According to orders, Sul and his Indians quickly outstripped the slower marching troops and rode north and west across the prairies, always keeping a wary eye out for sign of the Comanches. One by one the Little Wichita, the Wichita, the Pease, and finally the Red rivers were crossed. When Sul's horse finally gained the north bank of the Red, the young Texan was in that "no man's land" of Indian Territory.

Once beyond Red River, Sul was to select a suitable site for a base camp. Guided by the Tonkawa chief Placido and the chiefs of the Tehuacanas, Ross halted his party on the south bank of Otter Creek near present Tipton, Oklahoma, and waited for Van Dorn. The military expedition arrived four or five days later.[11] On September 26, still planning to push on to the Canadian, the commander put his men to work building a picket stockade, called Camp Radziminski. While the troops labored at the construction of the stockade, the Indian scouts prowled the prairie searching for sign of their quarry. Meanwhile, Sul's position of command—he was given the courtesy title of "Captain"—enabled him to associate with both officers and men of the U.S. contingent and win their confidence and respect.[12]

Two Wichita warriors, Nasthoe and his son, eventually roamed some one hundred miles north and east near present Rush Springs,

[10]Zachariah Ellis Coombes, *The Diary of a Frontiersman, 1858–1859,* p. 2; Wilbur S. Nye, *Carbine and Lance: The Story of Old Fort Sill,* p. 23; Robert J. Hartje, *Van Dorn: The Life and Times of a Confederate General,* p. 63.

[11]Deposition of Lawrence S. Ross, Greer County case, pp. 953–55. J. W. Williams traces the route of the expedition in "The Van Dorn Trails," *Southwestern Historical Quarterly* 44 (January, 1941): 321–43.

[12]Van Dorn's report, September 26, 1858, in U.S. Congress, House, *Annual Report of the Secretary of War,* 35th Cong., 2d sess., 1858–59, *House Executive Documents,* 2, pt. 2: 268–69; *Austin Southern Intelligencer,* November 3, 1858. See also Hartje, *Van Dorn,* pp. 64–65.

Oklahoma, where a Wichita village huddled amid its cornfields on the banks of Rush Creek. Upon approaching the camp, the two scouts were surprised to find that besides the domed grass huts and cornfields of the Wichitas, large numbers of Comanche tepees, temporarily camped at the permanent Wichita village, straggled along the banks of the stream. Many ponies grazed on the outskirts of the Comanche camp; the scouts estimated at least five hundred.[13]

In the camp itself Comanche and Wichita mixed freely, trading, gambling, and feasting. The Comanches, unknown to Major Van Dorn, had just concluded a treaty with U.S. representatives at nearby Fort Arbuckle and were celebrating.[14] Scouts had brought word of Van Dorn's presence on Otter Creek, but the Comanche chiefs were not particularly concerned. If blue-coated troopers were operating north of the Red River, they were friendly. Or so decided the chiefs, and the feasting, fun, and festivities went on unabated.

Nasthoe and his son hid until dark, then sought the huts of the Wichita chiefs. There they learned that the Comanches represented different bands commanded by several illustrious chiefs, including the notorious Buffalo Hump, fresh from recent depredations in Texas. Drawn by blood kinship, Nasthoe warned the Wichitas of the soldiers' plans before he and his son slipped off into the night. The scouts returned to Radziminski late on September 29, two days after Sul's twentieth birthday, and reported at once to their war leader. Sul then went to Van Dorn's quarters, where he informed the officer of the scouts' find. What he did not know was that the distance the scouts represented as forty miles was in reality almost one hundred.[15]

At first Van Dorn was suspicious of the scouts and their report, but Ross did not doubt their loyalty.[16] The young civilian soon convinced the military man to make a forced march to the Comanche camp and attack at daybreak, when a raid would be least expected. Van Dorn did

[13] Nye, *Carbine and Lance*, p. 24; report of Charles G. Whiting, captain, Second Cavalry, October 2, 1858, *Annual Report*, 35th Cong., 2d sess., 1858–59, *House Executive Documents*, 2, pt. 2: 269; Randolph B. Marcy, *Thirty Years of Army Life on the Border*, p. 159.

[14] General David E. Twiggs, commander of the Department of Texas, learned of the treaty only after Van Dorn's departure (Twiggs to Army Headquarters, October 7, 1858, *Annual Report*, 35th Cong., 2d sess., 1858–59, *House Executive Documents*, 2, pt. 2: 267).

[15] Nye, *Carbine and Lance*, p. 24; Whiting, October 2, 1858, *Annual Report*, 35th Cong., 2d sess., 1858–59, *House Executive Documents*, 2, pt. 2: 269.

[16] Whiteside, "Life of Lawrence Sullivan Ross," p. 15. This information came from an interview with Harvey Ross, son of Sul Ross, July 12, 1938.

not need much convincing. He immediately ordered the four cavalry companies and Ross's Indians to prepare for a short campaign. Van Dorn also ordered the supplies and extra horses and mules enclosed in the stockade. The infantry force remained as guards. Within the hour the party—some three hundred men in all, including J. T. Ward, the sutler—was ready to leave Radziminski. The troops and Sul's Indians rode eastward through the darkness.[17]

The raiding party rode most of the night, halting only when necessary to rest the horses. Dawn brought disappointment: the Comanche camp was not in sight. By questioning the scouts more closely, the two commanders then learned that a day's ride still lay before them. Van Dorn determined to press on and moved his troops forward throughout the day, despite the weariness of men and horses. In about thirty-eight hours they covered the ninety-odd miles between Radziminski and the Wichita village, passing through what is now Fort Sill.

Daybreak on the frosty first morning of October found the regulars and their auxiliaries moving toward the Comanche camp through a veil of chill fog. Men, saddle weary after more than fifteen hours of continuous riding, peered through the thick fog, hoping to see some signs of their goal. There were none, and it seemed they had passed the village in the night. Then Sul's scouts reported that the command was approaching the camp.

Van Dorn halted his force and made his dispositions. Sul and his Indians were to drive off the Comanche ponies. One company of the cavalry would attack the lower part of the village; the other three under his command would hit the upper. When the bugler sounded the charge, everyone would ride into the camp at a gallop in order to attack before the Comanches could act. The major also directed Sul to keep the Indian auxiliaries on the right of the troops once the attack began so that during the fighting they would not be mistaken for the foe.

Formed in columns of two, the four companies abreast with the Indian auxiliaries off to the right, the troopers readied for the onslaught. On command, they moved their horses forward, crossing four ridges before the clustered tepees loomed before them through the thinning haze. Then the bugle notes rang out.[18]

---

[17] Nye, *Carbine and Lance*, p. 24; Van Dorn's report, October 6, 1858, extra edition, *Dallas Herald*, October 10, 1858; Ross's own account, in Elizabeth Ross Clarke, "Life of Sul Ross," Ross Family Papers, Texas Collection, Baylor University, Waco, Texas (hereafter cited as Ross Family Papers, Baylor), p. 49.

[18] Nye, *Carbine and Lance*, pp. 25–26. Van Dorn has been castigated for his "bru-

Weapons out and ready, the troopers "poured down into the enemies' camp in the most gallant style." At the same time, Sul and his
Indians galloped recklessly across the broken country to drive off the
Comanche ponies. In doing so they separated the now aroused warriors from most of their war horses. Sul saw to it that the herd was
stampeded beyond reach of the camp and guards placed around it;
then, collecting the balance of his command, he rode to assist the
troopers in the brisk fighting taking place in the camp. Although surprised, the Comanche warriors nevertheless mounted a good defense,
fighting like tigers to allow their families to escape. (The Wichitas had
already fled or were hiding nearby.) The Comanches fought desperately while the fog, mixed now with powder smoke, became so dense
that vision was obscured.[19]

It was through this fog and smoke that Sul discovered a large party
of fugitives fleeing from the camp. He yelled for help in heading them
off and whirled his horse to race after them. In the confusion only three
men—Lieutenant Cornelius Van Camp, Private Alexander, and a
Caddo scout—heard and rallied to him. The four galloped after the
fugitives to find the group consisted only of women and children. Sul
told the others to let them go and then realized that one of the ragged,
dirty, terror-stricken girl children was white.

"Grab her!" he yelled to the Caddo. The Indian did so. For a few
moments the Caddo had his hands full as the little captive, terrified by
the commotion in the camp and the presence of a strange warrior and
still stranger white men, screamed and struggled to get free.[20]

The recapture of the little white girl so engrossed them that Ross

tal attack upon a defenseless Comanche camp" after the signing of the Fort Arbuckle
treaty (Annie Heloise Abel, *The American Indian as Slaveholder and Secessionist: An
Omitted Chapter in the Diplomatic History of the Southern Confederacy*, p. 55). However, it must be remembered that Van Dorn's superiors knew nothing about such an
agreement until after the expedition's departure.

[19] Van Dorn's report, *Dallas Herald*, October 10, 1858; Clarke, "Life of Sul Ross,"
Ross Family Papers, Baylor, pp. 49–50; Ross to Victor M. Rose, October 13, 1880, Victor
M. Rose Papers, Kathryn Stoner O'Connor Collection, from private collection, Dr. and
Mrs. Malcolm D. McLean, Arlington, Texas (hereafter cited as Rose Papers, O'Connor
Collection); Nye, *Carbine and Lance*, pp. 26–27.

[20] Clarke, "Life of Sul Ross," Ross Family Papers, Baylor, pp. 49–50; Ross to Rose,
October 13, 1880, Rose Papers, O'Connor Collection. This child was about eight at the
time of her rescue. At first she was thought to be the daughter of Cynthia Ann Parker,
who was at that time still with the Comanches (Coombes, *Diary of a Frontiersman*, p.
14).

and his companions suddenly found themselves cut off from the main body of soldiers by a force of about twenty-five warriors. Loosing a shower of arrows, the Comanches swept forward. Van Camp tumbled from his saddle, dead—pierced through the heart.[21] Also hit, the cavalryman Alexander fell before he could fire his carbine, but the Caddo, still holding the white girl, was miraculously unharmed. Sul swung his Sharps around to return the fire, but the percussion cap snapped and the weapon misfired. At the same time a Comanche arrow transfixed Sul's shoulder. While he reeled in the saddle, a warrior snatched up Alexander's carbine and shot Ross point-blank. For a split second their gaze locked and Sul recognized the warrior as Mohee, a Comanche he had known since childhood.[22]

Blood pouring from his wounds, Sul slipped from his saddle to the ground, landing with his six-shooter under him. He lay stunned for an instant, his arm and side partially paralyzed, then saw a gleam of metal as Mohee drew a scalping knife and sprang toward him with a yell. Though seriously injured and swiftly slipping into unconsciousness, Sul knew that he must act quickly if he was not to die by Mohee's hand. He painfully turned himself and fumbled at his holster, struggling ineffectively to draw his revolver with his other hand. There seemed to be no hope, and Sul thought his time had come.

In another instant Mohee would have been upon him, but just then the Comanches spied an approaching party of cavalry. Called away by his chief, the warrior reluctantly turned from his fallen and helpless foe and bounded off. Before Mohee could reach the safety of surrounding brush, Lieutenant James P. Major galloped up and killed him with a load of buckshot. The Comanche fell on his face only a few feet from his intended victim.[23]

Sul heard the shouts of the cavalrymen and the whoops of his In-

[21] Clarke, "Life of Sul Ross," Ross Family Papers, Baylor, p. 50. More than twenty years later, Ross remembered the "feelings of horror that took possession of me when I saw the arrow sent clear up the *feather* into the body and heart of the gallant young Van Camp" (Victor M. Rose, *Ross' Texas Brigade: Being a Narrative of Events Connected with Its Service in the Late War Between the States*, pp. 175–77; Ross to Rose, October 13, 1880, Rose Papers, O'Connor Collection).

[22] Clarke, "Life of Sul Ross," Ross Family Papers, Baylor, pp. 50–51; Ross to Rose, October 13, 1880, Rose Papers. A fault of the Sharps was that the percussion cap "frequently did not explode" (Frederick Law Olmsted, *A Journey Through Texas: Or a Saddle-Trip on the Southwestern Frontier*, p. 74).

[23] Clarke, "Life of Sul Ross," Ross Family Papers, Baylor, p. 51; Ross to Rose, October 13, 1880, Rose Papers, O'Connor Collection.

dians through the red haze of pain swiftly engulfing him and knew that
victory was theirs. As the sounds of battle grew fainter and fainter, he
was aware of Caddo John, one of his father's wards, bending anxiously
over him. Opening Sul's hunting shirt, Caddo John found that Ross
had sustained two wounds of four holes, both caused, he thought, by
the same .58-caliber Springfield ball. In addition to the wound pierc-
ing the shoulder, which was bleeding freely, Ross had been shot
through the body, the bullet entering the chest and exiting out the
back between the shoulder blades. John probed the wounds with a
scrap of silk handkerchief and his ramrod, then washed, dressed, and
bandaged them. Then he placed Sul on his horse and returned to the
rear, where the expedition surgeon was treating the other wounded,
among them Major Van Dorn.[24]

Meanwhile the battle continued, lasting in all between an hour
and a half and two hours. When Comanche resistance finally ceased,
white losses were four dead with twelve wounded, including the two
commanders and Ward, the sutler. Comanche casualties totaled fifty-
six—later seventy—dead, among them several women who had fought
beside their husbands. Many more were wounded. Despite this
slaughter, Buffalo Hump and most of his warriors managed to escape.[25]

While troopers rounded up three hundred of the Comanche
horses, other bluecoats fired the lodges. In all, 120 tepees were
burned, along with the Comanches' "ammunition, cooking utensils,
clothing, dressed skins, corn and subsistence stores" not appropriated
by the soldiers. Those who escaped "did so with the scanty clothing
they had on, and their arms." Within a few hours only ashes and the
dead remained to mark the site of the former encampment.[26]

For five agonizing days Sul lay under a post oak on the battlefield,
too severely injured to be moved. Although no vital organ had been

[24] Hobart D. Ragland, *The History of Rush Springs*, p. 77. The army doctor com-
plimented the Indian on his medical skill and tried to find out what foreign substance he
had put in the wound, but the Caddo would not tell him. It was probably *pouip* or *Yerva
del Indio*, an Indian "wonder drug" (Ragland, *History of Rush Springs*, p. 77; Jean Louis
Berlandier, *The Indians of Texas in 1830*, p. 88).

[25] Van Dorn's report, October 5, 1858, *Annual Report*, 35th Cong., 2d sess.,
1858–59, *House Executive Documents*, 2, pt. 2: 272; Nye, *Carbine and Lance*, p. 29;
Van Dorn's report, *Dallas Herald*, October 10, 1858; Hartje, *Van Dorn*, pp. 66–69. William Cloud, another participant, called the Rush Springs battle "a great fight and a complete one" (*Austin Southern Intelligencer*, November 3, 1858).

[26] Van Dorn's report, *Dallas Herald*, October 10, 1858. Van Camp's body was sent
back to Lancaster, Pennsylvania, for burial (Ragland, *History of Rush Springs*, p. 16).

touched by the ball that had torn through his body, the shock of the wound was great. For a time it seemed as though the young Texan's first command would be his last, but finally he rallied. Van Dorn was in better, but still serious, condition. While the U.S. forces remained on the battlefield, the commander prepared a recommendation addressed to the secretary of war and signed by the officers of his command, "asking the promotion of Captain Ross, and his assignment to duty in the regular army." As soon as the two wounded commanders were strong enough to attempt the long journey back to Fort Belknap, they were placed in mule litters and the entire party retraced its steps to Camp Radziminski. The other wounded were removed to Fort Arbuckle.[27]

The trip to Radziminski was an agonizing one to Sul, suffering from the painful body wound that had become infected. Thinking he was dying, he begged his Indian friends to kill him and end his torture and misery. His father's wards paid no heed to his feverish pleas and acted with great wisdom in treating the rankling wound. To ease their injured war leader when traveling over especially rough or broken terrain, the agency Indians bore him upon their own shoulders. Radziminski was reached at last, and there the escort procured a horse-drawn ambulance, enabling the wounded to make the rest of the journey to Fort Belknap in comparative comfort.[28]

Sul arrived at the agency on October 18, looking, in the eyes of the government schoolteacher, "verry [sic] much wasted by fatigue and his wound" but still "full of life and fun." He found news of the battle had preceded him, with reports that he was "as brave and daring as if trained and raised in War." His father had also learned of his injuries. Thinking Sul had been taken with the rest of the wounded to Fort Arbuckle, Shapley Ross departed for the fort and thus missed his son's arrival. It was October 26 before Sul was well enough to start the long journey back to civilization.[29]

[27] William B. Philpott, ed., *The Sponsor Souvenir Album and History of the UCV Reunion, 1895*, p. 98; Clarke, "Life of Sul Ross," Ross Family Papers, Baylor, pp. 53–54; Van Dorn's report, October 11, 1858, *Annual Report*, 35th Cong., 2d sess., 1858–59, *House Executive Documents*, 2, pt. 2: 275.

[28] Whiteside, "Life of Lawrence Sullivan Ross," p. 18; Ross to Rose, October 13, 1880, Rose Papers, O'Connor Collection. Whiteside cites as her source an interview with Sul's son, Harvey. The story was handed down in the family. The *Houston Chronicle*, February 17, 1929, cites Sul's nephew, Clint Padgitt, as a source.

[29] Coombes, *Diary of a Frontiersman*, pp. 7, 13, 22. Shapley returned a week before Sul's departure for Waco. According to a family tradition, Sul was carried home on a

War Department officials applauded Van Dorn's Wichita village campaign as a decisive step toward final subjugation of the ferocious Comanches. The Texas press, however, was less enthusiastic, noting on November 3 that the results of the battle "will, probably, be a cessation of depredations upon the border settlements for a time at least, and an end of the war should the blow be followed by active, energetic operations." Even this guarded optimism was overset when, a few days later, Sul stopped by Dallas on his way east from the Brazos Agency and reported that since Van Dorn's fight with them, the Comanches had stolen about one hundred head of horses from ranches and settlements in northern Texas.[30]

Without discounting the apparent military value of the battle, the Wichita campaign resulted mainly in fame for the two commanders, Van Dorn and Ross. The Mississippian was lionized and was for a time the toast of the army. For Sul Ross the campaign, besides a serious bloodletting, resulted in public recognition of his courage and ability as a military leader. It was the beginning of his career as a soldier, and he was later to consider the event "the most creditable incident of all relating to myself."[31]

More important to Ross's later Civil War service, of the officers of the Second Cavalry who were along on this expedition, four—Van Dorn, Captain Nathan G. Evans, Lieutenant James P. Major, and Lieutenant Charles W. Phifer—became Confederate general officers in the war. He would serve under or with all of them again.[32]

Once back in Waco, where he could recuperate under the watchful eye and tender care of his mother, Sul found his name in print. His friend Charles Pryor, editor of the *Dallas Herald*, had published Van Dorn's Wichita village report as an extra edition on October 10. *Herald* headlines described the action as a "Great Indian Battle" and a "Glorious Victory Over the Comanches." Other participants in the battle

stretcher (Coombes, *Diary of a Frontiersman*, p. 16; *Houston Chronicle*, February 17, 1929).

[30] Hartje, *Van Dorn*, p. 69; *Dallas Herald*, November 3 and 10, 1858.

[31] Nye, *Carbine and Lance*, p. 30; Hartje, *Van Dorn*, p. 68; *Austin State Gazette*, November 13, 1858; Adam Rankin Johnson, *The Partisan Rangers of the Confederate States Army*, p. 29; Ross to Victor M. Rose, July 4, 1881, Lawrence Sullivan Ross Letters, Barker Texas History Center, University of Texas at Austin.

[32] Rose, *Ross' Texas Brigade*, p. 159; George F. Price, *Across the Continent with the Fifth Cavalry*, pp. 23, 26–31.

wrote of what they had seen and of "Captain" Ross's role in the fight. In Sul's opinion, this growing fame more than balanced the other pay, "a dangerous gun shot wound," received for his services.[33]

Praise soon came from yet another source. While he was still convalescing at home, Ross received a highly complimentary letter from Commanding General Winfield Scott, promising the venerable veteran's friendship and assistance in pursuing a military career.[34] This proposal was tempting, offering as it did a direct commission in the regular army to a young man just twenty years of age and without any formal military training. If Sul had chosen to use it, Scott's help would have served him as a springboard to a career in the U.S. Army.

As in 1856, Ross faced a decision that would have changed, at least temporarily, the course of his life. But despite the persuasiveness of Scott's missive, powerful negative factors had to be considered. A young man of integrity, with a realistic view of his own accomplishments, Ross felt that his youthful experience, however praiseworthy, was not sufficient to prepare him for the responsibilities of an officer's commission. Then, too, he lacked several months in finishing his college course and wished to complete his A.B. degree. Finally, it is likely he was influenced in his decision by his matrimonial hopes.[35]

Of all the words of praise and admiration coming his way since the Wichita village fight, none were sweeter than those from Elizabeth Dorothy Tinsley, the dark-haired, bright-eyed daughter of a neighboring planter. Already he planned someday to make her his wife. Perhaps it was his determination to make his mark for Lizzie's sake that turned Sul's steps away from a military career and back to the university, although it might well have been his reluctance to subject her to the dreary and lonely existence he knew to be the lot of an army wife. Whatever his reasons, Ross declined to seek a regular army commis-

---

[33]*Dallas Herald*, October 10, 1858; *Austin Southern Intelligencer*, November 3, 1858; Ben C. Stuart, "The Texas Indian Fighters and Frontier Rangers" (M.A. thesis, Barker Texas History Center, University of Texas at Austin, 1916), p. 89. Sul Ross was also mentioned in the speech of John H. Reagan concerning Indian depredations in Texas, given before the House of Representatives on February 24, 1859 (*Dallas Herald*, April 6, 1859).

[34]Clarke, "Life of Sul Ross," Ross Family Papers, Baylor, pp. 53–54; Whiteside, "Life of Lawrence Sullivan Ross," p. 20. An attempt has been made to locate Van Dorn's letter to the secretary of war and Scott's letter to Ross, but it has not proved successful.

[35]Clarke, "Life of Sul Ross," Ross Family Papers, Baylor, p. 54.

sion. As soon as he could travel, he returned to Florence, where he graduated the following summer.[36]

[36] Ibid.; Ross to Rose, October 13, 1880, Rose Papers, O'Connor Collection; Clarke, "Life of Sul Ross," Ross Family Papers, Baylor, pp. 53–54; *Nashville Christian Advocate*, July 28, 1859; *San Antonio Daily Express*, November 22, 1908. Neither Van Dorn nor Lieutenant Colonel Robert E. Lee of the Second Cavalry brought his wife and family to the Texas frontier (see Hartje, *Van Dorn*, p. 55; Douglas Southall Freeman, *Robert E. Lee: A Biography*, I, 360).

☆ 4 ☆

First Ranger Command

AFTER his graduation from Florence Wesleyan, Sul Ross returned to
Texas. It was still his ambition to participate in the protection of the
frontier, although he found the circumstances of 1859 much changed
from those of a year earlier. Van Dorn's expedition had brought no lasting respite to the frontier. Indeed, Comanche horse-stealing raids had
recurred even before Ross recovered enough from his Wichita village
injuries to start back to Waco. The second week in November, hostile
red men again swooped down on the Brazos Reserve and made off with
160 head of horses.[1]

Ferocious attacks with accompanying atrocities continued as the
old year faded: timorous settlers in present Brown, Lampasas, and San
Saba counties fled while braver or more foolhardy neighbors "forted
up." A ranger captain operating around San Saba, reporting the de-
population of the area, remarked, "The people will retreat still further
unless immediate protection is afforded."[2]

But Comanche vengeance was not satisfied by a scattering of
horse-stealing and scalp-lifting raids, especially after a second Van
Dorn–agency Indian expedition in the spring of 1859. After one foray,
a Mexican boy recaptured from the Comanches reported that ten na-
tions of hostiles were joining in a covenant to fight "Van Dorn, Texas
and the Indians that fought under Van Dorn. . . . The first fight is to
be on Van Dorn and the friendly Indians, and the nearest white settlements to Van Dorn's battleground."[3]

---

[1] Zachariah Ellis Coombes, *The Diary of a Frontiersman, 1858–1859*, pp. 21, 29.

[2] John Williams to Governor Hardin R. Runnels, October 25, 1858, Texas Indian
Affairs Papers, 1835–60, Texas State Archives, Austin, Texas (hereafter cited as Indian
Affairs Papers); Hillary Ryan to Runnels, October 30, 1858, Indian Affairs Papers.

[3] Robert J. Hartje, *Van Dorn: The Life and Times of a Confederate General*,
pp. 71–73; Kenneth F. Neighbours, *Indian Exodus: Texan Indian Affairs, 1835–1859*,
pp. 130, 135; *Austin State Gazette*, October 1, 1859.

Not only were the Comanche predators again active at the time Ross returned, but the situation regarding the friendly remnant tribes had also drastically changed. Intensified Comanche raids only inflamed the hatred of white settlers living near the reserves. Many whites resented the presence of the red men on principle; others coveted the reservation land. Still others were convinced that agency Indians were in league with the hostiles and that stolen horses belonging to local settlers could be found among reservation pony herds. Unscrupulous whites thriving on horse stealing, robbery, and murder added their misdeeds to actual Indian raids and, like the hostiles, took care to throw as much of the blame as possible upon the reservation tribes. Even those settlers of some conscience were not above planting evidence to incriminate the agency Indians and force their removal.[4]

Pouring oil on the rapidly spreading flames of white suspicion and animosity was John R. Baylor, former agent at the Upper (Comanche) Reserve. Following his dismissal from service in May, 1857, Baylor's self-imposed mission had been to incite the white settlers against the reservation Indians and the government agents. At first, Baylor occupied himself with "addressing mass meetings, promoting petitions, and carrying on a newspaper campaign of recrimination." Later he published, first at Jacksboro and then at Weatherford, a racist newspaper called the *White Man*, which carried "inflammatory articles calculated to keep the public mind agitated."[5]

The result of this agitation by Baylor and others was the so-called Reservation War and the expulsion of the remnant tribes from Texas. Law-abiding citizens witnessed such atrocities as vigilantes murdering helpless and aged Indians, U.S. troops firing on white men to protect red men, and vindictive settlers preying on harassed tribesmen as they were hurried out of the state by regular troops and Texas Rangers.[6]

---

[4]John S. Ford, *Rip Ford's Texas*, p. 454; James Buckner Barry, *A Texas Ranger and Frontiersman: The Days of Buck Barry in Texas, 1845–1906*, p. 104; James Pike, *Scout and Ranger: Being the Personal Adventures of James Pike of the Texas Rangers in 1859–60*, p. xiv; Joseph B. Thoburn and Muriel H. Wright, *Oklahoma: A History of the State and Its People*, I, 288; Neighbours, *Indian Exodus*, pp. 125–26.

[5]Neighbours, *Indian Exodus*, pp. 118–19. During the Civil War, while Baylor was Confederate military governor of New Mexico Territory, he proposed to end Indian troubles there once and for all by poisoning the pernicious Apaches. This suggestion cost him his command (William C. Nunn, ed., *Ten Texans in Gray*, pp. 12–15).

[6]Neighbours, *Indian Exodus*, pp. 131–39; Rupert N. Richardson, *The Frontier of Northwest Texas, 1846 to 1876: Advance and Defense by the Pioneer Settlers of the Cross Timbers and Prairies*, pp. 195–212.

About the time Lawrence Sullivan Ross, A.B., was returning to Texas from Alabama, his father and two of his brothers were riding north with Shapley's persecuted wards. Although Sul had not been involved in the Indian removal controversy, he was to find that the incident affected the rest of his Indian-fighting career. For one thing, once the buffers of the two reservations were removed, the frontier counties of Texas felt the full fury of widespread attacks—and would continue to suffer for another fifteen years. Sul Ross would have ample opportunity to take part in state actions against the red marauders. On the other hand, young Ross was to experience white animosity both as a son of former agent Shapley Ross and as a Texas Ranger.[7] His battle to gain recognition in the state service of Texas would be a far from easy one.

It has been suggested that Sul Ross began his ranger career after his return to Texas in 1859, but no evidence in the available ranger papers appears to support such a claim. Although it is possible that he served in a company of mounted volunteers in a capacity other than as an officer, the muster roll of such an organization has not been found.[8]

It is likely that more mundane matters occupied Ross from the summer of 1859 to the spring of the next year, when he commanded his first ranger company. His health was still precarious; fatigue and a spell of cold rain in May, 1860, were enough to bring on a serious bronchial attack. Sul may well have spent much of the remainder of 1859 recovering from the wound received in the Wichita village fight. Also, at some time, probably upon his return from the university, Ross interested himself in helping search for the family and friends of the little white girl recovered from the Comanches. Although a diligent search was made, neither kin nor even any knowledge of the child's history was ever brought to light. Sul therefore "adopted, reared, and educated" her; she was named Lizzie Ross in honor of his sweetheart, Lizzie Tinsley, to whom he was then engaged.[9]

---

[7]Thoburn and Wright, *Oklahoma*, I, 292; Neighbours, *Indian Exodus*, p. 140; Pike, *Scout and Ranger*, p. xiv.

[8]William B. Philpott, ed., *The Sponsor Souvenir Album and History of the UCV Reunion, 1895*, p. 98. The Adjutant General Papers are sketchy at best. Only one box of pre-1860 correspondence still exists, and no other materials are extant for the period from 1846–61 (Carol J. Carefoot, archivist, Texas State Library, Austin, Texas, February 13, 1975, personal communication).

[9]Benjamin Franklin Gholson Recollections, Barker Texas History Center, University of Texas at Austin (hereafter cited as Gholson Recollections), p. 53; Captain Willis Lang Diary, Barker Texas History Center, University of Texas at Austin (hereafter cited as Lang Diary), pp. 5–6; Ross to S. A. Cunningham, May 14, 1894, Ross Family Papers,

However Sul Ross spent his time before April of 1860, it is known that by spring of that year he was fired by an ambition to help defend the frontier. All hands skilled in the use of rifle and revolver were needed as never before. Murder, rape, and robbery were rife, and the situation was rapidly becoming critical. Continued depredations and the increasingly frantic outcries of harassed citizens greeted the accession of Sam Houston to the governorship.

Although Houston was suspected by many of being an Indian sympathizer because he had lived with the Cherokees as a young man, he acted with characteristic forcefulness. In order that the outrages could be avenged and the forays halted, the frontier counties were directed to form "minute companies of fifteen men each." Arms and ammunition were also purchased with state funds and distributed to the citizens of the frontier counties to assist them in self-defense.[10]

On March 17, 1860, Colonel Middleton T. Johnson of Tarrant County was authorized by Governor Houston to "raise a sufficient number of mounted rangers to repel, pursue, and punish" the Indians then ravaging the northern and northwestern settlements of the state. Johnson, a former ranger of considerable reputation, sent out the call for volunteers. Five companies, hailing from McLennan, Dallas, Fannin, Collin, and Tarrant counties, initially answered his call.[11]

When the Waco company was raised by Captain J. M. Smith, Sul Ross enlisted. His ranger career began auspiciously, for of the three officers selected by the company, Ross was designated first lieutenant. There were also two second lieutenants (senior and junior), eight noncommissioned officers, a surgeon, and eighty-four privates. Before the company's departure for the frontier, the women of Waco presented the men with a beautiful banner made entirely of ribbon, which Lieu-

Texas Collection, Baylor University, Waco, Texas; Dudley G. Wooten, ed., A Comprehensive History of Texas, 1685–1897, II, 342.

[10] William C. Crane, Life and Select Literary Remains of Sam Houston of Texas, pp. 631–33.

[11] Ibid., p. 633; Marcus J. Wright, Texas in the War, 1861–1865, p. 116; Crane, Sam Houston of Texas, p. 633. Frederick Law Olmsted wrote of the rangers, "Their wild life and exciting combats were as romantic and attractive to adventuresome young men as any crusade of old." He noted that their pay was $25 a month, that rations of "hard bread and pork" or "fresh beef, flour, rice, sugar, and coffee" were issued every four days except when on a scout, and that the rangers "carried no tents and seldom employed baggage-wagons" (Olmsted, A Journey Through Texas: Or a Saddle-Trip on the Southwestern Frontier, p. 300).

tenant Ross accepted on behalf of his comrades. Another year would see a great many such musters, presentations, and acceptances by Texas forces, but this time under another flag.[12]

It was April 23 before the expedition at last departed. If the men could have been observed on the march, they probably would have fit the description of another group given by one of the rangers:

Imagine . . . men dressed in every variety of costume, except the ordinary uniform, armed with double-barreled shot guns, squirrel rifles, and Colt's six shooters, mounted on small, wiry, half wild horses, with Spanish saddles and Mexican spurs; unshaven, unwashed, undisciplined, but brave and generous men, riding pell-mell along roads, over the prairies, and through the woods, and you will be able to form a correct conception of a squad of Texan Rangers on the march. In such a band it is impossible to distinguish officers from privates, as the former have no distinct dress; and all act alike.[13]

While the bulk of the command traveled to Fort Belknap, the rendezvous point, Ross went ahead of the main party on another route. Eager as he was to fight hostile Indians, business demanded his attention. Sul rejoined the company at his father's ranch in Young County on the second of May. The next day Smith led his men to within three miles of Belknap, where they joined the other four companies. Soon afterward two additional companies arrived, bringing the regimental total to seven.[14]

The men loitered in camp while Smith and the other company commanders consulted before organizing the regiment. Rather than waste the lengthening spring days in idleness, Sul obtained permission to take twenty-five men on a scout to the Little Wichita. Whatever hopes he may have had of being the first to engage the hostiles were soon dashed. When he and his party returned to camp five days later, they had nothing to report except that they had killed some buffalo. What was even more exasperating, Ross learned that during his absence Indians had killed two men on nearby Elm Creek.[15]

These early operations set the tone for the entire campaign. On May 18 the seven companies mustered on the parade ground of Fort

[12] Lang Diary, pp. 1–2. For a discussion of the antebellum rangers, see Mark E. Nackman, "The Making of the Texas Citizen Soldier, 1835–1860," *Southwestern Historical Quarterly* 78 (January, 1975): 231–53.

[13] Lang Diary, p. 2; Pike, *Scout and Ranger*, pp. 21–22.

[14] Gholson Recollections, p. 53; Lang Diary, pp. 2–3; Crane, *Sam Houston of Texas*, p. 633.

[15] Lang Diary, pp. 4–5.

Belknap and then proceeded to the election of the necessary field officers. Captain Smith secured the desired position of lieutenant colonel, leaving his command vacant. Ross's comrades felt him most deserving of Smith's title, but this triumph was considerably lessened by
an acute attack of bronchitis, which struck on May 19. When the Waco
company held an election to fill the post of captain, Ross was ill enough
to cause concern, although he was no doubt cheered by the knowledge
that he won the captaincy without opposition.[16]

Although the new captain hoped to remain in camp with his men,
his condition soon became alarming enough to require his removal to a
nearby house. Though improving, Ross was still confined to his bed on
May 22 when Lieutenants Lang, Kelliher, and Gault met with him to
formulate company regulations. Two days later, when the company received orders from regimental headquarters to prepare for a review,
Sul was still too ill to rise. By the next morning, May 25, he was just
able to sit a horse. Although Ross went into town for the review, he was
too weak to appear on parade, and when the muster was over he remained in Belknap while his men proceeded to another campsite
nearby.[17]

All this was hardly an encouraging way to begin his career as a
Texas Ranger captain. Then, too, the growing problems of company
headquarters demanded Sul's attention. Ross soon found problems he
had not foreseen connected with command. Boredom born of inactivity engulfed the men. Some of the rangers found a hidden cache of
whiskey and became hilariously drunk; more quarrelsome members
found release from frustration in fist and blade. Even formerly con-
tented souls complained of short rations and bad water. Meanwhile,
headquarters changed its policies from day to day, giving rise to justi-
fiable criticism. To add a further blow to wavering ranger self-esteem,
Colonel Johnson departed for Galveston to take a wife while the whole
frontier was crying out against Indian depredations.[18]

The rangers wasted the first nine days of June in camp while Ross
struggled to deal with other problems crowding upon him. There were
headaches enough for any commander, let alone a young man of twenty-
one. During a drunken shooting spree one ranger wounded another,
although fortunately not seriously. Still another man deserted or was

[16] Gholson Recollections, pp. 53–54; Lang Diary, p. 5.
[17] Lang Diary, pp. 5–6.
[18] Ibid., pp. 6–7.

murdered by local desperadoes. To add to Ross's difficulties, at that same time Sul himself was experiencing the bitterness of an attack on his integrity. The whites in the area, especially those followers of John R. Baylor, resented his appointment as captain and lost no opportunity to exhibit their hostility.[19]

For one thing, Patrick Murphy and other ruffians responsible for the Reservation War and the removal of the remnant tribes considered themselves Ross's enemies and began to make trouble for the young captain. Murphy was an especially dangerous man, being one of those involved in the assassination of chief Indian agent Major Robert S. Neighbors at Belknap in September, 1859.[20] Unwilling to end his career with a load of buckshot in the back as Neighbors had done, Ross took a friend with him when he visited Murphy to discuss their differences. Fortunately these differences were resolved amicably; the showdown between Ross and Murphy ended with the captain and his friend taking supper with the Irishman.[21]

But this bloodless meeting between the two did not end the strong undercurrent of resentment directed toward Ross and his rangers by other members of the community. Once while he and a detachment were pursuing a raiding party fresh from depredations on the Trinity River, Ross and his men rode up to a house to get some water from the well. The mistress of the house came out at their approach and asked if they were going after the Indians. The ranger in the advance politely answered that they were. She then wanted to know whose company it was. The Waco Company of Captain Ross was the young man's proud reply, but he and the others were momentarily taken aback by the harridan's reaction to this information: "'I wish the Injuns may scalp the last one o' you,' she shouted in a shrill voice. The men all broke out into a laugh, which only increased her indignation; and as long as we were within hearing distance, her voice rang out maledictions upon our heads, and upon the heads of every friend of Captain Ross."[22] Sul had laughed, but no doubt the bitter words rankled. Although young, he had already shed blood in defense of his state, and

[19] Ibid., p. 7; Pike, *Scout and Ranger*, p. 71.

[20] While Murphy held Neighbors in conversation, Murphy's brother-in-law Edward Cornett shot the former agent from concealment (see Neighbours, *Indian Exodus*, p. 138; and Pike, *Scout and Ranger*, p. xvi).

[21] Lang Diary, p. 7.

[22] Pike, *Scout and Ranger*, pp. 71–72.

yet the people he was prepared to fight for again hated him because his father had been agent at the Brazos Reserve.[23]

This unreasoning hatred was also extended to the other members of the regiment. At the same time, the citizens' hostility evoked reciprocal ill feeling among the men they depended upon for protection. As the days passed, this spirit of mutual distrust and animosity grew. No doubt it was with great relief that Ross got his company into the saddle and onto the trail on June 10. By then Lieutenant Colonel Smith had formulated a plan of campaign against the Comanches: the rangers would move north to old Camp Radziminski, where they would rendezvous with Peter Ross's spy company of warriors from the old Brazos Reserve. Then the Texans, aided as in the past by friendly Indians, would search out and destroy the enemy.[24]

Until that time, ranger life as experienced by Captain Sul Ross had been far from carefree. But as the command rode north, he was able to relax and enjoy with the rest of his men the beautiful scenery and the pleasures of buffalo running and wild-horse hunting. After Independence Day Colonel Smith called the commissioned officers to a council of war, where he laid before them evidence indicating the Kickapoos had recently stolen horses and murdered two families in Texas. The consensus was "to wipe them out."[25]

Considering his ambition to distinguish himself as a ranger, Sul Ross was probably eager for the fray as three hundred Texans prepared to attack the hostile camp. Here were all the adventure and fun of military life without the burdensome drills and discipline of the regular army. Excitement reigned in the ranger camp as the regiment readied itself for action. But unknown to the Texans, the hostile tribesmen, including Comanches and Kiowas, had been warned of their plans. The second day out from their base camp, the men of Ross's company were chagrined to find the prairie ablaze ahead of them. They rode forward to investigate and found the other companies of the regiment drawn to the same spot. Further inquiry showed the fires had been recently and deliberately set.[26]

---

[23] The whites thought Sul would be soft on the hostiles because he had lived with Indians on the Brazos Reserve (see John M. Elkins, *Indian Fighting on the Texas Frontier*, p. 32).

[24] Lang Diary, p. 8.

[25] Ibid., pp. 9–12.

[26] Ibid., p. 12; Gholson Recollections, p. 54.

At mid-summer in an extremely dry year, there was no hope of halting the spread of the roaring flames. Soon the area between Red River and the Arkansas was a smoking, blackened desert. This disastrous prairie fire, occurring at a time when even the usual water holes were dry, all but ended the expedition's hope of chastising the hostiles. On July 12, after another conference with his officers, Smith decided to abandon the mission.[27]

Apparently ill again, Ross returned to the Washita Indian Agency near Fort Cobb with a few other sick men. Although he could not take field command himself, he sent Lieutenants Lang and Kelliher with thirty-one men on a scout to the Canadian River. They found "all . . . desert, burnt and barren." Neither Indians nor other living things were to be seen. This time the red men, acting in harmony with the environment, had been victorious.[28]

Johnson's regiment spent the rest of its time in the field scouting, wherever the men could find grass enough to support their mounts. Until the scouts found Indian sign there was little for the men to do but hunt, launder their ragged clothing, repair their equipment, and entertain themselves as best they could. This recreation was as varied as the men themselves. Often the "elevated feelings of youth" broke forth in song and the usual frontier horseplay. One evening the "boys had perfect revival in the form of skylarking" by throwing their comrades one after another into a nearby creek. Even Captain Ross was not exempt; in the spirit of frontier democracy he had to take his dunking in the muddy waters of the creek with the rest of his men.[29]

When the muddy waters at last lost their charms, the rangers turned to amusement of a different nature. From somewhere one of the men produced a violin, and as the moon shone brightly, the sounds of music and dancing filled the camp. It was a strange scene for the wilderness. The appearance of the party was grotesque enough to make anyone smile, for some of the dancers had discarded their boots, while others pranced barelegged in their shirttails. Since no women were present, some of the rangers had to assume the role of female dancing partners.[30]

[27] Gholson Recollections, pp. 54–55; Lang Diary, p. 13.
[28] Lang Diary, pp. 13–14, 16.
[29] Gholson Recollections, p. 55; Lang Diary, pp. 19–21.
[30] Lang Diary, pp. 21–22.

While the rangers frolicked at their camp in Indian Territory, a storm of trouble that would soon engulf them was brewing in Texas. As that year's critical presidential election approached and the fabric of the union began to disintegrate, political controversy between unionists and the states' rights party became even bitterer. Governor Sam Houston was a known unionist; he was also considered an Indian lover. Political animosity from Houston's enemies, many of them both avowed secessionists and Indian haters, colored evaluation of the governor's policies, including the activities of the rangers. It did not help the case of Johnson's regiment that the unit was proving ineffective. Scattered raiding parties were still coming into Texas; citizens far from the scene of action and not aware of the circumstances could not understand why the troops had not destroyed the hostiles.[31]

As might be expected, criticism poured in from all sides. In July a public meeting was held in Parker County to deal with Indian depredations in surrounding counties. At that time, indignant settlers drew up a number of resolutions for presentation to the governor. One such resolution stated that the protection offered the "frontier by the State government . . . is a humbug and deserves the condemnation of all honest men." Another suggested that the citizens petition Governor Houston "to withdraw the regiment of rangers from our frontier." Meanwhile, other citizens pointed out that Baylor and his cohorts had killed all the Indians to date in Texas "since Houston's army was raised."[32] As far as Houston's enemies were concerned, there was never any mystery as to who was responsible for this state of affairs. The culprit was the governor, who "never had the most remote intention of punishing the Indians."[33]

Houston's enemies were soon reinforced in their opinion. On August 26, 1860, Johnson's regiment disbanded.[34] While the men were making their various ways home, the ubiquitous Baylor was preparing

[31] *Austin State Gazette*, October 6, 1860.

[32] Ibid., July 24, 1860; *Clarksville* (Tex.) *Standard*, July 20, 1860.

[33] *Austin State Gazette*, July 24, 1860. When the *Austin Southern Intelligencer* accused the *Gazette* of doubting the courage and honor of the Texas regiment, *Gazette* editors answered: "We have denounced the policy pursued by Governor Houston, and we believe it meets with the universal reprobation of the men in our army, but all we have said of the latter has been in their commendation and praise. They have repeatedly been spoken of by us as gallant men, and able to do full justice to the frontier, if permitted by Governor Houston" (*Austin State Gazette*, August 11, 1860).

[34] Lang Diary, pp. 27–30.

an editorial bombshell, which was published at Weatherford on September 13. According to Baylor, Colonel Johnson's regiment had been the "most *stupendous sell* ever practiced on a frontier people." By its failure, the regiment had brought reproach to the name of Texas Ranger and "emboldened our enemies by demonstrating that Rangers are *perfectly harmless.*" Although Baylor indulged in a great deal of mirth at the expense of old Colonel Johnson and his new wife, he also hinted that he and his adherents intended to hang any of the rangers unlucky enough to fall into their hands. Baylor's statements in the *White Man* were bad enough, but ranger prestige was further reduced by criticism from their own ranks. One of the returning men described an Indian raid in Palo Pinto County and sarcastically noted, "This is the way that Governor Houston protects the bleeding frontier."[35]

What Sul Ross thought of the activities of Johnson's regiment is not known. Apparently he was not proud of his first ranger company, for he does not seem to have mentioned it in later years.[36] Certainly the failure of the campaign and the adverse publicity connected with it did not win him public appreciation. Neither did it lessen his growing reputation as an Indian lover. As far as the frontier was concerned, Sul Ross still had to prove himself.

This exculpation would not come easily, for there were dark hints from the Baylor crowd that Sul's name stood at the head of the list of candidates who deserved to hang. Despite the threats of Baylor and his friends, Ross stopped off at the family ranch in Young County before starting back to Waco. He rejoined his company en route on August 31 and reached Waco the morning of September 7. Captain Shapley Ross mustered the men out of service by calling the roll. There was no other ceremony. Sul Ross's first ranger command was over.[37]

As the confidence and hope expressed by Governor Houston in the success of the Johnson expedition died in the derisive laughter of the *White Man*, the chief executive again turned his attention to the plight of the suffering frontier. Although no Indian depredations were being reported at the moment, the frontier counties had to be defended, and it was necessary for the government to get another mili-

[35] *White Man*, September 13, 1860; *Austin State Gazette*, September 29, 1860.

[36] Few, if any, authors of earlier accounts mention this episode in Ross's life. Generally, they begin his ranger career with the formation of his second company in the fall of 1860.

[37] Lang Diary, pp. 30–32; *White Man*, September 13, 1860.

tary force into the field as quickly as possible. Greatly mortified by the poor management exhibited by Colonel Johnson, Houston looked elsewhere for the necessary leadership ability.[38] He found it in Lawrence Sullivan Ross.

[38] Crane, *Sam Houston of Texas*, p. 633; Houston to Middleton T. Johnson, November 3, 1860, in Amelia W. Williams and Eugene C. Barker, eds., *The Writings of Sam Houston*, VIII, 176–77.

☆ 5 ☆

The Battle of Pease River

On September 11, 1860, Governor Sam Houston authorized Sul Ross to raise a company of sixty "mounted volunteers" for "service in the neighborhood of Belknap." His orders were to "guard the passes leading into the country, and should Indians get into the settlements" he was to "attack, and if possible destroy them."[1]

This new commission came as a surprise to Sul. Though unexpected, this reiteration of the executive's faith in his ability was welcome. Ross wrote his acceptance on September 18, acknowledging the honor so conferred upon him and promising to have the men "in the field ready for action" with the "least possible delay."[2]

As directed by Houston, Ross raised his company in Waco the first week in October and set off for Fort Belknap, arriving on October 17. Word of his coming had preceded him. On October 13, four hundred people met at the county seat of Palo Pinto for a barbecue honoring some local pro-Baylor volunteers. At that time the citizens passed a resolution requesting "Capt. Sull [sic] Ross to resign his captaincy and leave the frontier." Eighty signers affixed their names to this document.[3]

Disregarding these rumblings from Palo Pinto, Captain Ross set about establishing his post in compliance with the orders given him by Governor Houston. Morale was high; Ross hoped to rid the frontier of

[1] Amelia W. Williams and Eugene C. Barker, eds., *The Writings of Sam Houston*, VIII, 139–40.

[2] L. S. Ross to Houston, September 18, 1860, Governor's Papers, Sam Houston correspondence, Texas State Archives, Austin, Texas (hereafter cited as Governor's Papers).

[3] Benjamin Franklin Gholson Recollections, Barker Texas History Center, University of Texas at Austin (hereafter cited as Gholson Recollections), p. 24; William C. Crane, *Life and Select Literary Remains of Sam Houston of Texas*, p. 633; James H. Baker Diary, 1858–1918, pt. 1, Barker Texas History Center, University of Texas at Austin (hereafter cited as Baker Diary), pp. 80, 166.

Indians before the company's term of enlistment expired. As before, he faced an uphill battle to win the approval of the majority of the settlers, who were convinced that the old reserve Indians were doing the raiding. Since Ross was known to be a friend of the reserve Indians, the people had no confidence in him. Wrote one citizen of Palo Pinto, "I hope the Capt. may accomplish some good, but if he does it will be an agreeable surprise to the frontier people."[4]

While sustaining a vote of no confidence from the civilians he was sworn to protect, Sul Ross again turned his attention to the problems of command. He kept scouting parties in the saddle constantly, and when Indian raiders did manage to penetrate his thinly stretched line of defense, he led the pursuit himself.[5]

It was about this time that Ross began planning to "carry the war" to the Comanche homeland, but before he could do so he found himself floundering in a sea of paperwork demanded by the governor. For one thing, the economy-minded state government hesitated to grant Ross all the provisions and materiel he deemed necessary for the maintenance of his men on the frontier. Upon their arrival at Fort Belknap the rangers found little or none of the ammunition, rations, equipment, and transportation promised them. Meanwhile, in order to obtain these necessities the young captain had to prepare accounts and vouchers and defend his conduct to Governor Houston.[6]

Although Ross was seemingly wasting much of his time in the unending drudgery of desk work, he was gaining invaluable experience in the practical aspects of military command. He was also learning to deal skillfully and diplomatically with his superiors, retaining their good opinion while championing the rightful needs of his men. At the same time he was gaining practical wisdom in the handling of his fellow frontiersmen, at best unruly soldiers. In those days of little discipline, quick tempers, and ready weapons, a commander had to be willing to risk his life to retain the respect of his men. As a ranger officer, Ross won and held the loyalty of his troops, although at some danger to himself.[7]

[4]Gholson Recollections, p. 24; Baker Diary, pt. 1, p. 178.

[5]Ross to Houston, November 19, 1860, Governor's Papers.

[6]Elizabeth Ross Clarke, "Life of Sul Ross," Ross Family Papers, Texas Collection, Baylor University, Waco, Texas (hereafter cited as Ross Family Papers, Baylor), p. 56; Williams and Barker, eds., *Writings of Sam Houston*, VIII, 140, 166, 174–75, 216; Houston to Ross, November 2 and 19, 1860, Governor's Papers.

[7]Ross to Houston, November 21, 1860, Governor's Papers; "Recollections of H. B. Rogers," in Gholson Recollections, p. 72.

All of this, even the necessity of maintaining his authority in the face of force, would be useful to Ross in the future, but at the moment he probably wished for a little more action against the enemy. He and the rangers got all they could ask for when a new series of Indian raids began in late November.

Autumn was a time particularly dreaded by the settlers of northwest Texas, for with the brightly lit nights of the harvest moon came the fierce Comanche. The raiding season of fall, 1860, began with a scattering of horse-stealing raids; on October 27, Ross, his rangers, and other citizens—some one hundred men in all—were in hot pursuit of a band of Indian horse thieves. But this was only the tuning up for what rapidly developed into a full symphony of horror. Large raiding parties fell upon the settlers of Parker, Young, Palo Pinto, and Jack counties in the last days of November. Led by the redoubtable war chief Peta Nocona, the Comanches murdered, raped, robbed, and mutilated their way across these counties. The raid climaxed in the savage murder of pregnant Mrs. Sherman, who was raped, tortured, scalped, and left to die.[8]

News of the Sherman atrocity reached Palo Pinto on November 28; within two days a citizen noted that "trains of wagons, miles in length are leaving this country for more secure abodes." Although some families stampeded for the safety of less exposed settlements, others prepared to fight it out. The large number of raiding warriors meant that the Texans could not muster sufficient strength to check their incursions and still protect the women and children on the lonely ranches. At best those settlers remaining had to hold their ground and hope to overtake the raiders on their retreat. When it seemed the worst was over, volunteer companies began organizing; that from Palo Pinto formed as early as December 2 under the command of Captain Jack Cureton.[9]

News of these "most appalling outrages" reached Austin on December 6. Governor Houston immediately authorized the raising of two twenty-five-man companies to cooperate with Ross. At the same time he informed Ross of his action, repeated his confidence in the

[8] Baker Diary, pt. 1, p. 182; John M. Elkins, *Indian Fighting on the Texas Frontier*, p. 30; W. C. Cochran Reminiscences, 1850–69, Barker Texas History Center, University of Texas at Austin (hereafter cited as Cochran Reminiscences), p. 10; Kenneth F. Neighbours, *Indian Exodus: Texan Indian Affairs, 1835–1859*, p. 140. For a highly colored version of the Sherman episode see John Graves, *Goodbye to a River*, pp. 132–39.

[9] Baker Diary, pt. 1, pp. 191–92, 193–98.

young Waco officer, and expressed his hope to soon hear of Ross's success.[10]

Meanwhile Sul Ross had plans of his own, returning to his idea of striking at the Comanche camps that served as bases for raiding parties. Accordingly, he had been on a scout with thirty-two men when the Nocona raids occurred. The captain and his men returned to their base to find the stricken counties in chaos and the more courageous citizens arming for a retaliatory campaign. More important to his future plans, Ross learned that a local posse had traced the Indian raiders to their winter village on Pease River. Because the camp was a large one, harboring at least five hundred warriors besides women and children, the whites wisely turned back for assistance.[11]

Since it was Ross's determination "to curb the insolence of these implacable hereditary enemies of Texas," he made plans to "carry the war into their own homes." In the meantime he sought to augment his small force of rangers. The situation on the frontier meant he could only take forty of his sixty-man force; therefore, he appealed to Captain Nathan G. Evans, commanding U.S. troops at Camp Cooper, for help. Evans, who had befriended Ross during the Wichita village campaign, responded by sending the ranger officer a detachment of twenty-one men from the Second Cavalry.[12]

At the same time Cureton and some sixty-eight citizens were preparing for a similar campaign; they too felt the need to increase the size of their force. Some of the party therefore proposed asking Ross for assistance. This suggestion was resented by the majority, but eventually the minority view prevailed. Ross agreed to the union of forces, saying in later years that he welcomed the aid of these "self-sacrificing patriots."[13] What he did not know (or chose to ignore) was that a large

[10]Crane, *Sam Houston of Texas*, p. 633; Houston to Ross, December 6, 1860, Governor's Papers; Williams and Barker, eds., *Writings of Sam Houston*, VIII, 215–16; Houston to Thomas Stockton, December 6, 1860, Governor's Papers, p. 217; Houston to William C. Dalrymple, December 6, 1860, Governor's Papers, pp. 217–18; Houston to James Buckner Barry, December 6, 1860, Governor's Papers, p. 218.

[11]Ross to Houston, December 8, 1860, Governor's Papers. According to another source, Ross learned the location of the Comanche camp from friendly Indians at Fort Cobb, who sent him the information via government beef contractors (Gholson Recollections, p. 25).

[12]Ross's own account, in Clarke, "Life of Sul Ross," Ross Family Papers, Baylor, p. 56; Ross to Houston, December 8, 1860, Governor's Papers. Baker Diary, pt. 1, p. 202, says "23 Dragoons"; Gholson Recollections, p. 25, says twenty soldiers counting the sergeant.

[13]Elkins, *Indian Fighting*, pp. 31–32; James T. DeShields, *Cynthia Ann Parker:*

number of Cureton's patriotic citizens protested joining forces with an officer who had a reputation as an Indian lover.

It was late afternoon on December 11 before Sergeant John W. Spangler and twenty troopers arrived from Camp Cooper. The party rode out the next morning. Traveling with the forty rangers and twenty-one soldiers were the ranger surgeon; Antonio (Anton) Martínez, Ross's Mexican cook; and a buffalo hunter of mixed blood known variously as John Socie or Stuart. Stuart knew the Pease River country and felt he could lead Ross's party directly to the site of the Comanche camp. Martínez had been included because he had been a Comanche captive and knew the location of the water holes.[14]

Ross and his party joined Cureton's group on December 13, although the combined forces did not begin the march until the next morning. In the van rode the scouts, followed by Ross and his rangers and Spangler and his troopers, while the citizen volunteers brought up the rear. Although Cureton was much older than Ross, he recognized that the special orders the young captain held from Governor Houston gave him the right of supreme command. Displaying great tact in a potentially stressful situation, Ross counseled often with the older captain. There was at least a temporary truce between the ranger-regular party and the civilians.[15]

Cold was the weather and so was the trail, but thanks to Stuart and Martínez pursuit was possible. Led by the guides, the party headed northwest across rising mesquite prairies intersected by slashing ravines and littered with outcropping rocks. At times the Texans had to pick their way carefully—the first day out, they traveled only fifteen miles. Cold weather, bad water, and poor grass added to the discomfort of man and horse.[16]

Fresh Indian sign became plentiful as the troops rode forward on their jaded horses. As the pursuit continued, Cureton's men, not as

---

The Story of Her Capture, pp. 50–51. Ross's friendly relations with the army probably did not help his public image; many citizens were still bitter over the fact that U.S. troops had resisted their attempts to wipe out the Brazos Reserve Indians during the Reservation War of 1859.

[14] Gholson Recollections, pp. 25–26, 70; M. L. Crimmins, "First Sergeant John W. Spangler, Co. H., Second United States Cavalry," *West Texas Historical Association Yearbook* 26 (October, 1950): 68–76; Rupert N. Richardson, ed., "The Death of Nocona and the Recovery of Cynthia Ann Parker," *Southwestern Historical Quarterly* 46 (July, 1942): 18.

[15] Gholson Recollections, p. 26; Baker Diary, pt. 1, p. 203.

[16] Baker Diary, pt. 1, pp. 203–204.

well mounted as the rangers and the regulars, began to find it increasingly difficult to keep up. Heavy rain followed by a brisk norther further cooled the martial ardor of the citizens.[17]

Soon after the Texans had gone into camp late the afternoon of December 18, two of Ross's scouts returned with exciting news. Only a few miles ahead they had found signs that four Comanches had recently skinned a polecat and then ridden upriver. A man of action with that sense of good timing essential to a successful military commander, Ross prepared to break camp and follow. Before doing so, he conferred with Cureton. The civilian leader informed the ranger captain that his horses were so weakened by overuse and poor forage that he could not hope to ride on until morning. Ross decided to take up the trail again with the understanding that Cureton and his men would follow as soon as possible the next day.[18]

Ross's party rode on through the failing light. When the men joined the other scouts they learned that even fresher sign had been found, indicating that the Comanche camp lay still further upriver but within striking distance. Ross gave the order to ride on. Daybreak found the saddle-weary Texans approaching the Pease and its tributary, Mule Creek, through a long valley. Ahead of them loomed a chain of rough hills.[19]

Suspecting Comanches to be nearby, Ross scouted ahead. At one place he urged his mount up the slope of a nearby hill. On the crest, fresh prints of unshod hooves greeted his eyes. The Indian vedettes had just departed. More carefully now, but with his approach screened by blowing sand, Ross rode a mile further on to another high point. As he gained the rise, he found what he was searching for. Only two hundred yards away, at the base of the hill, a large Comanche hunting camp was spread out along the banks of Mule Creek.[20]

Effectively concealed by the norther blowing clouds of sand, Ross was able to study the arrangement of the camp and the nearby terrain without fear of discovery. His soldier's eye showed him how the little valley could be made into a trap. Then Ross saw something else: the dismantling of tepees and the packing of ponies told him the Coman-

[17] Ibid., pp. 206–208; Gholson Recollections, p. 26.

[18] Gholson Recollections, p. 27; Baker Diary, pt. 1, p. 208.

[19] Gholson Recollections, pp. 27–28; Richardson, ed., "Death of Nocona," p. 16.

[20] Ross's own account, in Clarke, "Life of Sul Ross," Ross Family Papers, Baylor, p. 57.

ches were breaking camp. As he watched, several squaws finished loading their packhorses and were preparing to depart with their husbands and children. The raiding party would have to act swiftly in order to catch the hostiles in the valley, for Ross knew his horses were too exhausted for a lengthy pursuit.[21]

Still screened by clouds of blowing sand, Ross signaled for his men to join him. When they did, he gave his orders: the guide would ride back after Cureton, and the sergeant and his men would circle around and close the line of retreat at the creek mouth while he led the rangers in a galloping charge down the ridge. He cautioned his men to be sure their weapons were ready and their saddle girths tight, then drew his own revolvers and spurred his mount down the slope. His rangers followed.[22]

The surprise thus planned was complete: the Comanches had no idea the enemy was near until the rangers topped the ridge and descended upon the disorganized camp, guns blazing. Many Comanches died "before they could prepare for defense." Others "fled precipitately right into the arms" of the sergeant and his cavalrymen.[23] Despite the element of surprise, however, the victory was not to be won without a fight. Several groups of Comanches had been riding westward away from the remaining tepees just as the rangers attacked. While the women and children galloped for safety, the warriors turned back. Under the direction of a chief wearing magnificent accouterments, these braves dismounted and, using their horses as breastworks, formed an irregular circle in front of the rangers. It was evidently their intention to hold back the whites until the others could escape.

Sul yelled for twelve of his best mounted men to ride west and close that route of escape before he turned his attention to directing the fighting at the circle. Warriors and horses fell under the Texans' deadly fire. Surrounded, the Comanches decided on desperate action. At a signal from their chief, they rose as one man, threw themselves on the nearest uninjured horses, and scattered.[24]

[21] Ibid.; Richardson, ed., "Death of Nocona," p. 16; Gholson Recollections, p. 28.

[22] Clarke, "Life of Sul Ross," Ross Family Papers, Baylor, p. 57; Gholson Recollections, pp. 28–29.

[23] Ross's own account, in Clarke, "Life of Sul Ross," Ross Family Papers, Baylor, p. 58.

[24] Ibid., pp. 59–60; Gholson Recollections, pp. 29–30; Richardson, ed., "Death of Nocona," pp. 17–18.

Ross, followed by his lieutenant, Tom Kelliher, galloped after a trio of fleeing Comanches, two of them riding double. The two Texans soon overhauled the single rider, and the captain was in the act of shooting when the Comanche reined in the horse and held up a child. Without another glance at the woman, Ross yelled to Kelliher to look after the squaw while he rode after the other two. From his costume, he knew one of the Comanches was the chief who had so ably directed the defense. Ross was determined to conquer this foe. The other, whose head was all that was visible above a buffalo robe, also appeared to be a man.[25]

Finally, Ross's swift horse carried him within range of the fleeing pair. He fired his six-shooter, killing the rear rider, who fell backwards, dragging the chief off the horse at the same time. It was only then Ross realized he had just killed a girl about the same age as his fifteen-year-old sweetheart.

There was no time for regrets, for the chief was on his feet and shooting arrows at the approaching horseman. Not wishing to repeat the Wichita village affair, Ross ducked low on his mount's neck. Then one arrow struck the ranger's horse, sending the animal into a frenzy of bucking. Other shafts flashed by too close for comfort. Ross held onto his saddle pommel with his left hand while snapping random shots at the warrior. One of these broke the Comanche's right arm, rendering his bow useless. As his angry horse quieted, Ross dismounted and shot the Comanche twice more, but still the chief did not fall. Instead, he "walked deliberately" to a small mesquite sapling, and leaning against it began to sing a "wild, weird" death chant.[26]

Just then Ross's Mexican servant, who could speak Comanche, came up with some of the rangers. Ross asked Martínez who the Indian was. Anton replied that he was Nocona. Ross then told the Mexican to tell the Comanche that if he would surrender he would not be shot any more, but the Indian "signalized his refusal with a savage attempt" to spear the ranger captain with his lance. Ross could only admire the chief's bravery and pity him, but by then Martínez was begging for permission to shoot Nocona, since his whole family had been massacred by this chief some years before. Reluctantly, Ross nodded, and

[25] Clarke, "Life of Sul Ross," Ross Family Papers, Baylor, p. 58.
[26] Ibid., pp. 58–59.

Martínez administered the coup de grâce. Only when his courageous foe was dead did Ross take the chief's buffalo horn headdress, shield, lance, bow, and gold ornaments as trophies.[27]

When Ross returned to the place where he had left Tom Kelliher and the woman, he found the lieutenant cursing wildly because he had almost injured his favorite horse running after an old woman. Ross turned his full attention for the first time to the woman. She was "very dirty and far from attractive in her scanty garments, as well as her person," but the moment he saw her blue eyes he knew she was not a Comanche. He gave orders for the woman and her child to be brought along.[28]

As the party rejoined the rest of the rangers and the troopers, the captain discovered a little Indian boy about nine years old hiding in the tall grass, expecting every moment to be killed by the white men who had raided his village. Ross took the little fellow up behind him on his horse and later carried him back to Waco, where "Pease," as he was called, became one of the family.[29]

Cureton's men rode in just as rangers and regulars returned to the Indian camp from their pursuit of the fleeing Comanches. Much to their chagrin, the volunteers arrived too late to have any part in the fighting or even in the scalping of the dead. When Cureton's men learned of the fight, they congratulated Ross and his men upon their good luck, especially since the victory had been won without one white casualty, not even a minor wound. Then, having expressed their con-

[27] Richardson, ed., "Death of Nocona," p. 19. For years a controversy has raged as to whether this chief was the real Nocona. Martínez, who had been Nocona's slave, identified the Indian as such and told the rangers how he had been captured and his parents murdered by Nocona in Mexico years before (Richardson, ed. "Death of Nocona," pp. 19–20). He also correctly identified the woman as Nocona's wife (Gholson Recollections, p. 34). However, Quanah Parker, the son of Nocona and Cynthia Ann Parker, always claimed that Nocona was not in camp at the time of the attack (see Frank X. Tolbert, *An Informal History of Texas: From Cabeza de Vaca to Temple Houston*, pp. 132–33).

[28] Clarke, "Life of Sul Ross," Ross Family Papers, Baylor, pp. 60–61. Charles Goodnight, who always (according to his own account) did things better, earlier, faster, or smarter than everyone else, claimed he was the first one to recognize the captured woman as white (J. Evetts Haley, *Charles Goodnight: Cowman and Plainsman*, p. 57).

[29] The Comanche lad remained with his adopted family, received a good education, and died a respected citizen of McLennan County (Clarke, "Life of Sul Ross," Ross Family Papers, Baylor, p. 61). Although he was given the choice of returning to his people, he always refused (Gholson Recollections, pp. 32–33). See also "Pease Ross," in Dayton Kelley, ed., *The Handbook of Waco and McLennan County*, p. 233.

gratulations, the citizens joined the rangers in plundering the Comanche camp and gathering up the spoils.[30]

This good feeling lasted only until the citizens had time to recall their previous animosity toward the rangers and the regulars and to think up new grievances. Then less generous members of Cureton's group began blaming Ross for pushing ahead. This sense of ill usage soon led them to whisper among themselves that Ross's men had appropriated all the captured Comanche horses for their own use and had misrepresented the number of hostiles they had killed.[31] When Ross announced that he was going to return to the settlements, Cureton's volunteers insisted on remaining behind. Doubtless many of the citizens were motivated by a sincere desire to follow up Ross's victory; some malcontents, however, appeared more concerned with discrediting, or at least rendering insignificant, the actions of the state and federal troops. Whatever their reasons for continuing in the field, the citizens were not successful in their quest, and the joint expedition ended, as it had begun, on a note of discord.

While the Texans celebrated their victory or brooded over their grievances, Ross and the more sober-minded members of the group tried to learn if any more Comanches were nearby. Both the woman and the boy told of a larger camp farther up the Pease. Not wishing for his command to fall victim to a surprise attack, Ross sent out scouts, who found the village, but it had been hastily abandoned.

That night the whites camped together on Mule Creek. The woman was fearful for her life, and it was only with difficulty that Ross and his companions convinced her that they meant her no harm. Still she continued in great distress. At last the Mexican interpreter succeeded in extracting the information that she feared for the lives of her two sons, Quanah and Pecos, who had been with her in the camp at the time of the ranger attack. The whites assured her that no boys had been killed, and thereafter she became more tractable.[32]

As the Texans gathered around the campfire that night, the main

[30] Elkins, *Indian Fighting*, p. 33; Baker Diary, pt. 1, p. 209. The apparent guilt of this particular band of Comanches was established when Ross's men found Mrs. Sherman's Bible in their camp (*Dallas Herald*, January 2, 1861).

[31] Baker Diary, pt. 1, pp. 209, 211–12. Evidently the citizens did not stop to consider the facts of the case: the Comanches were breaking camp when Ross attacked, and if the captain had waited for Cureton's men, the hostiles would have already departed.

[32] Gholson Recollections, pp. 31–32, 36; Clarke, "Life of Sul Ross," Ross Family Papers, Baylor, p. 61.

topic of conversation was the question of the woman's identity. Through Martínez, Ross questioned the sullen captive. She knew neither her name nor where she had come from, but upon further interrogation she was able to recall some circumstances surrounding her capture as a child. These facts generally coincided with what Ross knew about the massacre at Parker's Fort in 1836 and the capture of Cynthia Ann Parker.[33]

When the captain and his men returned to their post on Elm Creek, Ross sent the woman and her child to the wife of Captain Evans at Camp Cooper and dispatched a messenger to Isaac Parker. Colonel Parker went to Cooper to identify the woman, but she had forgotten her people as well as her mother tongue. Then Parker happened to mention that his niece's name had been Cynthia Ann. At that the blue eyes lit up, the woman slapped her chest and said, "Me Cincee Ann." The lost Cynthia Ann Parker was found after almost twenty-five years.[34]

The battle of Pease River won Sul Ross enduring fame. His aggressive tactics of carrying the war to the Comanche fireside (as it had long been carried to that of the white) ended charges of softness in dealing with the Indians. Texas and especially Waco rang with sincere if incorrect praise of the "gallant Waco Rangers" and their "brave young Commander" who had brought about the "entire extermination of the band that had perpetuated the more than savage barbarities." Except for Ross's most inveterate foes, most Texans would have agreed with the editorial suggestion of giving "all honor to the boys and their gallant Captain."[35]

Although Sul did not end Comanche hostilities as some historians claim, Indian raids did not reach their full force again until the Civil War had drained most able-bodied men from the frontier. Then the dread raiders struck again and again until 1875, when the last band, led

[33] Ross's own account, in Clarke, "Life of Sul Ross," Ross Family Papers, Baylor, p. 61; Gholson Recollections, pp. 33, 34, 36; *Dallas Herald*, January 2, 1861.

[34] Clarke, "Life of Sul Ross," Ross Family Papers, Baylor, pp. 61–62. For a more detailed consideration of Cynthia Ann's capture as a child, her life with the Indians, and her unhappiness after her return to the white world, see DeShields, *Cynthia Ann Parker*; and Paul I. Wellman, "Cynthia Ann Parker," *Chronicles of Oklahoma* 12 (June, 1934): 163–71.

[35] (Waco) *Southwest*, January 16, 1861. Commented one critic: "Ross got the honor of capturing Cynthia Ann Parker when Captain Jack Cureton should have had the honor and credit for the capture, as Cureton was the man that gathered the company of 95 men and started on the trail of the Indians. Ross joined him with only forty men after Cureton was several days on the trail" (Cochran Reminiscences, p. 11).

by Quanah Parker, son of Cynthia Ann, finally surrendered to reservation life.[36]

By that time, Sul Ross, no longer a soldier, was setting his feet on the lower rungs of the ladder of statesmanship that would eventually lead him to the highest elected office in the state. According to one contemporary, it was "this Pease River fight and the capture of Cynthia Ann Parker that made Sul Ross governor of Texas."[37] Praise from high state officials also helped to win the young ranger captain recognition and was invaluable in pursuing a political career later.

Governor Houston, to whom Ross had dispatched his report of the battle along with the trophies taken from the dead chief, expressed great satisfaction at the young captain's victory. However, the chief executive had more than praise for the young ranger captain: he had another job for Ross. Notifying the young man that he would be speaking in Waco on New Year's Day, Houston asked Ross to meet him there. When Sul did so, the governor proposed to give him another commission when his current one expired. He instructed Ross to disband his present company, give the men a chance to reenlist, and then recruit enough rangers to increase his company to eighty-three members. Written orders would follow shortly, the governor promised.[38]

These written orders, or rather Houston's failure to send them as promised, were to play a part in Ross's resignation from the rangers. According to one source written many years later, Ross declined Houston's offer in January and took immediate steps to free himself from the rangers because of his state's trend toward secession. Ross's actions and correspondence on the subject, however, do not support this argument. Although a Southerner with strong convictions supporting states' rights, Ross was no fire-eater. In this he followed the leadership of Houston himself, whom he greatly admired.[39] Like other moderate Southerners, Ross apparently adopted an attitude of wait-and-see.

[36] One such nineteenth-century account claimed that Ross and his men recovered more than eight hundred stolen horses (John Henry Brown, *Indian Wars and Pioneers of Texas*, p. 317).

[37] Cochran Reminiscences, p. 11.

[38] J. W. Wilbarger, *Indian Depredations in Texas*, p. 239; Gholson Recollections, pp. 40–41; Llerena Friend, *Sam Houston: The Great Designer*, p. 334; Clarke, "Life of Sul Ross," Ross Family Papers, Baylor, pp. 67–68; Ross to Houston, February 12, 1861, Governor's Papers.

[39] Gholson Recollections, p. 41; Clarke, "Life of Sul Ross," Ross Family Papers, Baylor, p. 75.

Meanwhile, in accordance with the governor's directions, he recruited twenty new men for his company and waited several days for the promised orders, but none came. At last he could wait no longer. Taking his recruits with him, the captain returned to his post in Young County.[40]

Since he was back at ranger field headquarters on January 14, 1861, it is not known if Ross voted in the election, held January 8, to select delegates for a secession convention. Perhaps, like Houston, he considered the election illegal, or perhaps Ross was waiting to see what the secession convention—and the executive—would do before determining his course of action. As the new year unfolded, disturbing news filtered into the frontier settlements from the state capital. Late in January the secession convention met and passed the Ordinance of Secession, which was to be presented to the voters on February 23, 1861. These stirring events demanded Sul's presence in Waco, and it was probably at this time that he determined to resign his commission and return home.[41]

Internal changes within the rangers helped him decide, for upon his return to Elm Creek, Ross had learned, much to his disquiet, that Captain William C. Dalrymple had been appointed colonel and aide-de-camp to Governor Houston and as such was commanding the rangers. Ross's experience, limited as it was, had taught him that such breaking of the chain of command lessened ranger effectiveness. Worse, however, was to follow. Ross was arranging the reorganization of his old company when Dalrymple arrived at the Elm Creek camp. The colonel, offended, professed to know nothing about Houston's verbal instructions to reorganize and apparently took Ross to task for disobeying orders. This misunderstanding, strengthened by the change in commander, provided Ross with an excuse to leave the rangers. He completed the reorganization of his company and returned to Waco with those of his men who did not choose to reenlist.[42]

On February 12 Ross wrote Governor Houston two letters. One

[40] Ross to Houston, February 12, 1861, Governor's Papers.

[41] James Buckner Barry, *A Texas Ranger and Frontiersman: The Days of Buck Barry in Texas, 1845–1906*, p. 125; C. W. Raines, ed., *Six Decades in Texas or Memoirs of Francis Richard Lubbock*, pp. 304–305; Dudley G. Wooten, ed., *A Comprehensive History of Texas, 1685–1897*, II, 86–88, 103–13; Friend, *Sam Houston*, pp. 330–37.

[42] Ross to Houston, February 12, 1861, Governor's Papers; William C. Dalrymple to Houston, February 15, 1861, Adjutant General Papers, Texas State Archives, Austin, Texas (hereafter cited as Adjutant General Papers).

merely reported the change of command to his successor; the other, somewhat aggrieved in tone, explained his reasons for resigning. Ross reminded the executive of the verbal orders he had received and touched briefly on his encounter with Dalrymple. He also balked at the idea of serving under Dalrymple, since he believed a ranger company could prove effective only as long as the captain was subject solely to the orders of the executive.[43]

Significantly, there is no mention in either letter of secession or the menace of approaching war. Perhaps the young soldier and the old statesman could no longer agree on the future role of the Lone Star State. Ross also may have wished to avoid a formal break with Houston over secession and used ranger affairs as an excuse to leave that branch of state service.

Houston received Ross's resignation on February 22. The governor immediately wrote Dalrymple, informing him of Ross's determination to quit the service, but added that he would not accept the resignation. He cleared the young captain of all blame in the misunderstanding between himself and the colonel. Houston then reminded Dalrymple that "the state of the Frontier demands good and efficient Officers and I find nothing in Capt. [sic] Ross to disapprove." So certain was Houston of Ross's return to duty that he gave Dalrymple specific orders to carry out when Ross returned.[44]

Next Houston turned his attention to persuading Ross to return to his command. He had, he said, always trusted Ross's "capacity as an officer" and his "deportment, as a soldier and a gentleman" had won his "entire approval." It was the governor's desire that Ross at once increase his "command to eighty-three, rank and file, and take the field again." In further recognition of Ross's services, Houston appointed him aide-de-camp with the rank of colonel. Perhaps the governor hoped in this way to keep Sul in Texas during the sectional strife then blazing into rebellion. An old campaigner, Houston likely guessed what horrors were in store for the harassed frontier counties once the hostile tribesmen were freed to begin their raids anew. But it was not to be. Sul Ross felt he owed his allegiance to his section as well as to his state. Support of the Southern states was, he felt, "the path of duty."[45]

[43] Ross to Houston, February 12, 1861, Governor's Papers.
[44] Houston to Dalrymple, February 22, 1861, Adjutant General Papers.
[45] Houston to Ross, February 23, 1861, quoted in Victor M. Rose, *Ross' Texas Brigade: Being a Narrative of Events Connected with Its Service in the Late War Between*

Adamant in his refusal to remain on the frontier while greater issues were at stake, Ross briefly returned to civilian life.[46] He enjoyed a few months free from the pressures of military service before enlisting in the Army of the Confederate States. During the next three years he rose from private to major, from major to colonel, and from colonel to brigadier general. The skill and habit of command of his Indian-fighting days were with him on battlefields from Arkansas to Georgia.

---

the States, pp. 161–62; Ross to Mrs. Ross, September 16, 1861, Ross Family Papers, Baylor.

[46] Ross to Victor M. Rose, October 5, 1880, Ross Family Papers, Baylor.

☆ 6 ☆

A Texan Rides to War

ON February 23, 1861, Texas voters went to the polls to ratify or reject the Ordinance of Secession. By the end of that day, 586 McLennan County citizens had cast their ballots in favor of secession, and only 191 voted against it. It is not known how Lawrence Sullivan Ross voted: perhaps by that time he had been convinced of the need for secession. Later he was to defend the crusade for Southern independence as the "cause of civic liberty and constitutional government." But whatever his thinking in February of 1861, Sul Ross was definitely interested in the outcome of the referendum.[1]

Politics notwithstanding, the former ranger captain was loyal to his state and section. Once the die was cast, he would throw in his lot with Texas whether as a sovereign republic or as a member of the Confederacy. His role was clear once the Lone Star State had declared itself out of the Union on March 2, 1861, and into the Confederacy three days later.[2]

As the secession drama on the Texas stage drew to its predictable conclusion, Ross turned to more personal matters. Bright eyes as well as politics engrossed his attention. These spring months of 1861, so crucial to Texas, were also of utmost importance to him, for they saw

---

[1] Marcus J. Wright, *Texas in the War, 1861–1865*, pp. 185, 199; Elizabeth Ross Clarke, "Life of Sul Ross," Ross Family Papers, Texas Collection, Baylor University, Waco, Texas (hereafter cited as Ross Family Papers, Baylor), p. 72. Apparently it was a point of honor, even with nonslaveholding Southerners, to resist Federal meddling in internal sectional affairs (see Richard M. Weaver, *The Southern Tradition at Bay: A History of Postbellum Thought*, p. 183).

[2] Clarke, "Life of Sul Ross," Ross Family Papers, Baylor, p. 75. A Texan first and a Confederate afterwards, Ross's loyalty to his section extended only so far. For example, by late September, 1861, he had made up his mind to resign his major's commission and return to Texas if Northern forces invaded the Lone Star State (Ross to Mrs. Ross, September 28, 1861, Ross Family Papers, Baylor).

the final wooing and winning of his beloved Lizzie Tinsley. Petite of figure, silvery of voice, and vivacious of manner, this charming Southern belle had the youth of Waco at her feet. Perhaps her face was a trifle too short and her chin too square for actual beauty, but her coloring was of the most envied Irish type—brunette hair and clear, fair complexion—while her large, luminous blue eyes could enthrall any male heart.[3]

Lizzie had been only eight when her wealthy physician-planter father, David Augustus Tinsley, moved from the old family plantation at Macon, Georgia, to Waco with his wife, children, slaves, and livestock. Purchasing forty acres roughly contiguous to the Ross farm as well as extensive acreage along the Brazos, Dr. Tinsley built a white-pillared, front-galleried mansion and settled down to raise cotton, corn, and thoroughbred horses. The young folk of Waco were always welcome at the hospitable planter's home, and there Sul Ross spent many happy hours in Lizzie's company. Their relationship matured through the years from boy-girl attachment to marital devotion, spanning a lifetime. By spring, 1861, Sul's long wait for his bride was almost over. May 28 was the chosen date for their wedding, but inevitably the demands of war intruded upon their happiness.[4]

When it was certain that war would result from secession, Confederate statesmen in Texas began warning of probable invasion from the north. State troops would be needed to resist this movement if and when it came. At the same time the Confederate government in Montgomery, Alabama, began to press Governor Edward Clark (who had replaced the contumacious Houston on March 16) to raise troops for Confederate service. At first the call for Confederate troops was for infantry, but mounted volunteers also prepared themselves for service.[5] Sometime during this period Peter F. Ross resigned his commission in

[3]Clarke, "Life of Sul Ross," Ross Family Papers, Baylor, p. 46; "Notes on Lawrence Sullivan Ross and Elizabeth Tinsley Ross," by Mrs. Peeler Williams, niece of Sul Ross, in her Family Scrapbook, private collection of Elizabeth Williams Estes, Lorena, Texas (hereafter cited as Family Scrapbook, Estes).

[4]Clarke, "Life of Sul Ross," Ross Family Papers, Baylor, pp. 44–45; Williams, "Notes," Family Scrapbook, Estes; Dayton Kelley, ed., *The Handbook of Waco and McLennan County*, p. 266; Marriage Records, McLennan County Courthouse, Waco, Texas, bk. 1, p. 32.

[5]William C. Nunn, ed., *Ten Texans in Gray*, pp. 26, 148; James M. Day, ed. and comp., *House Journal of the Ninth Legislature Regular Session of the State of Texas, November 4, 1861–January 14, 1862*, p. 25; E. B. Long, *The Civil War Day by Day: An Almanac, 1861–1865*, p. 60.

the state troops and returned to Waco to raise a company for war service. Among the privates who presented themselves for enlistment in Pete's company was his brother Sul.

Part of the anxiety in Texas over the Union preparations for invasion from Indian Territory stemmed from fear of what role the various tribes would play in such a venture. The hostile tribes like the Comanches, Kiowas, and Kickapoos would remain hostile; on the other hand, many members of the Five Civilized Tribes—Choctaws, Cherokees, Seminoles, Creeks, and Chickasaws—were slaveholders and hence disposed to be sympathetic toward the Confederate cause. The question uppermost in Texan minds was what to expect of the remnant tribes so recently and brutally expelled from the state.[6]

Sul Ross was also watching the frontier. He recognized the need to make treaties with all tribes in order to ensure the safety of the frontier and brought this need to the attention of Governor Clark. At the same time Earl Van Dorn, who had transferred his allegiance from the United States to the Confederacy and had traded his brevet major's rank and a company in the Second Cavalry for a colonel's stars and command of Texas, turned his attention to the problems of the frontier. He also urged the sending of a peace commission, especially to the reserve or remnant tribes at their reservation near Fort Cobb, and he suggested Sul Ross as the person best qualified to conduct the necessary negotiations. Colonel James E. Harrison of Waco added his support to the plan.[7]

Thus prompted, Clark wrote Ross on May 15, 1861, commissioning him to proceed immediately to Indian Territory to assure the reserve Indians of the "friendship and good will of Texas and the Confederate States." Clark reminded Ross that securing the "active cooperation or at least the friendly inactivity" of the reserve Indians was of "peculiar importance to us in the present crisis."[8]

---

[6]Long, *Civil War Day by Day*, p. 67; various letters to Governor Edward Clark, especially A. G. Walker, Birdville, Tarrant County, Texas, May 8, 1861, in Governor's Papers, correspondence, May–July, 1861, Texas State Archives, Austin, Texas (hereafter cited as Governor's Papers).

[7]Robert J. Hartje, *Van Dorn: The Life and Times of a Confederate General*, pp. 79–80; Edward Clark to L. S. Ross, May 15, 1861, executive documents, Governor's Papers; Victor M. Rose, *Ross' Texas Brigade: Being a Narrative of Events Connected with Its Service in the Late War Between the States*, p. 162. Harrison served as a Confederate commissioner to the Creeks and the Choctaws (Wright, *Texas in the War*, p. 81).

[8]Clark to Ross, May 15, 1861, executive documents, Governor's Papers.

Ross replied on May 23, 1861. He reminded Clark that the state government had failed to pay many of those same Indians for their services rendered as scouts for Colonel Johnson's regiment the summer before. Unless he was authorized to assure them "that there is a prospect of getting this pay, very soon," Ross warned, he could "not hope to meet with much success." He also stated that it would be necessary to guarantee the reserve Indians "ample protection" from their enemies, the Comanches. In the meantime, he planned to leave for Indian Territory on June 3.[9]

An unusual press of government business prevented Clark from replying until June 6, when he wrote Ross that those Indians who had served the state troops as scouts were entitled to their pay, but that they would have to wait until "the Treasury is in funds. At present it has none."[10]

Meanwhile, the long-awaited day had come for Sul to claim his bride. Little is known about the actual nuptials, although history records that the ceremony was performed at the Tinsley home by U. C. Spencer, the local Methodist minister. Following the general custom in the South at that time, the ceremony probably took place in the early evening and was followed by an elaborate supper. The next day it was customary for the entire bridal party to travel to the home of the groom for more feasting and entertainment. Usually the bridal week was spent visiting relatives and friends, although in Sul and Lizzie's case this pleasantry was cut short by the groom's departure on his mission for the state government.[11] Regretfully leaving his tearful bride with her parents, Ross set his face toward Indian Territory.

Upon his arrival at the Washita Agency, Ross found his journey to conciliate the remnant tribes had been unnecessary. Southern commissioners had already approached these tribes, and a preliminary treaty had been signed on May 15, 1861.[12] At first it appeared Ross had cut short his honeymoon for nothing. While at the agency, however,

[9] Various letters to Governor Clark, Governor's Papers.

[10] Various letters to Governor Clark, executive documents, Governor's Papers.

[11] Clarke, "Life of Sul Ross," Ross Family Papers, Baylor, p. 69; Marriage Records, McLennan County, bk. 1, p. 32; Everett Dick, *The Dixie Frontier: A Social History of the Southern Frontier from the First Transmontane Beginnings to the Civil War*, pp. 136–37; *Waco Tribune-Herald*, October 30, 1949. It is interesting to note that Sul was marrying into plantation society, as his father had done.

[12] Considering the depleted condition of the state treasury at that time, this early action by the Confederacy was for the best (William W. Newcomb, Jr., *The Indians of*

he learned from a white trader named Shirley that the "wild" (non-Penateka) Comanches had expressed a desire to come to an agreement with the hated *tejanos*. Their people would be at a designated point on Red River until the end of July, the Comanche chiefs told Shirley, and asked that they be met there by an agent from Texas authorized to treat with them.[13]

Ross realized that if the Comanches could be persuaded to refrain from raiding Texas settlements, troops needed for protection of the frontier could be used elsewhere. He returned to Texas, visited Austin, and laid his argument before Governor Clark. As before, the plethora of government business claimed the executive's attention, and Ross went back to Waco without having accomplished his mission. It was July 17 before he heard from Clark, who stated his determination to adopt and carry out Ross's suggestions regarding the Comanches. The governor asked if there was still time to meet with the hostiles and, if so, whether Ross would undertake the mission.[14]

Shirley, Ross replied, had informed the Comanches that it would be impossible for a commissioner from Texas to meet them so soon and had asked them to remain in the area until their request could be passed along to the state authorities. The young Texan was optimistic about his chances of arranging a permanent treaty, but he reminded Clark that for the successful accomplishment of his mission he would need authority to draw on either state or Confederate funds. Similarly, he suggested that the governor notify the Confederate secretary of war of their plans and secure the secretary's approval and assistance in order "to prevent a conflict of appointments as before."[15]

This time Clark sent Ross the necessary credentials. Again Sul left Lizzie's side to ride north on behalf of Texas. Upon his arrival in Gainesville, Ross learned that Indian Commissioner Albert Pike was en route to the Washita Agency on a similar mission for the Confederacy. Believing it best that Texas stay in the background and allow the Confed-

---

Texas, from Prehistoric to Modern Times, p. 258; Captain James J. Diamond to Colonel W. C. Young, July 3, 1861, Governor's Papers).

[13] Ross to Victor M. Rose, October 5, 1880, Ross Family Papers, Baylor; Ross to Clark, July 17, 1861, Governor's Papers.

[14] Ross to Rose, October 5, 1880, Ross Family Papers, Baylor; Clark to Ross, July 13, 1861, executive documents, Governor's Papers.

[15] Ross to Clark, July 17, 1861, Governor's Papers.

erate government "to assume the responsibility and expense," Ross turned back without announcing the purpose of his mission.[16]

Following his return to Waco, Ross had a few days with Lizzie before again taking up the duties of a soldier. Toward the middle of August, Pete Ross's company answered the call of Colonel B. Warren Stone of Dallas for a cavalry regiment to serve in Missouri with General Ben McCulloch. Time had come at last for Private Ross to say farewell to domestic tranquillity and to embark upon what would prove to be the most arduous, danger-filled four years of his life. Leaving his wife with her parents, he rode to the rendezvous point with the Waco company.[17]

In his devotion to what he construed as duty, Sul Ross was like so many thousands of other young soldiers, both Northern and Southern, hastening to war during the spring and summer of 1861. As far as experience was concerned, he was better prepared than most for the hardships of campaigning and the horrors of combat.[18] Despite this experience, however, he exhibited the same naiveté shown by so many others in thinking the conflict would be short.[19]

When the Waco company reached Dallas, Ross learned that it would be more than a week before the mustering officer could arrive from San Antonio. Obtaining leave from his obliging brother, Sul slipped back to Waco to spend a few last bittersweet days with his "dear Lizzie." He returned to camp on September 1 to find his name being "actively canvassed" for the position of major. He consented to "run the race through."[20]

[16] Ross to Rose, October 5, 1880, Ross Family Papers, Baylor. Pike signed a treaty with the "wild" tribes in the Leased District, Indian Territory, on August 12, 1861 (Annie Heloise Abel, *The American Indian as Slaveholder and Secessionist: An Omitted Chapter in the Diplomatic History of the Southern Confederacy*, p. 200).

[17] *Dallas Herald*, August 14, 1861; Clarke, "Life of Sul Ross," Ross Family Papers, Baylor, p. 69. For a general discussion of the recruitment and use of Texas cavalry, see Stephen B. Oates, *Confederate Cavalry West of the River* (Austin: University of Texas Press, 1961).

[18] See William Clyde Billingsley, ed., "'Such Is War': The Confederate Memoirs of Newton Asbury Keen," pt. 1, *Texas Military History* 6 (Winter, 1967): 242–46.

[19] Ross to Mrs. Ross, September 7, 1861, Ross Family Papers, Baylor.

[20] *Dallas Herald*, August 21 and 28, September 4, 1861; Ross to Mrs. Ross, September 1, 1861, Ross Family Papers, Baylor. Ross's Civil War correspondence began with this letter of September 1, 1861, and continued until January 12, 1865. In all there are fifty-four letters.

With the arrival of the mustering officer, the ten companies that were to form what was then known as Stone's regiment and only later designated as the Sixth Texas Cavalry set about organizing and mustering into service. The Waco company organized as G Company on September 7, the men enlisting for twelve months.[21] When formed, the regiment, which drew men from the counties of Bell, Cherokee, Collin, Dallas, Grayson, Henderson, Kaufman, McLennan, Rusk, Tarrant, and Van Zandt, boasted a total of eleven hundred fifty members.[22] This process, along with drills, parades, and visits by local women, reporters, and distinguished civilians, occupied the men through September 12.

Meanwhile Ross continued his campaign for major, probably assisted by the glowing account of his Indian-fighting career then appearing in the *Dallas Herald*.[23] At the same time, he was getting acquainted with Colonel Stone. His first impression was of a man in every way "worthy & competent" to fill the position of regimental commander. On September 13, when the men balloted on their regimental officers, Ross easily defeated his two opponents for the office of major by a margin of three to one. Indeed, he had reason to feel proud of his success, for one of his opponents had been a grayheaded Mexican war veteran of some prominence in the Dallas area.[24]

When the regiment took up the line of march on September 16, Major Ross commanded the advance division of three companies.

<hr/>

[21] *Dallas Herald*, September 11, 1861. The muster-in roll lists Private Lawrence Sullivan Ross, age twenty-three, as enrolled on that date. His horse, which he was to furnish with the understanding that the government would reimburse him for its loss, was valued at $150 and his equipment, including a double-barreled shotgun and a six-shooter, at $50 (Unpublished Muster Rolls, Sixth Texas Cavalry, General Services Administration, National Archives, Washington, D.C. [hereafter cited as GSA, NA]).

[22] Rose, *Ross' Texas Brigade*, p. 36; *Dallas Herald*, August 28 and September 4, 1861.

[23] According to the *Dallas Herald*, September 11, 1861, there were "no better soldiers of their age in Texas than Pete and Sul Ross."

[24] Ross to Mrs. Ross, September 7, 1861, Ross Family Papers, Baylor; Ross to David Augustus Tinsley, September 13, 1861, Ross Family Papers, Baylor. Ross made more of an impression on his comrades than he realized. Noted one soldier, "I with others was introduced to L. S. Ross before this election & was very favorable [*sic*] impressed with the fine looking L. S. Ross" (L. H. Graves Diary, May 1, 1861–April 1, 1864, McLean Collection, Arlington, Texas [hereafter cited as Graves Diary], p. 26). Photocopy of typescript prepared by Margaret Stoner McLean from the originals loaned by the late Kathryn Stoner O'Connor, Victoria, Texas.

Colonel Stone and Lieutenant Colonel John S. Griffith each followed with a similar contingent. Almost immediately an incident occurred, which, for the time, cooled Ross's military ardor. A member of the Methodist Church, which opposed dram-drinking, Sul experienced great "surprise and mortification" when he reported to Stone and found his commanding officer "too drunk to be capable of transacting any business whatever." Far worse, however, was that Stone had become drunk with the men under his command. Ross knew the colonel consequently could not "hope to command the respect or receive the proper obedience to his authority" from those same men in the future.[25]

Despite his fears that the regiment would "not achieve many gallant victories," the young major assumed the burdensome responsibility of preparing the men for the next day's march. Once the command was fairly on the road, Sul's equanimity returned. As the pangs of homesickness lessened, his natural fighting spirit and love of action flamed up. News from Missouri was cheering: the Texans optimistically hoped to winter in Saint Louis. The rumor of a possible Confederate invasion of Kansas further raised his spirits, and the pleasures and problems of command soon demanded his full attention.[26]

These problems were manifold; the lack of supplies was the most serious. For some time the shortage of supplies had reduced the men of Stone's regiment to rations of poor beef and flour so wormy that it had to be sifted before use. Besides the shortage of food, ammunition was almost completely lacking. At one time the regiment had scarcely enough to load the weapons of the guard—while rumors hinted of coming trouble with the tribes in Indian Territory still loyal to the Union.[27]

Stone's regiment finally arrived at McCulloch's headquarters near Maysville, Arkansas, around the middle of October. There the Texans found reports that McCulloch was preparing to carry the war into Kansas, that den of Jayhawkers (antislavery guerrillas) and horse thieves. Like many other Texans of his time, Ross considered Kansas a breeding ground for much of the sectional trouble. He anticipated "a great deal of sport" in the coming campaign and hoped that McCulloch's

[25] Ross to Mrs. Ross, September 16, 1861, Ross Family Papers, Baylor.

[26] Ibid., September 28, 1861, Ross Family Papers, Baylor.

[27] Ibid., October 5, 1861, and Ross to D. A. Tinsley, October 4, 1861, both in Ross Family Papers, Baylor.

Confederates would keep the Jayhawkers so busy defending their own homes that "they will not find time to plunder others."[28]

Before the Confederates could move against the Kansas Jayhawkers, word came of the retreat of General Sterling Price and his army from Lexington, Missouri. Union General John C. Frémont and thirty thousand troops were rumored to be in pursuit of the retreating Southerners. McCulloch put himself at the head of a force of cavalry that included Stone's regiment and pushed toward Carthage, Missouri. There the Confederates met Price's force, but Frémont had dropped behind, and his position could not be located with any accuracy.[29]

McCulloch wanted accurate information about the enemy and he wanted it quickly. A former Texas Ranger, he knew where to look among his troops for men of suitable skill and daring. Sul Ross was the man he chose for command of his scouting force, for, as the general told the former ranger, he knew from Ross's history in Texas that Ross "would find Frémont's army if they were still upon Missouri soil." But when time came for the scout, Ross was detained on duty in the rear of the army, and neither he nor the Sixth had any part in the skirmish that followed. It is hard to say whose disappointment was greatest— that of the young major, who was to have commanded the scouting party, or that of Stone's men, who were "all over a fire" for a chance to get at the Yankees.[30]

Stifling his disappointment, Ross waited with his men in Neosho, Missouri. Events there soon gave him something else to think about. For one thing, Ross was present when the secessionist members of the Missouri legislature, meeting in extralegal session, voted that state out of the Union. For another, the arrival of nearly nude Missouri troops made him appreciate Texas' generosity in supplying its soldiers.[31]

A man of genial good humor, Ross never let his mind linger long on unpleasant circumstances over which he had no control. Neverthe-

---

[28] Ross to Mrs. Ross, October 14, 1861, Ross Family Papers, Baylor; Rose, *Ross' Texas Brigade*, p. 37.

[29] Ross to Mrs. Ross, October 28, 1861, Ross Family Papers, Baylor; Rose, *Ross' Texas Brigade*, p. 38; Franz Sigel, "The Pea Ridge Campaign," in *Battles and Leaders of the Civil War*, ed. Robert Underwood Johnson and Clarence Clough Buel, I, 314; Albert Castel, *General Sterling Price and the Civil War in the West*, pp. 57–58.

[30] Ross to Mrs. Ross, October 28, 1861, Ross Family Papers, Baylor; Max S. Lale and Hobart Key, Jr., eds., *The Civil War Letters of David R. Garrett Detailing the Adventures of the 6th Texas Cavalry, 1861–1865*, p. 34.

[31] Ross to Mrs. Ross, October 28, 1861, Ross Family Papers, Baylor.

less, he was enough of a realist to deplore the want of harmony evident between Generals Price and McCulloch, whose "petty quarrels and jealousies" prevented them from active cooperation.[32] This lack of co-ordination was nowhere more evident than in the Confederate intelligence system. It was not known if Frémont had crossed the Osage River on his advance from Saint Louis; neither was there any information as to the size of his force. Price demanded that McCulloch join him in a concerted attack on the Union army, while the Texan refused to do so without more information. In order to gain this information, McCulloch again ordered Major Ross on a scout, but this time the general saw to it that the former ranger was unhampered by any other duty.

The general's confidence was not misplaced. Twice during the first two weeks of November the young major led scouting parties near Springfield. Each time Ross succeeded in slipping within the Union lines, gathering much valuable information, and getting his force out again before Federal troops sent to capture him could close their trap. These scouting expeditions were the making of his reputation in both armies.[33]

All the information acquired by Major Ross on this reconnaissance mission had indicated that Federal forces in Springfield under General David Hunter, Frémont's successor, were only waiting for orders to move south. This he reported to McCulloch. That officer and Price, however, were still trying to agree on where their forces should engage the advancing foe. Price wished to attack the enemy while still in Missouri, lest his troops refuse to fight outside the state. More cautious or less optimistic than Price, McCulloch wanted to await the Yankees' coming in the strategically advantageous Boston Mountains area of northern Arkansas. As things turned out, McCulloch did not get a chance to test the strength of the defensive position he had chosen; Hunter hastily retreated toward Saint Louis on November 9.[34]

By then winter was closing in; mid-October brought weather cold enough for Ross's taste. Clothing and boots of many of the Texans were wearing out and forage for their horses was becoming scarce. While

[32] Ibid.
[33] Clarke, "Life of Sul Ross," pp. 80–83, and Ross to Mrs. Ross, November 5, 1861, both in Ross Family Papers, Baylor; Castel, *General Sterling Price*, p. 60.
[34] Castel, *General Sterling Price*, pp. 59–60; Sigel, "The Pea Ridge Campaign," I, 314.

Price's troops reoccupied Springfield, McCulloch ordered his troops
back to the Arkansas River, where suitable shelters were erected for
men and horses. Arrangements were also made to furlough four men in
every company and an appropriate number of officers. On November
26, 1861, Ross obtained a sixty-day leave of absence. He left almost
immediately for Texas.[35]

When Ross rejoined his regiment in early 1862, he found the military situation rapidly changing. Revitalized Union troops under the
command of General Samuel R. Curtis were again pushing toward
Springfield, causing Price to abandon the city and fall back to join Mc-
Culloch in Arkansas. By February 18, the bluecoats, some twelve thousand strong, had reached Sugar Creek, a small stream in northwestern
Arkansas near a rise in the ground known as Pea Ridge. Nearby stood a
tavern and Butterfield Stage station decorated with elk horns. Meanwhile, Price joined McCulloch in the Boston Mountains region to the
southwest of Elkhorn Tavern.[36] Cooperating at last, the Confederate
commanders sought a chance to drive the enemy back into Missouri.
One thing was obvious—Federal supply lines were greatly extended.
This was an irresistible temptation to enterprising cavalry commanders. Late in February McCulloch unleashed Sul Ross and more than
five hundred troopers on a raid behind enemy lines. Ross was to recon-
noiter, destroy supply trains, and otherwise harass the Federal rear.
He and his men performed their assigned task admirably.

Swinging wide to the east of Curtis's army, Ross's cavalrymen
(Texas Rangers, the enemy persisted in calling them) thundered north
and west into Missouri and swooped down on the Federal rear. Near
Keetsville, seventy miles behind enemy lines, Ross's men raided a
Union supply train. Although the Confederate raiders narrowly missed
capturing two Northern generals, the rebels did net eleven other prisoners, liberated over sixty horses and mules for Confederate service,
and destroyed several wagonloads of commissary supplies.[37]

        [35]Ross to D. A. Tinsley, October 15, 1861, and Ross to Mrs. Ross, October 14,
1861, both in Ross Family Papers, Baylor; Rose, *Ross' Texas Brigade*, pp. 40–41; Billingsley, ed., "'Such Is War,'" pt. 1, pp. 243–44; Samuel B. Barron, *The Lone Star Defenders: A Chronicle of the Third Texas Cavalry, Ross' Brigade*, p. 62; Graves Diary,
p. 40; Field and Staff Muster Roll, Sixth Texas Cavalry, November and December, 1861,
Military Service Record for L. S. Ross, from Unpublished Muster Rolls, GSA, NA.
        [36]Hartje, *Van Dorn*, p. 112; Sigel, "The Pea Ridge Campaign," I, 314–17.
        [37]Billingsley, ed., "'Such Is War,'" pt. 1, pp. 247–48; Ross to Mrs. Ross, March 1,
1862, Ross Family Papers, Baylor.

This raid further enhanced Ross's growing reputation. In the official report of the action, Colonel Stone waxed eloquent in praise of his young subordinate, saying he could not "too highly estimate the chivalry and gallantry of this intrepid, daring knight, nor too highly appreciate the prudence and administrative ability of this officer."[38]

Hardly had Major Ross recovered from the fatigue resulting from this raid when the Confederate Army received its marching orders. Major General Earl Van Dorn had assumed command of Price's and McCulloch's combined forces on March 3, 1862. He was confident that his sixteen thousand troops—mixed infantry, artillery, and cavalry, including one thousand assorted Confederate Indians under the command of General Albert Pike—could surprise and easily crumple the extended Federal line.[39]

During the two-day march to the Yankee encampment on Sugar Creek, severe weather and lack of supplies sapped the strength of the advancing Confederates. It did not help that Van Dorn, by training a cavalry officer, consistently overmarched his infantry. Even Stone's troopers were worn down by exposure and weakened by the lack of food.[40]

Just as the famished, weary Texans were preparing to eat the dry corn and turnips they had been able to forage, General McCulloch appeared at regimental headquarters on the night of March 6. It was the intention of the commanding general to send McIntosh with Stone's and Elkanah Greer's Texas cavalry regiments around the rear of the enemy to block Curtis's escape route and cut his supply lines. Raiding was what the Texans did best, and they started promptly at the designated hour, but about half a mile down the road the order was countermanded.[41]

Van Dorn had decided to execute a flanking movement, planning to pass with Price and McCulloch and their troops around Pea Ridge by the Bentonville-Keetsville Detour Road and attack Curtis's army from the rear. In this way the Confederates would avoid making a

[38] U.S. War Department, *The War of the Rebellion: A Compilation of the Official Records of the Union and Confederate Armies*, ser. 1, VIII, 302.

[39] Sigel, "The Pea Ridge Campaign," I, 319, 334, 337; Hartje, *Van Dorn*, pp. 120–23.

[40] Hartje, *Van Dorn*, p. 127; Ross to D. A. Tinsley, March 13, 1862, Ross Family Papers, Baylor; Barron, *Lone Star Defenders*, pp. 67, 77.

[41] Ross to D. A. Tinsley, March 13, 1862, Ross Family Papers, Baylor.

frontal assault on the strong Federal entrenchment along Sugar Creek.[42]

Stone's regiment received orders to march at 8:00 A.M. As the Texans rode to the detour, Major Ross was shocked to see the Confederate infantry in squads of fifties and sixties lying on the roadside "overcome with hunger and fatigue." It was then his spirits began to fail, and he feared the result of an engagement with a well-organized, strongly posted enemy while "those men upon which the commanders rely most" were too exhausted to reach the battlefield.[43]

The young major had good reason to fear the coming engagement. Van Dorn's strategy was detected, allowing Curtis time to swing his army around. Also, the flanking movement took more time than had been expected. At dawn on March 7, McCulloch's troops were just entering the detour. Some five miles of rough road still separated them from Price's Missourians. Thus it was when the battle opened before noon, the Confederates found themselves fighting on two widely separated fronts.[44]

To add to Confederate difficulties, the Union commander sent Colonel Peter Osterhaus with a force of cavalry, infantry, and artillery to engage McCulloch before he could reach Price. Osterhaus was forming his troops northwest of Leetown, the only settlement in the Pea Ridge area, when the Federal movement was detected by McCulloch's scouts. Led by their brigadier, the five cavalry regiments left the road and swung southeast to face this new enemy threat. Formed in columns of four, the horsemen began their advance through a heavily wooded area toward Leetown to the accompaniment of distant artillery fire.[45]

As the front ranks emerged from the timber, the rebel cavalrymen found the enemy on their right flank. A three-gun battery was placed behind a rail fence while a bluecoat cavalry regiment waited in support. With a "rumbling noise like the heavens had split open," the Federal battery opened fire.[46]

[42] Ibid.; Sigel, "The Pea Ridge Campaign," I, 320–22; Hartje, Van Dorn, pp. 133, 144.

[43] Ross to D. A. Tinsley, March 13, 1862, Ross Family Papers, Baylor.

[44] Billingsley, ed., "'Such Is War,'" pt. 1, p. 250; Hartje, Van Dorn, p. 144.

[45] Hartje, Van Dorn, pp. 140–41; Sigel, "The Pea Ridge Campaign," I, 321; U.S. War Department, Official Records, ser. 1, VIII, 303; Barron, Lone Star Defenders, p. 67.

[46] U.S. War Department, Official Records, ser. 1, VIII, 301; Barron, Lone Star Defenders, p. 68; Billingsley, ed., "'Such Is War,'" pt. 1, p. 250.

The next instant the impetuous McIntosh led his troops against the line of enemy pieces with their supporting cavalry. Major Ross was in command of the Sixth's first battalion in this charge. The Iowa cavalrymen bravely rode forward to counter this wave of yelling, whooping gray troopers, but they were brushed aside as the Confederates raced on to jump their horses over the fence and overrun the battery.[47]

Ross halted at the guns long enough to accept the surrender of the officer in charge, and then he and his men "put right in after" the Yankee cavalry. The chase was an exhilarating one—on the Texans galloped, firing into the ranks of the retreating enemy until the fleeing bluecoats led their pursuers within musket shot of massed Union infantry with supportive artillery. Then it was the turn of Ross and his men to "advance backwards." The gallant major did not gallop from the field when "shell, round shot, and grape shot came whizzing in terrific peals" toward him, but he admitted to walking his horse "very fast" until out of range.[48]

As the fighting became general near Leetown, the other cavalry regiments were dismounted to support the infantry. Only the Sixth remained on horseback in the reserve. Although the men of Stone's regiment were exposed to enemy fire as the battle lines wavered back and forth that March afternoon, they took no other part in the fighting.[49]

Shortly after the Sixth reformed following the charge on the battery, McCulloch and then McIntosh were killed. Colonel Stone sent Ross to bear the news to Van Dorn and to request new orders. Again the major's frontier training served him well as he made his way around the opposing armies to Van Dorn's position near Elkhorn Tavern. Ross obtained the commander's orders for the next day, then rode through the night to deliver them to Colonel Greer of the Third Texas Cavalry, who had succeeded to command of the western wing. It was the next morning before the weary young officer rejoined his regiment.[50]

With the deaths of McCulloch and McIntosh, the Confederate attack on the west fell apart. Although Van Dorn impetuously renewed his assault on the eastern side of the ridge the morning of March 8, the

[47] Ross to D. A. Tinsley, March 13, 1862, Ross Family Papers, Baylor; Barron, *Lone Star Defenders*, p. 68.

[48] Ross to D. A. Tinsley, March 13, 1862, Ross Family Papers, Baylor.

[49] U.S. War Department, *Official Records*, ser. 1, VIII, 303; Graves Diary, p. 68.

[50] U.S. War Department, *Official Records*, ser. 1, VIII, 303; Ross to D. A. Tinsley, March 13, 1862, Ross Family Papers, Baylor.

battle was lost.[51] Recalling the engagement several days later in a letter to his father-in-law, Ross placed the blame for the defeat on Van Dorn. Not only had the time and place for the battle been wrong—the major noted ironically that the defeat at Federal hands came at the "very position Gen McCulloch had selected last fall"—but the Mississippian had been guilty of mismanagement. The general had overmarched and underfed his troops before the struggle, and he had also neglected to inform his subordinates (other than McCulloch and McIntosh) of his plan of attack. "We whipped ourselves," Ross asserted.[52]

Van Dorn's failure to secure a victory at Pea Ridge (or Elkhorn Tavern, as the Confederates called it) made it impossible for Southern troops to try to hold Missouri any longer. The Confederates retreated deeper into Arkansas. Later that same month, Van Dorn received orders to bring his troops across the Mississippi to aid the army of General Albert Sidney Johnston, then in retreat following the loss of Forts Henry and Donelson.[53]

In early April the twelve-month cavalry regiments, including Stone's, were sent to Des Arc, Arkansas. Because of the scarcity of forage, these troops were dismounted and their horses sent back to Texas. This was not accomplished without some protest by the men, who regarded the action as a flagrant "breach of faith."[54]

From Des Arc the dismounted and disgruntled cavalrymen were forwarded to Memphis, Tennessee, by steamboat. Arriving with his regiment some two weeks after the battle of Shiloh, Ross found the city filled with the wounded from that encounter. He noted approvingly

[51] It was from lack of food that the defeated rebels suffered most. Barron witnessed the shooting of a hog; starving men hacked apart the carcass and marched on eating the "raw bloody pork without bread or salt" (*Lone Star Defenders*, p. 73).

[52] Ross to D. A. Tinsley, March 13, 1862, Ross Family Papers, Baylor. For a capsule account of the battle, see D. Alexander Brown, "Pea Ridge," *Civil War Times Illustrated* 6 (October, 1967): 4–11, 46–48. The Sixth's losses were light: Colonel Stone reported only nineteen men killed, wounded, or missing (U.S. War Department, *Official Records*, ser. 1, VIII, 304).

[53] Thomas L. Snead, "The First Year of the War in Missouri," in Johnson and Buel, eds., *Battles and Leaders*, I, 227.

[54] Rose, *Ross' Texas Brigade*, pp. 63–64. After all, at this time "no Texan walks a yard if he can help it" (James Arthur Lyon Fremantle, *The Fremantle Diary, Being the Journal of Lieutenant Colonel James Arthur Lyon Fremantle, Coldstream Guards, on His Three Months in the Southern States*, ed. Walter Lord [Boston: Little, Brown, 1954], p. 58; Albert H. Allen, ed., *Arkansas Imprints, 1821–1876*, p. 202).

that the women of the city devoted their time to nursing the sufferers and cautioned Lizzie for his sake to try to do the same.[55]

It was also while the Sixth was camped at Memphis that news reached the troops of the passage by the Confederate Congress of the Conscription Act of April 16, 1862. This law provided, among other things, for a three-year extension of the terms of service for the troops under arms. It also allowed for the reorganization of companies, battalions, and regiments with the return of old officers or the election of new ones.[56]

With the passage of the Conscription Act of April, 1862, Sul Ross's first term of service as a Confederate soldier ended. He had won considerable fame as scout and raider and would soon win more acclaim as field commander. He and his men would serve on foot throughout the momentous spring, summer, and early fall of 1862, winning fresh laurels on new battlefields as infantry riflemen. Not until mid-October would the men of the Sixth Texas be reunited with their horses, and by then Major Ross would be the respected and popular colonel of the regiment.

[55] Ross to Mrs. Ross, April 22, 1862, Ross Family Papers, Baylor.
[56] Wilfred Buck Yearns, *The Confederate Congress*, p. 65.

☆ 7 ☆

Colonel of the Sixth

In the eyes of the men of the Sixth Texas Cavalry, the Conscription Act of 1862 had one virtue at least—it gave them Sul Ross as their regimental commander in place of Colonel Stone. Seeking an appointment to brigadier general under the provisions of the act, Stone had left his regiment in Memphis and hastened to Richmond. Since he did not expect failure, he declined to campaign for reelection for colonel and thus left the field open for Ross.

Stone's action pleased the men of the Sixth, who demanded that Major Ross seek regimental command. Although Sul could have easily defeated the other contender, Lieutenant Colonel John S. Griffith, he did not wish to best his friend, who earnestly desired the position. Ross also shrank from the responsibility inherent in the position. But despite the fact that he told his men he "did not want the position and would not have it," the Texans stubbornly maintained they would elect him over his protest.[1]

The question of regimental command was still at a stalemate when the Sixth received orders to proceed to Corinth, Mississippi, to join the army commanded by General Pierre G. T. Beauregard. His army had retreated there the second week in April. Since Beauregard desired reinforcements as quickly as possible, the rebel high command decided to send the Texans and other troops from Van Dorn's army to Corinth by rail.

So overburdened was the Memphis and Charleston Railroad by the exigencies of transporting so many men at once that when the hour came for the Sixth to leave for Corinth, only flatcars were available. Many of the Texans had their first experience of railway travel when

---

[1] Ross to Mrs. Ross, April 22, 1862, Ross Family Papers, Texas Collection, Baylor University, Waco, Texas (hereafter cited as Ross Family Papers, Baylor).

they boarded twenty flatcars pulled by a single decrepit locomotive, and the ensuing teeth-rattling, bone-shaking two-day ride was one few of them ever forgot.[2]

When the rickety locomotive at last drew its soldier-laden train of flatcars into the depot at Corinth, the Texans saw an appalling sight, which must have unnerved all but the most stout-hearted. In contrast to the tender care being shown the sick and wounded in Memphis, most of the sufferers in Corinth were lying unattended outside—on the depot platform and along the roadbed or in boxcars on the sidings. Unfortunately, the circumstances surrounding the arrival of the Sixth proved to have ominous significance. Men sickened and died as measles, mumps, and malaria swept the idyllically beautiful but unsanitary camps. Poor rations and bad water did their part to undermine further the health of the army.[3]

Meanwhile military life went on. It was while at Corinth, which Ross described as a "malorious sickly spot, fitten only for aligators and snakes," that the Conscript Act went into effect. On May 8, 1862, Ross found himself elected colonel despite his protests against the use of his name in connection with "that responsible office."[4]

The summer that followed was a frustrating one of illness, deprivation, and infantry drill, but it brought maturity to the young former ranger captain. As he had foreseen, multiple responsibilities and perplexities accompanied field command. Sickness was prevalent. At one time Ross estimated that only half of the men of his regiment were fit for duty. He himself was not immune.[5]

Despite feeling "very puny and unwell," Ross would not neglect

---

[2] William Clyde Billingsley, ed., "'Such Is War': The Confederate Memoirs of Newton Asbury Keen," pt. 2, *Texas Military History* 7 (Spring, 1968): 46–47.

[3] Kate Cumming, *Kate: The Journal of a Confederate Nurse*, pp. 27–30, 36; Billingsley, ed., "'Such Is War,'" pt. 2, p. 47. For a romantic view of the Confederate camp at Corinth, see the chromolithograph after the Conrad Chapman painting reproduced in *The American Heritage Picture History of the Civil War*, pp. 376–77.

[4] U.S. War Department, *The War of the Rebellion: A Compilation of the Official Records of the Union and Confederate Armies*, ser. 1, X, pt. 2, pp. 548–51; Samuel B. Barron, *The Lone Star Defenders: A Chronicle of the Third Texas Cavalry, Ross' Brigade*, pp. 80–83; Ross to Mrs. Ross, May 16 and June 14, 1862, Ross Family Papers, Baylor. Colonel Stone failed to secure his promotion to brigadier general and returned to Texas, where he eventually served with the Second Regiment of Texas Partisan Rangers (Marcus J. Wright, *Texas in the War, 1861–1865*, pp. 31, 125).

[5] Ross to Mrs. Ross, May 16, June 14, and June [July] 2, 1862, Ross Family Papers, Baylor.

his duties. There was not much he could do about the poor rations issued his men, or the foul water they were forced to drink, but at least Ross could try to provide his nearly destitute men with clothing. After one review in which one-third of his men appeared barefooted and another group lacking uniform trousers drilled in their underdrawers, Colonel Ross wrote a "very saucy note" to the generals detailing the wrongs inflicted upon his Texans. This boldness resulted in a new supply of clothing.[6]

In addition to the ever-present problem of supplies, there was the difficulty of transforming undisciplined cavalry into disciplined infantry. Ross devoted much time to drilling his regiment, as did brigade commander General Charles W. Phifer, who set about with "untiring energy" to make soldiers "out of wild Texas boys."[7]

While the men were learning the rudiments of infantry tactics, their colonel was increasing his military knowledge and already high reputation. The Sixth was involved in several skirmishes as the Confederates retreated south along the Mobile and Ohio Railroad following their withdrawal from Corinth on May 29–30, 1862, and each time Ross showed skill and daring in command.[8] It was soon apparent to his superiors that Sul Ross was developing into a fine regimental commander. Since General Phifer was often absent, Ross as senior colonel frequently commanded the brigade. So pleased were both his superiors and his subordinates that his name was suggested for promotion to brigadier general more than once during the summer of 1862.[9]

Also indicative of Ross's growing military maturity and of the trust his superiors had in him was the selection of the Sixth to be remounted. Of the eight or ten different cavalry commands dismounted at Des Arc, Ross's regiment was the only one to be so favored at that time. General Price informed the young colonel that he was expecting "something brilliant" from the Texans when they received their horses.[10]

---

[6] Ibid., June 14, 1862, Ross Family Papers, Baylor.

[7] Billingsley, ed., "'Such Is War,'" pt. 2, p. 50; Ross to Mrs. Ross, June 14, 1862, Ross Family Papers, Baylor.

[8] In an unusually sentimental mood, Ross noted that he spent his first wedding anniversary under heavy fire. Then, lest he cause Lizzie to "take a little cry" at this reference to a happier hour, he filled the rest of his letter with amusing anecdotes about the activities of his men.

[9] Ross to Mrs. Ross, June 5 and 14, July 20, August 25 and 27, 1862, Ross Family Papers, Baylor; Victor M. Rose, *Ross' Texas Brigade: Being a Narrative of Events Connected with Its Service in the Late War Between the States*, p. 164.

[10] Ross to Mrs. Ross, August 10, 1862, Ross Family Papers, Baylor; Max S. Lale and

But hard marching and harder fighting as infantry lay ahead of the Texans before the desired horses would reach Mississippi. According to orders issued by Braxton Bragg, commanding general in the west who was then preparing an invasion of Kentucky, it was imperative to the Confederate cause that the Army of the West prevent Union forces in Mississippi from reinforcing General Don Carlos Buell in central Tennessee. In mid-September Price led his seventeen thousand troops against the garrison of Iuka, Mississippi, as a preliminary step in thwarting such a juncture.[11]

As Price's veterans marched north, Ross's dismounted troopers were observed in the ranks by Dabney H. Maury, their division commander. Maury, a West Pointer, described the Texans as "one of the finest bodies of men ever seen in any service." The men performed ably in battle, but on the march they were completely undisciplined. Their colonel was judged "a very handsome, poetical-looking young fellow with voice and manner gentle as a woman's, and the heart of a true soldier of Texas." Every garden patch and orchard they passed drew the cavalrymen from the ranks, and Maury and his staff spent much time and effort in ordering stragglers back to the column.[12]

In spite of this distracting extra attention bestowed upon his men by Maury and his staff, Ross's outlook on life was more sanguine than it had been all summer. Above all, he was more hopeful of an early ending of the war than he had been in months. In June, while he was battling a debilitating fever, even rumors that France had recognized the independence of the Confederacy failed to excite him. While others were wagering that peace would be proclaimed in thirty days, Ross saw "no probability of the War terminating much short of so many years."[13]

Hobart Key, Jr., eds., *The Civil War Letters of David R. Garrett Detailing the Adventures of the 6th Texas Cavalry, 1861–1865*, p. 65.

[11] U.S. War Department, *Official Records*, ser. 1, XVII, pt. 1, pp. 376–82, 706–709, pt. 2, pp. 62–140; Thomas L. Snead, "With Price East of the Mississippi," in *Battles and Leaders of the Civil War*, ed. Robert Underwood Johnson and Clarence Clough Buel, II, 725–27, 730, 732–34, 736; Mark Mayo Boatner III, *The Civil War Dictionary*, pp. 428–29; Albert Castel, *General Sterling Price and the Civil War in the West*, pp. 96–97.

[12] Dabney H. Maury, *Recollections of a Virginian in the Mexican, Indian, and Civil Wars*, pp. 174–75.

[13] Ross to Mrs. Ross, June [July] 2, 1862, Ross Family Papers, Baylor. At one point Ross's spirits were so low he wrote to Lizzie that he "would give almost any consideration to touch the west bank of the Missi. [*sic*] River again" (June 14, 1862, Ross Family Papers, Baylor).

As long as his physical condition remained unstable, Ross experienced bouts of homesickness in addition to general depression. As his health improved, he recognized the folly of yielding to melancholy and freed himself from dark moods by "engaging in hard work for a time, such as drilling for two or three hours in the hot sun." But even knowledge of this cure for the blues could not help him understand why the high command wasted most of the summer in inactivity. He could see only one positive factor in the delay: the Confederates were becoming, thanks to the "strict tutorage" of General Braxton Bragg and others, "most effectively disciplined and skilfully [sic] drilled."[14]

News of other Confederate successes—those of cavalry raiders John H. Morgan in Kentucky and Nathan B. Forrest in Tennessee—raised Ross's spirits. This confidence received an additional boost from the orders to remount his men, and by late August, Ross was predicting that in less than two months the stars and bars of the Confederate flag would wave on the north bank of the Ohio River. Ross's optimism remained high as Price's troops headed toward Iuka, a fashionable watering place on the Memphis and Charleston Railroad. The Confederates entered the town September 14, right behind the evacuating Yankee garrison. Large amounts of welcome commissary and other stores fell into rebel hands.[15]

While Price's men feasted on captured delectables, Union General U. S. Grant sent five divisions under Edward O. C. Ord and William S. Rosecrans to attack the Missourian from two sides before he could be reinforced. In order to extricate his troops from Iuka before the trap could be closed, Price set Maury to hold off Ord's advance while Henry Little's division attacked Rosecrans, who blocked the route of retreat.[16]

Ord failed to press his advantage, so during the heavy fighting between Little and Rosecrans, Maury's men—Ross's impatient Texans among them—were held in reserve. At first the colonel thought his chances for "a share of the danger" were slight. Then a regiment of Arkansas sharpshooters deployed at a distance opened fire on the Tex-

[14] Ross to Mrs. Ross, June [July] 2 and July 20, 1862, Ross Family Papers, Baylor.
[15] Ibid., July 29 and August 25, 1862; and Ross to D. A. Tinsley, August 28, 1862, both in Ross Family Papers, Baylor; Robert G. Athearn, ed., *Soldier in the West: The Civil War Letters of Alfred Lacy Hough*, p. 77.
[16] Boatner, *The Civil War Dictionary*, p. 428; Castel, *General Sterling Price*, pp. 100–101.

ans, their own men. One Arkansas rifleman took "three fair shots" at Ross; fortunately the man's aim, even at one hundred thirty yards, was not good. The incensed Texans begged their commander for permission to return the fire, but he refused. Recognizing the obvious disorganization of the sharpshooters, Ross had his men prepare to charge them with fixed bayonets. The Arkansas troops gave way and ran in the face of such steely resistance. For the Sixth, the rest of the Iuka fight was only anticlimax.[17]

Following the stalemate at Iuka, the Confederates continued their retreat along the Mobile and Ohio Railroad until they reached Baldwyn, Mississippi, on September 25, 1862. Since the regimental officers received marching orders after only a few days of rest, Ross concluded that they were going "back to try it over again."[18]

He was correct in his guess. Within a week, Van Dorn had assumed command of his and Price's combined forces. As in March, Van Dorn had grandiose plans for attacking and defeating the enemy. He would rush his twenty-two thousand troops northward to Corinth, then held by Rosecrans and fifteen thousand Federal troops, and destroy the bluecoat army before Grant could send in reinforcements from the scattered Union outposts in Tennessee. Capture of this heavily garrisoned railroad and highway center would enable the Confederates to reestablish themselves in middle Tennessee in accordance with Bragg's plan.[19]

Great were the odds against success. In order to approach Corinth the Confederates would have to cross two sizable rivers, the Hatchie and the Tuscumbia, and traverse fifteen miles of dusty roads. If they expected to take Rosecrans by surprise, they would have to strike swiftly—in ninety-degree heat and at a time when many local wells were low or dry. Once they had overcome the obstacles of distance and time, the rebels would have to face the fortifications they had constructed that spring. Within those earthworks lay two more lines of defense, but it is unclear if the Confederate commanders even knew of

[17] Ross to Mrs. Ross, September 24, 1862, Ross Family Papers, Baylor. The sharpshooters belonged to the brigade of William L. Cabell, who was, according to Ross, "so drunk as to be unable to distinguish even the Men of his own Brigade from the enemy."

[18] Ibid.

[19] William S. Rosecrans, "The Battle of Corinth," in Johnson and Buel, eds., *Battles and Leaders*, III, 738, 743, 745–46; U.S. War Department, *Official Records*, ser. 1, XVII, pt. 1, p. 377; Robert J. Hartje, *Van Dorn: The Life and Times of a Confederate General*, pp. 214–15.

their existence. As at Elkhorn Tavern, Van Dorn was not only poorly informed about the actual enemy position but he was also keeping much information he did have to himself.[20]

Despite these problems, Van Dorn's plan prevailed. On the second of October the main body of troops crossed the Hatchie River at Davis's Bridge and moved toward the bridge over the Tuscumbia. Here a skirmish flared up between the Confederate vanguard and Yankee cavalry. When the Confederates halted that evening, Corinth was only ten miles away, but Rosecrans had been apprised of their approach.

The Mississippian had his troops on the march before daybreak the next morning. When the actual attack began shortly after ten, Van Dorn's right division under General Mansfield Lovell engaged the enemy first. As the fighting became general, Ross's Texans were in the thick of the battle. Attacking ferociously, Phifer's brigade drove the Federals in their center back past the old Confederate fortifications to their second line of defense—nine guns placed on a hill and supported by infantry. As the regimental bugler sounded the charge, the "noble little band" of dismounted cavalry gave "one wild shout for Texas" and dashed toward the Federal line. Grapeshot, shell, and minie balls filled the air, but although men and officers dropped on all sides, the Sixth did not falter. On the Texans swept, led by their colonel, who was sometimes on horseback, sometimes on foot, but always in the vanguard. "It was a fearful charge," recalled one of the participants, "but on we went . . . up to the very mouth of the battery when the gunners and infantry fled away and left it in our possession."[21]

After the capture of the guns by the Sixth, the Federals fell back on their final line of defense and manned the siege guns and other heavy artillery. Ross and his Texans were then one-half mile in front of the Confederate lines and only three hundred yards from the enemy. The colonel formed his men under the brow of a hill and sent a messenger to his brigade commander for orders. General Phifer directed him to hold the hill at all costs until fresh troops could reach him.[22]

Fifteen minutes passed, but the promised reinforcements did not

[20] Hartje, *Van Dorn*, p. 220; Castel, *General Sterling Price*, pp. 108, 111; John Milton Hubbard, *Notes of a Private*, p. 42.
[21] Castel, *General Sterling Price*, pp. 109–11; Billingsley, ed., "'Such Is War,'" pt. 2, p. 52–53; *Dallas Herald*, November 8, 1862.
[22] *Dallas Herald*, November 8, 1862.

arrive. Then Ross detected a movement in the enemy troops as about one thousand men sallied out of the works. Anxiously the colonel scanned the Confederate rear for signs of the fresh troops promised by Phifer. There were none. When it became evident that the Federals were flanking his men and that no assistance was coming, Ross reluctantly gave the order to withdraw.[23]

While the weary troops settled down to snatch what rest they could, the commanding general laid his plans. The battle would begin before dawn with an artillery barrage. General Louis Hébert would initiate the attack on the Confederate left; then he would be joined by the right under Lovell and the center under Maury. To John C. Moore's and Phifer's brigades of Maury's division went the honor of assaulting the enemy line at its most heavily defended points—Batteries Robinett and Williams—and breaking through into the town.[24]

As at Elkhorn, Van Dorn decided to engage his troops without detailed reconnaissance as to the strength of the enemy position. The more thoughtful among Ross's Texans, having contemplated the strength of the Federal works during the brief time spent at the outpost, had doubts about their future.[25] At the same time, Sul Ross had not won his reputation as a scouting officer without being able to determine accurately the strength of an enemy position, and he was concerned by what he had seen at Robinett. He had noted the "bastions and breastworks" and the presence of a three-hundred-yard-wide belt of fallen trees and abatis guarding the approach to the ditch and earthworks. Over this his men would have to charge in the face of enemy marksmen while enduring the fire of "siege guns and heavy field pieces." He knew the next day's battle would be desperate, if not hopeless, and he entertained little expectation of surviving a frontal assault on Robinett.[26]

[23] Ibid.

[24] Hartje, *Van Dorn*, p. 228.

[25] L. H. Graves Diary, May 1, 1861–April 1, 1864, McLean Collection, Arlington, Texas (hereafter cited as Graves Diary), p. 80. Photocopy of typescript prepared by Margaret Stoner McLean from the originals loaned by the late Kathryn Stoner O'Connor, Victoria, Texas. See also *Dallas Herald*, November 8, 1862.

[26] *Dallas Herald*, November 8, 1862; Elizabeth Ross Clarke, "Life of Sul Ross," Ross Family Papers, Baylor, p. 87. Ross had good reason to feel concern. One expert has estimated that in a 350-yard infantry charge on a battery of smoothbore artillery, the pieces could get off eleven rounds of canister in just over three minutes (see Jack Coggins, *Arms and Equipment of the Civil War*, p. 76).

Daylight came, but the fighting on the left did not begin. At last the dilatory Hébert presented himself at his commander's headquarters as too ill to direct his division. While Van Dorn transferred the command of the eastern wing to General Martin E. Green, Maury's division moved forward. Soon the rebel center was engaged in force but without support.[27]

In one last desperate effort to take the town, Van Dorn ordered Maury's men to storm the Federal defenses. With a yell, Moore's brigade raced to take Robinett. Spearheading this attack was the Second Texas Infantry, commanded by Colonel William P. Rogers, who was killed on the parapet of Robinett. Almost immediately following Rogers's attack, Phifer's brigade swept toward the same goal. Disregarding the hail of rifle and artillery fire raking their ranks, the rebels rushed toward the works with a tremendous yell. Men of the Sixth succeeded in scrambling into the eastern edge of Robinett, where they used bayonets and clubbed muskets to drive the Federal defenders from their stronghold and to take the guns. For a few moments the shot-riddled banner of the dismounted cavalrymen waved proudly on the crest of the enemy earthworks.[28]

It was during this charge on Robinett that Ross's white mare managed to unseat her rider and bolt, causing the report to spread through the ranks that he had been killed. But he reached the fortifications safely and was rallying his shattered regiment when Union reinforcements rushed to the scene. Within minutes the gray-coated ranks, terribly thinned by that time, crumpled and rolled back. Failing in this last attempt to take and hold the town, Van Dorn ordered a withdrawal.[29]

At nightfall the defeated, disorganized Confederates halted at Chewalla, Tennessee, ten miles northwest of Corinth. For a time it looked as if Van Dorn's army would escape without further opposition,

---

[27] Billingsley, ed., "'Such Is War,'", pt. 2, p. 53; Hartje, Van Dorn, p. 229.

[28] Glenn W. Sunderland, "The Battle of Corinth," Civil War Times Illustrated 6 (April, 1967): 35; Rosecrans, "The Battle of Corinth," II, 751; Ross's own account, in Dallas Herald, November 8, 1862; A. W. Sparks, The War Between the States as I Saw It: Reminiscences Historical and Personal, p. 275.

[29] Monroe F. Cockrell, ed., The Lost Account of the Battle of Corinth and Court-Martial of General Van Dorn, p. 31; Ross to J. A. Pryor, Dallas Herald, November 8, 1862. Confederate ferocity in the fighting around Corinth convinced many Federals that the rebels were influenced by some kind of stimulant, and rumors circulated that Van Dorn made his men drink a mixture of whiskey and gunpowder before fighting (John K. Bettersworth, ed., Mississippi in the Confederacy as They Saw It, I, 97).

but this was not to be. When the Confederates arrived at Davis's Bridge over the Hatchie River the morning of October 5, they found a Union force of sixty-five hundred men in possession of the west bank. To add to their difficulties, from the rear came reports of pursuit. Unless another escape route could be found, the rebels would be trapped at the bridge.[30]

While scouts searched for and located another crossing, Van Dorn sent a token force of infantry, cavalry, and artillery to contest the Yankee advance. Among the troops assigned this task were survivors of Maury's division, which included Ross and the Sixth. Temporarily assuming command of the brigade in the absence of Phifer, who was ill, Ross arrived with his seven hundred riflemen just as the three-hundred-man remnant of Moore's brigade and six field pieces on the west bank of the Hatchie were being hard pressed by the enemy. Throwing his troops into the fight, first on the west bank of the river and then, after an orderly withdrawal, on the east, Ross cooperated with Moore and later with Cabell in holding back the powerful Yankee advance.[31]

Generals Van Dorn, Price, and Maury "witnessed the unequal contest" between the small Confederate rearguard and the larger Union force "with great anxiety." As they watched, Ross and the men of his command won new glory on the banks of the Hatchie. Moore's men gave way, and for almost three hours the men of Phifer's brigade held at bay ten times their number, repulsing three major enemy assaults.[32] Maury was particularly impressed by the behavior of Ross and his Texans at Corinth and at Hatchie Bridge. When the War Department called upon Maury to report the name of the officer who had been especially distinguished at Corinth and the Hatchie, he replied with that of Lawrence Sullivan Ross. It was this gallant action that won the young colonel his later promotion to brigadier general.[33]

[30] U.S. War Department, *Official Records*, ser. 1, XVII, pt. 1, pp. 392–93; Boatner, *The Civil War Dictionary*, p. 177.

[31] U.S. War Department, *Official Records*, ser. 1, XVII, pt. 1, pp. 394–95; *Dallas Herald*, November 8, 1862; Hartje, *Van Dorn*, pp. 236–37.

[32] *Dallas Herald*, November 8, 1862. See also Pryor to Ross, in Rose, *Ross' Texas Brigade*, pp. 165–66.

[33] *Dallas Herald*, November 8, 1862; U.S. War Department, *Official Records*, ser. 1, XVII, pt. 1, pp. 394–95; Maury's letters of October 6, 1863, in Rose, *Ross' Texas Brigade*, pp. 165, 168. The Sixth lost 148 men in the Corinth campaign—55 killed, 63 wounded, and 30 missing (William F. Fox, *Regimental Losses in the American Civil War, 1861–1865*, p. 566).

Van Dorn withdrew his army deeper into central Mississippi. Within a few weeks of the battle at Corinth, the Sixth's long-awaited horses arrived and the regiment was transferred to the cavalry brigade of Colonel William H. ("Red") Jackson. This West Pointer from Tennessee had both youth and frontier experience in common with Ross, and the two were close friends.[34]

Remounting and transferral to service under Jackson were good news. Change in command meant he would have to reapply for leave to return to Texas that winter, but Ross's friend and immediate superior evidently saw no reason why he should not be allowed to do so. The first week in November Sul Ross went on detached service, which included a furlough in Texas.[35]

Mid-January found Ross en route to rejoin his regiment. He always found return to duty painful after being at home, and this time his homesickness was acute. Twice while still on the road, he wrote Lizzie. Of these letters, one was an outpouring of love and longing. "The call of duty alone prompted me to leave you when my heart and all my feelings rebelled against it. But I trust I may see the hour, when I shall reach home, to be absent from you no more."[36]

When the colonel rejoined his men, he found the Sixth had not been idle during his absence. In late December Van Dorn carried out a daring raid on the Union supply depot at Holly Springs, Mississippi. The rebels destroyed an estimated $1.5 million worth of military stores being stockpiled for General Ulysses S. Grant's overland advance on Vicksburg. The attack was enough to make Grant change his plan of approach to the river citadel.[37]

In addition to this action, Ross learned that more positions had been shuffled in the higher echelons. The dashing Van Dorn, now

[34] Dabney H. Maury to Captain James M. Soughborough, A.A.G., October 20, 1862, in Military Service Record for L. S. Ross, from Unpublished Muster Rolls, General Services Administration, National Archives and Records Service, Washington, D.C. (hereafter cited as GSA, NA); Boatner, *The Civil War Dictionary*, p. 433; Clarke, "Life of Sul Ross," Ross Family Papers, Baylor, p. 88.
[35] U.S. War Department, *Official Records*, ser. 1, XVII, pt. 1, p. 382; undated newspaper clipping in Family Scrapbook of Mrs. Peeler Williams, private collection of Elizabeth Williams Estes, Lorena, Texas; *Mobile Advertiser and Register*, October 25, 1862; Ross Military Service Record, GSA, NA. Ross accompanied his wounded brother home (see "The Killing of Chief Peta Nouona," *Frontier Times* 4 (December, 1926): 43.
[36] Ross to Mrs. Ross, January 24, 1863, Ross Family Papers, Baylor.
[37] U.S. War Department, *Official Records*, ser. 1, XVII, pt. 1, pp. 503, 508–509, pt. 2, p. 463.

chief of cavalry in the west, was preparing to move into central Tennessee to aid Bragg, who was facing Rosecrans's army following the fighting at Stone's River. It was the intention of General Joseph E. Johnston, commanding general in the west, that Van Dorn's troopers should disrupt enemy communications and prevent the transferral of Union troops from western to central Tennessee.[38]

After a fatiguing march the cavalry command reached Columbia, Tennessee, before Washington's birthday. The rest of February was spent skirmishing with small enemy parties. On March 5, 1863, Van Dorn's corps, consisting of the cavalry divisions of Forrest and Jackson, surrounded a Union reconnaissance force of one brigade of infantry and one of cavalry at Thompson's Station near Spring Hill, Tennessee. In this engagement the Sixth fought dismounted, and with the other Texas cavalry regiments they made three assaults with drawn revolvers on the enemy line before carrying the Federal position. The rebels netted about twelve hundred prisoners when the infantry surrendered following the escape of the bluecoat cavalry and artillery.[39]

Following Van Dorn's victory at Thompson's Station, Ross noted that "scarcely a day passes but we have a fight." During this time Ross was often in command of the Texas Cavalry Brigade, which had been organized in Mississippi under Colonel John W. Whitfield of the Texas Legion. Whitfield, twenty years older than Ross, his second brigade officer, was a veteran of the Mexican War and had served in the U.S. Congress as a representative of Kansas Territory. As colonel of the Legion, he had performed bravely at Elkhorn Tavern and at Iuka.[40]

It soon became evident that Whitfield liked to enjoy the privileges of rank while delegating the responsibilities to others. Although he seldom complained, Ross wrote home that Whitfield had been "frolicing [sic] around seeing his friends & enjoying himself and scheming" to get an appointment as brigadier general while leaving his second in command "all the work to do. . . . He complains of Rheumatism & thus get[s] to Richmond."[41]

But while Whitfield "schemed" in Richmond for a promotion,

[38] Ibid., pt. 2, pp. 832–33, 835, 838.

[39] Lale and Key, eds., *Letters of David R. Garrett*, p. 73; U.S. War Department, *Official Records*, ser. 1, LII, pt. 2, pp. 75, 116–18, 122–24; Dudley G. Wooten, ed., *A Comprehensive History of Texas, 1685–1897*, II, 620.

[40] Ross to Mrs. Ross, April 12, 1863, Ross Family Papers, Baylor; Wright, *Texas in the War*, p. 96.

[41] Ross to Mrs. Ross, April 12, 1863, Ross Family Papers, Baylor.

Ross was gaining further useful knowledge of brigade command. He got along with the men under him as well as with his superiors, and at any moment he could get from the generals of his corps "such an endorsement as would ensure" his own set of wreathed stars. But with all his work as well as the responsibilities of command weighing on his shoulders, Ross was not quite sure he wanted a promotion—yet. Besides, he disliked having to ask "an office of anyone," as Whitfield most certainly was doing.[42]

Meanwhile, the Texas Brigade was seeing plenty of action. Skirmishing opened the third week in March; on April 10, 1863, Van Dorn's corps engaged the enemy in what came to be known as the First Battle of Franklin. Although the Texans were dismounted and deployed in line of battle several times, they were held in reserve during most of the fighting.[43]

It is evident from Ross's description of the affair that he considered the engagement of little significance. He had no way of knowing that the day's fighting marked the close of the first half of the war, nor could he foresee that he and the Texas Brigade would return to Franklin some twenty months later. Far more important, however, was the murder of Captain S. L. Freeman, chief of Forrest's artillery, after he had surrendered.[44] This marked a change in the conduct of the war; thereafter, combat in Ross's field of operations would become increasingly brutal.

But for the moment the glow of chivalry continued to gild the realities of war. Shortly after the battle of Franklin, Van Dorn's corps held a review at Spring Hill, which was reported by a correspondent of the *Mobile Register and Advertiser*. Although the spectacle of "the high-spirited boys, the dancing horses, the gleaming guns and glittering sabers" was of interest to the *Register* reporter, his true skill rested in sketching word portraits of officers and men. Forrest, Jackson, Frank C. Armstrong, and George B. Cosby were briefly described, but it is interesting to note that the reporter's interest was caught and held by the approach of the Texas Brigade.

---

[42] Ibid. The Texas Brigade was made up of the Third, Sixth (when not on detached service), Ninth, and Twenty-seventh Texas cavalry regiments. The Twenty-seventh was also known as the First Texas Legion (Wright, *Texas in the War*, pp. 91, 96).

[43] Ross to Mrs. Ross, April 12, 1863, Ross Family Papers, Baylor.

[44] Robert J. Willett, Jr., "The First Battle of Franklin," *Civil War Times Illustrated* 7 (February, 1969): 18, 22; Ross to Mrs. Ross, April 12, 1863, Ross Family Papers, Baylor.

Here come those rollicking, rascally, brave Texans; and there at their head is a young man apparently twenty-eight years of age, with wavy black hair, black moustache, an olive complexion, fine expressive features and graceful form. This is Colonel Ross, of the Sixth Texas. . . .

What singular looking customers those Texans are, with their large brimmed hats, dark features, shaggy Mexican mustangs, and a *lariet* [*sic*] . . . around the pummel of their saddles. They are said to be unmerciful to prisoners, but are a tower of strength when there is a fight on hand.[45]

This entertaining event held at Spring Hill was the last corps review ever attended by Van Dorn. On May 7, 1863, the Mississippian was murdered by a citizen whose wife he had supposedly seduced.[46] Van Dorn's death caused reorganization and reassignment of the Confederate cavalry command. Forrest retained his division to operate in Tennessee while Jackson's division marched to the assistance of beleaguered Vicksburg, then threatened by Union troops under Grant and William T. Sherman. The Texans occupied a position on the right of Johnston's army, which was seeking to break through Grant's encirclement to join forces with John C. Pemberton's gray-coated defenders within the river citadel. Although about forty miles from Vicksburg, Ross could hear the "constant & terrific bombardment."[47]

Ross came under fire from another direction about this same time when he found himself involved in a squabble over who was to command the Texas Brigade. Whitfield's jaunt to Richmond had paid off, and he had received his appointment to brigadier general. Returning to Tennessee shortly before Jackson's division left for Vicksburg, the new general resumed command of the Texans. But Jackson considered Whitfield "entirely unfit for cavalry" and requested that Joseph E. Johnston relieve him from duty and once and for all assign Ross to command the brigade. Johnston complied with the request, but Whitfield was not to be ousted without a struggle. He immediately appealed his case to the secretary of war. There the matter stood while the other, greater battle for Vicksburg raged.[48]

Despite this tension about brigade command, Ross and his Texans

[45] Personne [pseud.], *Marginalia: Or, Gleanings from an Army Note-Book*, pp. 168–70.

[46] For a detailed discussion of the mystery surrounding the murder of Van Dorn, see Hartje, *Van Dorn*, pp. 307–23.

[47] Ross to Mrs. Ross, June 9, 1863, Ross Family Papers, Baylor. There is a monument to Ross on the grounds of Vicksburg National Military Park.

[48] Ross to Mrs. Ross, June 9, 1863, Ross Family Papers, Baylor. The *Mobile Adver-*

remained active in the weeks before the fall of Vicksburg. "We worry them at all times," he wrote of the enemy near his position, "and keep them closely confined within their lines." When the Federals did manage to slip out of the Confederate encirclement, they usually preyed on the local civilians. This infuriated Ross. The young man who had grown up amid the horrors of Indian warfare admitted that he never before had witnessed "such sights of desolation & consequent beggary & ruin" and did all he could to punish those responsible.[49]

With the surrender of Vicksburg on July 4, 1863, Grant and Sherman forced Johnston to retreat beyond Jackson, Mississippi. The Texas Brigade was among the Confederate cavalry units disputing Sherman's advance into central Mississippi, but the triumphant Whitfield had been reinstated in command. For some weeks from mid-July to mid-August, Ross commanded an independent detachment made up of the Sixth plus a battalion and a company drawn from other commands. Then, in order to have full benefit of Ross's services at the brigade level, Major General Stephen D. Lee, new cavalry commander in Mississippi, detached the Sixth from Whitfield's brigade and, joining it with Colonel R. A. Pinson's First Mississippi Cavalry, created a new brigade especially for Ross's command. At the same time, Lee too began pressing Richmond for an appointment for the Texan.[50]

Late in September, Ross's brigade, with 894 men present for duty, was ordered to Pontotoc, Mississippi, where it received reinforcements bolstering its total strength to 1,100 men. On October 25, 1863, Johnston directed 2,500 of the best troopers from Ross's, Samuel W. Ferguson's, and James R. Chalmer's commands to ready themselves for a raid into central Tennessee. The objective was to cooperate with the commands of Philip D. Roddey and Joseph Wheeler in breaking the railroads in the rear of Rosecrans's army, then besieged by Bragg at Chattanooga.[51]

---

tiser and Register, June 24, 1863, sounded a slightly different note, saying that the loss of Whitfield was very much regretted. The reporter admitted that Ross was "a young officer of very superior qualifications."

[49] U.S. War Department, Official Records, ser. 1, LII, pt. 2, p. 477, XXIV, pt. 2, p. 226; Ross to Mrs. Ross, June 9, 1863, Ross Family Papers, Baylor. Ross's anger was typical of the psychological shock experienced by chivalrous Southerners who embraced the idea of total war for the first time (Richard M. Weaver, The Southern Tradition at Bay: A History of Postbellum Thought, pp. 66–68).

[50] Graves Diary, pp. 107–10; Ross to Mrs. Ross, August 25, 1863, Ross Family Papers, Baylor; U.S. War Department, Official Records, ser. 1, XXX, pt. 4, p. 656.

[51] Graves Diary, pp. 113–14; U.S. War Department, Official Records, ser. 1, XXX, pt. 4, pp. 704, 724; Rose, Ross' Texas Brigade, p. 121.

When the order came from general headquarters, Ross wrote Lizzie that his brigade was "just starting on a grand raid" through Tennessee. As she was soon to bear their first child, he was anxious to hear from her, but he knew it would be many long weeks before her letters could reach him.[52]

The campaign that followed began inauspiciously. Eventually Wheeler's command was ordered back to Chattanooga, leaving Lee's troops (including Ross's brigade) to deal with Federal reinforcements under Sherman working their way along the Memphis and Charleston Railroad toward the invested city. At Tuscumbia, Alabama, the last week in October, Ross's brigade encountered the rear elements of Sherman's troops. The Texan colonel immediately "inaugurated a system of surprises, attacks, etc., [sic] that annoyed the enemy intolerably." For six days ten thousand Yankees resisted, but were finally forced back across the Tennessee River and eventually withdrew to Corinth.[53]

Succeeding in this limited objective, which failed to affect the outcome of the siege at Chattanooga, the Confederates returned to northern Mississippi. Nevertheless Ross had good reason to feel proud of his men. A war correspondent praised the colonel and his troopers, saying that when Ross's men charged, "something has to give way, and somebody is sure to get hurt." Noting that the rebels always went into a fight with a yell, the reporter added that after such a charge, "more than one Yankee has been found literally scared to death."[54]

Skirmishing continued throughout November. Late that month the long-awaited letters from home arrived, but they contained saddening news: Sul and Lizzie's first child was dead.[55] But there was little time for grief or even for rest from the demands of command. A few days later Lee's troopers rode north again, this time headed for the section of railroad recently rebuilt by Sherman linking the Yankee gar-

[52] Ross to Mrs. Ross, October 4, 1863, Ross Family Papers, Baylor. It is possible that Lizzie suffered a miscarriage in early 1862, but this is only conjecture. Ross was a true Victorian when it came to prudishness of expression, and his mention of her "illness" is oblique.

[53] John P. Dyer, *From Shiloh to San Juan: The Life of "Fightin' Joe" Wheeler*, p. 109; *Mobile Advertiser and Register*, November 22, 1863; Graves Diary, pp. 117–18; Rose, *Ross' Texas Brigade*, p. 121; Lale and Key, eds., *Letters of David R. Garrett*, pp. 87–88.

[54] *Mobile Advertiser and Register*, November 21, 1863.

[55] Ross to Mrs. Ross, November 29, 1863, Ross Family Papers, Baylor. Ross Family records do not record the name or sex of the child, so it is probable the baby was stillborn or died immediately after birth.

risons of Memphis and Corinth. Early in December, Ross's men met the
enemy at Salisbury, Tennessee, routed their slightly superior force,
and drove the Yankees out of town. That night the Texans and Pinson's
Mississippians ripped up rails and burned ties in the manner later to
be perfected by Sherman's bummers.[56]

The smoldering remains of a wrecked railroad marked their trail
as the Confederates turned westward. At Moscow, Tennessee, on December 3, 1863, Ross's brigade and another rebel unit encountered
Federal cavalry commanded by Colonel Edward Hatch. Hatch, who
recently had boasted he could whip the Confederates, was crossing his
brigade of four regiments over a bridge spanning Wolf River when the
gray-coated horsemen approached. Ross attacked the Federals with
such ferocity that many Union cavalrymen plunged their horses off the
bridge in order to escape.[57]

After displaying such "dash and gallantry" at Moscow, Ross's brigade was ordered back to Mississippi. Lee had finally succeeded in
ousting Whitfield from command of the Texas Brigade and having Ross
permanently appointed brigade commander. At the same time prominent civilians of the area, among them Joseph Davis, brother of the
president, as well as various military men, had expressed a desire for
Ross's promotion. The wheels of officialdom were at last in motion.[58]

As December came to a close, so did a major phase of Sul Ross's
Confederate military career. Perhaps it was best that there was no seer
present to graphically describe what lay ahead. For Ross would indeed
receive his brigadier's wreaths early the next year, thus becoming the
ninth youngest general officer in the Confederacy.[59] But he would also
have to struggle almost continuously against the spirit of discontent in
his command. Ross would continue his illustrious career, leading the

[56] Lale and Key, eds., *Letters of David R. Garrett*, p. 88; U.S. War Department,
Official Records, ser. 1, XXXI, pt. 1, pp. 588–90; Ross to Mrs. Ross, December 16,
1863, Ross Family Papers, Baylor.

[57] U.S. War Department, *Official Records*, ser. 1, XXX, pt. 4, p. 147, XXXI, pt. 1,
p. 586; Lale and Key, eds., *Letters of David R. Garrett*, p. 88.

[58] U.S. War Department, *Official Records*, ser. 1, XXXI, pt. 3, p. 794; Ross to Mrs.
Ross, December 16, 1863, Ross Family Papers, Baylor; Colonel Giles S. Boggess to M.
D. Graham, December 5, 1863, and Graham to Jefferson Davis, December 21, 1863,
both in Ross Military Service Record, GSA, NA.

[59] Author's own computation, based on data from Ezra J. Warner, *Generals in
Gray: Lives of the Confederate Commanders*.

brigade that would bear his name safely through the carnage of the Yazoo City, Atlanta, and Franklin-Nashville campaigns. But the cost in lives of his friends, neighbors, and fellow soldiers would be heartbreaking, and his own health would finally give way under the strain. There would be much to dare and much to suffer before the "path of duty" would lead Sul Ross back to Texas.

☆ 8 ☆

Ross's Texas Brigade

EARLY in October, 1863, Major General Stephen D. Lee, commanding Confederate cavalry in Mississippi, penned a troubled letter to Secretary of War James A. Seddon. The problem uppermost in Lee's mind was the "efficiency of the most reliable troops" under his command—the Texas cavalry brigade of General John W. Whitfield. For some time Whitfield's feeble health had kept him from active field duty. Far worse, trouble was brewing in the three Texas regiments forming the brigade. The men of the First Texas Legion, the Third Texas, and the Ninth Texas were "in a manner dissatisfied."[1]

In the past this dissatisfaction had been sporadic, affecting the Texas cavalry regiments only at intervals. Usually discontent arose out of crises connected with command policies. Changes of type and length of service, field of operations, and commanders, as well as the policy of granting furloughs, at one time or another had caused friction between the Texas troops and the Confederate headquarters.[2]

By autumn of 1863 the situation was becoming critical, for Texan discontent was growing. Lee warned Seddon that "unless a proper Officer is assigned to their command and one popular with them, they surely will cross the river." To counteract the dissension in the Texas

---

[1] Stephen D. Lee to James A. Seddon, October 2, 1863, copy in Ross Family Papers, Texas Collection, Baylor University, Waco, Texas (hereafter cited as Ross Family Papers, Baylor).

[2] Victor M. Rose, *Ross' Texas Brigade: Being a Narrative of Events Connected with Its Service in the Late War Between the States*, pp. 63–64; Wilfred Buck Yearns, *The Confederate Congress*, p. 65; William Clyde Billingsley, ed., "'Such Is War': The Confederate Memoirs of Newton Asbury Keen," pt. 2, *Texas Military History* 7 (Spring, 1968): 56; Samuel B. Barron, *The Lone Star Defenders: A Chronicle of the Third Texas Cavalry, Ross' Brigade*, p. 146; U.S. War Department, *The War of the Rebellion: A Compilation of the Official Records of the Union and Confederate Armies*, ser. 1, XXXI, pt. 1, p. 576.

Brigade, Lee urged the promotion of Colonel Lawrence Sullivan Ross
to brigadier general and the assignment of Ross to permanent brigade
command.[3]

On October 29, Whitfield left his brigade for Texas. Since Ross
was then operating against the enemy in northern Alabama and western Tennessee, command of the Texas Brigade went temporarily to
Colonel Hinchie P. Mabry of the Third Texas. Mabry found he had his
hands full, for discord continued to seethe throughout the ranks.[4]

Such was the situation when Colonel Sul Ross arrived at the Texan
camp near Queen's Hill, Mississippi, on December 16. Following his
successful raid into Tennessee, Ross had returned to Mississippi. At
Grenada he had received orders from General Lee to proceed south at
once and take command of the Texas Brigade. So urgent was the matter
that Ross left the Sixth Texas and First Mississippi regiments to follow
later while he traveled by the Mississippi Central Railroad to Jackson
and thence to his new command. Lee accompanied him.[5]

To further counteract discontent, Lee outlined a mission for the
brigade. Several thousand muskets awaited shipment across the Mississippi: Ross and his brigade were requested to cross a portion of the
desperately needed arms above Vicksburg. Ross was to take with him a
section of artillery, for once the arms were safely across, he could use
his own judgment about interfering with Yankee shipping.[6]

The Sixth Texas rode in on December 21. The next day the command moved out, bound for the vicinity of Greenville via the Yazoo
delta. Wet freezing weather, bottomless roads, and the poor condition
of the arms train hindered the progress of the mission. Wagons and
artillery pieces bogged down in the icy quagmire despite the impress-
ment and use of ox teams. By herculean labors Ross got his artillery to
Garvin's Ferry on the Sunflower River. A drop in temperature on the

---

[3] Lee to Seddon, October 2, 1863, Ross Family Papers, Baylor. To an extent this
discontent was present in the Sixth (Max S. Lale and Hobart Key, Jr., eds., *The Civil
War Letters of David R. Garrett Detailing the Adventures of the 6th Texas Cavalry,
1861–1865*, p. 77).

[4] Rose, *Ross' Texas Brigade*, p. 112; Homer L. Kerr, ed., *Fighting with Ross' Texas
Cavalry Brigade, C.S.A.*, pp. 102–103.

[5] U.S. War Department, *Official Records*, ser. 1, XXXI, pt. 1, p. 586; Ross to Mrs.
Ross, December 16, 1863, Ross Family Papers, Baylor. On December 21, 1863, the officers of the First Mississippi Cavalry sent a committee to wait on Ross and extend the
regiment's regrets at losing him as commander and wishes for his continued success.

[6] U.S. War Department, *Official Records*, ser. 1, XXXI, pt. 3, pp. 841–42.

night of December 31 froze the wagon train in the mud five miles to the rear of the main body of horsemen, making further progress impossible.[7]

The officer in charge of the arms train wished to abandon the expedition, but Ross would not give up so easily. The brigade, which had already crossed the Sunflower, dismounted, recrossed, and walked back to the train, where each enlisted man took two and each officer three muskets to carry back to their horses. Then the guns were carried on horseback the remainder of the distance to the Mississippi River.[8]

Other difficulties faced the Texans when they reached the Mississippi. The weather continued bitterly cold, while the river ran high. Skiffs had to be secured. All this was hindrance enough, but because of prowling Federal gunboats the arms could be ferried across the river only at night. Despite these almost insurmountable difficulties, Ross's men succeeded in crossing about fifteen hundred of the muskets during a three-night period.

Once the arms were safely across, Ross turned his attention to disrupting navigation of the river. The single artillery piece that had been able to keep up was placed on the bank of the river as some enemy shipping approached. One transport was disabled by artillery fire, but it was towed off by another craft before the Texans could capture it. Since some of his men were barefooted and all were suffering from exposure and hunger, Ross led his forces back into the interior, where shelter and rations were available.[9]

While the Texans were retracing their steps through the swamps and canebrakes, a courier reached Ross's headquarters with orders for the brigade to take up position near Benton, Mississippi. A large enemy force was being concentrated at Vicksburg and it was necessary that the Yazoo River and the Mississippi Central Railroad be guarded from attack. The Texans reached Benton on January 20. Four days later Ross turned command of the brigade over to Mabry and headed for

[7] Ibid., pp. 841–42, 879–80, XXXIV, pt. 2, pp. 810, 811; Kerr, ed., *Fighting with Ross' Cavalry*, pp. 103–104.

[8] U.S. War Department, *Official Records*, ser. 1, XXXII, pt. 2, p. 823, XXXIV, pt. 2, pp. 862–1000; Kerr, ed., *Fighting with Ross' Cavalry*, pp. 105–107. The cold was intense and many troopers suffered frostbite.

[9] U.S. War Department, *Official Records*, ser. 1, XXXIV, pt. 2, pp. 862–1000; Kerr, ed., *Fighting with Ross' Cavalry*, pp. 106–107; Barron, *Lone Star Defenders*, p. 176.

Sul Ross as a teenager. *Courtesy of the Texas Collection, Baylor University.*

Left: Cynthia Ann Parker and her infant daughter Prairie Flower soon after the Battle of Pease River. *Author's collection, original in the Texas Collection, Baylor University. Right:* Ross monument on the Vicksburg, Mississippi, battlefield. *Courtesy of Confederate Research Center, Hill Junior College.*

Left: Brigadier General L. S. Ross. *Courtesy of Confederate Research Center, Hill Junior College. Right:* Elizabeth Tinsley Ross during the Civil War era. *Courtesy of Dr. and Mrs. Neville P. Clarke, private collection.*

Ross about the time of his governorship. *Courtesy of the Library of Congress*.

Ross's office as governor. *Left to right:* George P. Finlay, Barnett Gibbs, Ross, H. M. Holmes. *Courtesy of Texas A&M University Archives.*

Texas capitol at its dedication, May, 1888. *Courtesy of Texas A&M University Archives.*

Ross's home as president of Texas A&M College. *Courtesy of Texas A&M University Archives.*

Texas A&M College campus about 1895. Ross Hall is on the right. *Courtesy of Texas A&M University Archives.*

Left: Elizabeth Tinsley Ross about 1880. *Courtesy of Mrs. Paul Mason, private collection. Right:* Lizzie Ross in later years. *Courtesy of Dr. and Mrs. Neville P. Clarke, private collection.*

Ross's funeral cortege, January 5, 1898. *Courtesy of Dr. and Mrs. Neville P. Clarke, private collection.*

Freshmen at Texas A&M University "washing Sully down." *Courtesy of Confederate Research Center, Hill Junior College.*

Lawrence Sullivan Ross bronze statue by Pompeo Coppini, Texas A&M University campus. *Courtesy of Confederate Research Center, Hill Junior College.*

Jackson's cavalry division headquarters, where news evidently awaited him of his promotion to brigadier general.[10]

Ross was back with his command by January 31, three days after the brigade drew blood in an engagement with a gunboat and transport near Mechanicsburg. In actions at Liverpool, Mechanicsburg, and Yazoo City, Mississippi, on February 3–5, Ross's men repulsed heavy attacks by Yankee infantry and cavalry cooperating with three gunboats.[11]

Since many of the Union troops were black, the citizens of Yazoo City credited Ross and his men with their deliverance. They exhibited their gratitude further by lavishly entertaining the Texans, from the new brigadier to the lowest private. Then the holiday came to an abrupt end. On February 3, 1864, troops under Major General William T. Sherman departed Vicksburg on a raid into central Mississippi aimed at capturing Meridian, an important rail and supply center. It was imperative that the Texas Brigade join the main body of Jackson's cavalry division east of the Pearl River as soon as possible.[12]

In the month-long Meridian campaign that followed, the outnumbered Confederates were able to do little to resist the Union advance. Except for the harassment of foragers and stragglers, the Confederates were unable to prevent the Union forces from wreaking vengeance upon citizens and destroying both private and public property. However, on February 16 at Marion Station just outside Meridian, Ross's Texans successfully checked the passage of a Yankee raiding column.[13]

This necessary diversion of Ross's cavalry into central Mississippi left the Yazoo country open to invasion. On February 9 a Union force of some sixteen hundred white and black troops, both infantry and cavalry, occupied Yazoo City. For the next nineteen days the bluecoats prowled the area, raiding as far east as the Mississippi Central Railroad

[10] U.S. War Department, *Official Records*, ser. 1, XXXIV, pt. 2, p. 862, XXXII, pt. 1, p. 365, pt. 2, pp. 513–14, 550, 624, 824–26; L. H. Graves Diary, May 1, 1861–April 1, 1864, McLean Collection, Arlington, Texas (hereafter cited as Graves Diary), p. 128. Photocopy of typescript prepared by Margaret Stoner McLean from the originals loaned by the late Kathryn Stoner O'Connor, Victoria, Texas; Kerr, ed., *Fighting with Ross' Cavalry*, p. 109.

[11] Kerr, ed., *Fighting with Ross' Cavalry*, p. 109; U.S. War Department, *Official Records*, ser. 1, XXXII, pt. 1, pp. 365, 826, pt. 2, pp. 830–31.

[12] Ross to Mrs. Ross, February 9, 1864, Ross Family Papers, Baylor; Barron, *Lone Star Defenders*, p. 177; Kerr, ed., *Fighting with Ross' Cavalry*, p. 111; Mark Mayo Boatner III, *The Civil War Dictionary*, pp. 543–44; U.S. War Department, *Official Records*, ser. 1, XXXII, pt. 1, pp. 174–75.

[13] *Mobile Register and Advertiser*, March 5, 1864.

and as far north as Grenada and Greenwood. This force stripped the
countryside of blacks, livestock, foodstuffs, and cotton. Added to the
horrors of civil war were the Southern nightmares of miscegenation,
racial strife, and servile insurrection. On the twenty-eighth the triumphant Yankee column returned to Yazoo City, leaving in its wake a trail
of misery and desolation that boded no good for the Federals once the
Confederates returned to the area.[14]

That afternoon a squadron of the First Mississippi Cavalry, African
descent, met a party of Texan scouts and pursued them to the rest of
the brigade's campsite near Benton. Ross ordered the Sixth and the
Ninth Texas to charge them; after the first volley a number of blacks,
recent recruits mounted on mules from the nearby plantations, "broke
in wild disorder." A running fight resulted that lasted until the few survivors reached the Federal fortifications at Yazoo City.[15]

The next four days passed in desultory skirmishing. The evening
of March 4 Brigadier General Robert V. Richardson and his five hundred fifty–man West Tennessee Brigade arrived, bolstering the combined Confederate force to thirteen hundred. Although Richardson
ranked Ross, he agreed to cooperate with the Texan as with an equal.[16]

The next morning the Confederates attacked, drove the enemy
from all but one redoubt, and in fierce, all-day hand-to-hand fighting
took the city, capturing many supplies and some prisoners. Ross demanded the "immediate and unconditional" surrender of the last redoubt, then occupied by the Eleventh Illinois Infantry and some black
troops. Surrender negotiations broke down when Ross would not "recognize negroes as soldiers," since two of his men had been brutally
murdered by black troops some weeks before.[17]

While Ross and the Union commanders "squabbled about the
terms of surrender" and the status of black soldiers, the Federal troops
gained reinforcements by the arrival of two transports loaded with in-

[14] U.S. War Department, *Official Records*, ser. 1, XXXII, pt. 1, pp. 320–26;
Thomas Gilliam to Victor M. Rose, June 30, 1881, Victor M. Rose Papers, Kathryn
Stoner O'Connor Collection, from private collection, Dr. and Mrs. Malcolm D. McLean,
Arlington, Texas; Kerr, ed., *Fighting with Ross' Cavalry*, pp. 112–13; Barron, *Lone Star
Defenders*, p. 182.
[15] U.S. War Department, *Official Records*, ser. 1, XXXII, pt. 1, pp. 320–23, 390;
Kerr, ed., *Fighting with Ross' Cavalry*, pp. 112–13; Barron, *Lone Star Defenders*,
pp. 181–82.
[16] U.S. War Department, *Official Records*, ser. 1, XXXII, pt. 1, pp. 385–90.
[17] Ibid., pp. 208, 385–87.

fantry. Not wishing to needlessly sacrifice the lives of their men, Ross and Richardson withdrew to Benton. The next day the Federal forces hastily departed Yazoo City, taking with them vivid recollections of Texan vengeance.[18]

Again the whites of Yazoo City enthusiastically welcomed their deliverers. The women of Yazoo County requested that the general and his brave men remain in the area, while other citizens showed their appreciation in more imaginative ways. One wealthy gentleman living nearby christened his newborn daughter "Texanna" in honor of the brigade. At the same time cakes, bouquets, calls, and invitations were showered upon the Texans.[19]

For several weeks the men basked in the growing warmth of the spring sun and in the praise of their Yazoo County friends. Man and mount alike welcomed this period of rest and recreation. But even as a mettlesome horse becomes difficult to handle with too much grain feeding and too little riding, the unruly element in the brigade made rest a prelude to restiveness. Ross's appointment as brigade commander had quieted much internal dissension, for the young officer was popular with his men. They appreciated the modest strength of his character, respected him for his leadership ability, and loved him for his courage and concern for their welfare. Ross's popularity soon bore fruit: on February 1, 1864, the Third Texas Cavalry "re-enlisted to a man."[20]

Although his appointment as commander had silenced the worst complaints and his tightened discipline had ended the worst infractions, Ross found he still had to deal with a spirit of unruliness among his men. To his great shame this rebellion manifested itself most strongly in his former regiment. In mid-March some one hundred fifty men of the Sixth Texas demonstrated against the appointment of an unpopular officer, Colonel Jack Wharton, to command their regiment. Ross at

[18] Ibid. The citizens told Ross that when his men attacked, the newest recruits among the black troops panicked and rode wildly through the streets yelling that "Old Ross" was coming (Ross to Mrs. Ross, March 19, 1864, Ross Family Papers, Baylor).

[19] "War Reminiscences. Petitions From the Citizens of Mississippi to Gen. Ross," undated clipping, in Ross Family Scrapbook, Mrs. Paul Mason Collection, College Station, Texas; citizens of Yazoo City to General L. S. Ross, February 6, 1864, Ross Family Papers, Mason Collection; Ross to Mrs. Ross, March 19, 1864, Ross Family Papers, Baylor.

[20] W. A. Callaway, "Incidents of Service," *Confederate Veteran* 28 (October, 1920): 372; U.S. War Department, *Official Records*, ser. 1, XXXII, pt. 2, p. 826.

tempted to identify and punish the men responsible, but was prevented by the general breakdown of respect for military authority in
his command. Finally the young general was forced to conclude that
his "command, influence, or authority" over his men did "not depend
on their respect for or fear of military law or authority, but simply their
love for me as an individual." It was a bitter awakening, and although
Ross accepted the facts of command as they were and channeled this
loyalty to himself into ways helpful to the Confederate cause, he was
ever afterwards haunted by the realization that should injury, death, or
even extended leave deprive the Texans of his leadership, most of his
men would desert.[21]

Had it not been for this mutiny of the Sixth, the time spent at
Yazoo City would have been without incident except for a brief campaign. As it was, only one battle—a raid on the Union-leased cotton
plantations at Snyder's Bluff—broke the interlude.[22]

That was late March. Early in April, Ross received orders to
march to western Tennessee to reinforce General Nathan B. Forrest's
cavalry command, but the order was countermanded en route and the
Texans were sent instead to Tuscaloosa, Alabama. From that point de-
tachments of the Sixth and the Ninth Texas operated against bush-
whackers, deserters, and other "tories" lurking in the northern part of
the state. Meanwhile Ross found himself among friends from college
days. A round of parties, a visit to his wife's relatives in Georgia, and a
sitting for a portrait in ambrotype occupied his days until the brigade
received its next orders.[23]

Again the Texans turned the noses of their horses west, and again
their hopes of returning to the Trans-Mississippi Department rose
high. At a review in Columbus, Mississippi, on April 13, Bishop-
General Leonidas Polk had promised to furlough the men by regiments as soon as possible. The first furlough had been delayed, but at
last the brigade was moving in that direction. Near Eutaw, Alabama,
these new orders were countermanded and Ross and his men sent to

[21] U.S. War Department, *Official Records*, ser. 1, XXXII, pt. 3, pp. 877–78; Ross
to D. A. Tinsley, September 14, 1864, Ross Family Papers, Baylor.

[22] U.S. War Department, *Official Records*, ser. 1, XXXII, pt. 1, p. 653, pt. 3,
p. 318; Kerr, ed., *Fighting with Ross' Cavalry*, p. 115.

[23] Kerr, ed., *Fighting with Ross' Cavalry*, p. 140; Barron, *Lone Star Defenders*,
186–87; Ross to Mrs. Ross, April 26, 1864, Ross Family Papers, Baylor. This ambrotype
is the best known of Ross's wartime portraits and shows the young general at the apex of
confidence and resplendency.

Montavallo and from there to Rome, Georgia. Johnston was already re-treating in the face of Sherman's drive south, and the gray-coated com-mander desperately needed as many men as he could muster.[24]

Ross's active role in the Atlanta campaign began the day after his command arrived in Rome, but it was May 17 before the Texans met the enemy in force. Dismounting at that time, the brigade drove the blue-coated skirmishers back and attacked a Federal infantry division. The Union troops fell back in confusion, leaving the victorious Texans in possession of the field until they were flanked by an overwhelming number of the enemy. It was a pattern often to be repeated in the cam-paign. More important, however, the skirmish at Rome marked the be-ginning of the brigade's one hundred days under fire.[25]

These 100 days under fire, or 112 by Ross's own count, involved eighty-six battles. Rome, Kingston, Etowah River, Racoon Creek, Stilesboro, Burnt Hickory, Dallas, New Hope Church, Lost Mountain, Big Muddy Creek, Sweet Water, Powder Springs, Lick Skillet, and Chattahoochee River—the roll call of place names marking skirmish sites of Ross's men could well be used to trace the relentless step-by-step advance of Sherman's western wing. Most of these engagements were minor, but claimed Texan lives and limbs just the same.[26]

Ross began the general battle (May 25–June 5) at New Hope Church, Georgia, when his skirmishers met Union troops on May 23. This action, however, was unusual; in the daily fighting the Texans generally followed a pattern of dismount, skirmish, fall back, mount, ride, dismount, and skirmish again. For days the soldiers saw more of earthworks and rifle pits than they did of their horses.[27]

Here and there an incident broke the monotony of dismounted service, scanty rations, pouring rain, and the unending rattle of small-

[24] Barron, *Lone Star Defenders*, p. 186, Kerr, ed., *Fighting with Ross' Cavalry*, pp. 138, 141; Ross to Mrs. Ross, April 26, 1864, Ross Family Papers, Baylor.

[25] Kerr, ed., *Fighting with Ross' Cavalry*, pp. 143–44; Graves Diary, p. 136; Bar-ron, *Lone Star Defenders*, p. 194; U.S. War Department, *Official Records*, ser. 1, XXXVIII, pt. 3, p. 899; Samuel G. French, *Two Wars: An Autobiography of General Samuel G. French* (Nashville: Confederate Veteran, 1901), p. 194; Kate Cumming, *Kate: The Journal of a Confederate Nurse*, pp. 121–22. One historian has estimated that Ross's brigade "averaged a fight a day for over three months" beginning with the fighting at Rome (see Allan C. Ashcraft, *Texas in the Civil War: A Résumé History*, p. 26).

[26] Kerr, ed., *Fighting with Ross' Cavalry*, pp. 142–69; U.S. War Department, *Offi-cial Records*, ser. 1, XXXVIII, pt. 4, pp. 731, 737, 764, 783, 786–87, pt. 5, pp. 861, 901.

[27] Billingsley, ed., "'Such Is War,'" pt. 3, p. 105; U.S. War Department, *Official Records*, ser. 1, XXXVIII, pt. 3, pp. 616, 618.

arms fire and the roar of cannonade. One day Ross, with some of General William J. Hardee's staff, was mortified to witness the "shameful conduct" of the men of the Third Texas who fled in a disorderly manner at the approach of the enemy. On another occasion the general himself barely escaped injury, capture, or death when he delayed on the skirmish line to read some letters newly arrived from home and was fired upon by Federal troops.[28]

The days dragged on, the fighting continued, and the Texans longed for a few days of rest and peace away from the firing line. Men remained under fire so long they became contemptuous of danger. But no matter how brave the soldiers and the commander, the strain of "fighting all the time" wore down all alike. Having an opportunity one day to look at himself in a mirror, Ross was surprised at the "care-worn and haggard" expression reflected there. He guessed he had aged ten years in eighteen months and admitted that he was nearly worn out by overwork. The reason for this overwork was that Generals Jackson and Johnston had great confidence in his command, and much of the other cavalry was considered worthless.[29]

This overwork increased during July when a two-pronged Union cavalry raid swept east and west around Atlanta in a bold attack on the remaining rail line south. Brigadier General Edward M. McCook with four thousand horsemen made up the western wing, while Major General George Stoneman and five thousand men formed the eastern. Sherman directed the two commands to meet at Lovejoy's Station and cooperate in destroying the railroad from that point to Macon, Georgia.[30]

Ross detected the Federal movement on July 22; by July 27 the Confederate command definitely knew what was in the wind. Major General Joseph Wheeler dashed to the east to intercept Stoneman. At the same time, Jackson, commanding the brigades of Ross and Colonel Harrison, rushed to head off McCook's raiders. Because the Federals had a twelve-hour start, they succeeded in destroying a Confederate

---

[28] U.S. War Department, *Official Records*, ser. 1, XXXVIII, pt. 4, pp. 766–67; Ross to Mrs. Ross, July 19, 1864, Ross Family Papers, Baylor.

[29] Ross to Mrs. Ross, July 7, 1864, Ross Family Papers, Baylor. For a later portrait made during the war that reveals Ross's weariness, see Dudley G. Wooten, ed., *A Comprehensive History of Texas, 1685–1897*, II, 620.

[30] U.S. War Department, *Official Records*, ser. 1, XXXVIII, pt. 1, p. 75; Jacob D. Cox, *Atlanta*, Campaigns of the Civil War Series, no. 9, pp. 181–82.

wagon train and wrecking portions of both the Macon and Western and Atlanta and West Point railroads before they were brought to bay.[31]

Meanwhile, the western pursuit party had been joined by Wheeler and some five hundred of his troopers who had already dealt with Stoneman. Late the evening of the twenty-ninth, Ross attacked the blue-coated column near Lovejoy's Station. Twice the Eighth Iowa Cavalry charged the Texans, trying to break through their encirclement, and twice were repulsed; the third time the Federals were able to punch through Ross's line and ride for the safety of the Chattahoochee River. Ross regrouped his men, remounted, and pounded after the raiders. The race ended at Newnan, Georgia, the next day when Wheeler's advance caught up with and attacked the enemy. Ross dismounted his brigade, sent his horses to the rear, and charged. At the same time other Confederate forces attacked.[32]

Seeing his command surrounded, McCook released his men to fight their way through as the opportunity presented itself. While one dismounted detachment of the Eighth Iowa Cavalry locked in fierce hand-to-hand combat with Ross's troopers, a larger contingent of the same command swept between the Texans and their horses. Another party of Federals surrounded the Texas headquarters staff, fighting desperately in the cut of a road. Ross himself was among the officers captured, but before he could be hustled off to McCook, Wheeler's men successfully counterattacked, rescuing commander, men, and horses.[33]

Remounting, the Texans moved to the rear of the enemy column in time to receive the surrender of a large portion of the Eighth Iowa. When the gains and losses of the action were totaled, Ross noted that his men had captured 587 prisoners, among them two brigade commanders and a number of field and company officers; the colors of the Eighth Iowa and Second Indiana cavalry regiments; two pieces of ar-

[31] U.S. War Department, *Official Records*, ser. 1, XXXVIII, pt. 2, pp. 761–62, pt. 3, p. 688, pt. 5, pp. 901, 907; Cox, *Atlanta*, pp. 182, 188; Barron, *Lone Star Defenders*, p. 199; Wright, *Texas in the War*, p. 81.

[32] U.S. War Department, *Official Records*, ser. 1, XXXVIII, pt. 3, pp. 955, 963–65; Billingsley, ed., "'Such Is War,'" pt. 2, p. 56, pt. 3, p. 111.

[33] U.S. War Department, *Official Records*, ser. 1, XXXVIII, pt. 2, pp. 762–63; report of Major Root, Eighth Iowa Cavalry, August 5, 1864, *Official Records*, ser. 1, XXXVIII, pt. 2, pp. 776–77; Ross's report, August 1, 1864, *Official Records*, ser. 1, XXXVIII, pt. 3, pp. 963–65; Wheeler's report, October 9, 1864, *Official Records*, ser. 1, XXXVIII, pt. 3, p. 955.

tillery; eleven ambulances; and a large selection of horses, equipment, and badly needed small arms. All this was at the cost of only five killed and twenty-seven wounded.[34]

After the breakup of the McCook raid, Ross's brigade remained in the area southwest of Atlanta. Desultory skirmishing continued until August 18, when Brigadier General Judson Kilpatrick's Yankee cavalry raided the Confederate railroad lifeline. Pushing past the pickets of the Sixth Texas at Sandtown, Kilpatrick's force of forty-five hundred men hit the Atlanta and West Point Railroad at Fairburn. Ross attacked the raiders the next morning. Repulsed by the greatly superior Federal force, Ross nevertheless continued skirmishing with the Federals until they reached Jonesborough on August 19. The next day a sizable Confederate force in addition to Ross's brigade surrounded Kilpatrick's men at Lovejoy's Station.[35]

Like McCook, Kilpatrick had no other choice but to fight his way out of the Confederate encirclement. Colonel Robert H. G. Minty, commanding the First and Second brigades, aimed his twenty-four-hundred-man force at the nearest part of the thinly stretched Confederate line. This happened to be Ross's brigade. As a softening-up measure before the dash for freedom, the Federal artillerymen fired into the lane behind the dismounted Texans, stampeding their horses. Then six regiments of Union horsemen charged Ross's men.

For an instant the Texans held the line, emptying their weapons at the steadily approaching column; then they turned as one man and ran for the rear. Before they could reach the goal, the Federal cavalry overran them.[36] Minty thought he had wiped the Texas Brigade from the face of the earth, but as soon as the Federal charge was safely past, General Ross and the brigade bugler appeared on the opposite side of the field. As the bugler sounded assembly, the Texans began straggling in from different directions. Total Texan losses in the entire Kilpatrick episode were only two killed, twenty wounded, and thirty captured. By August 22 Ross's men were back in line and ready for duty.[37]

[34] Ross's report, U.S. War Department, *Official Records*, pt. 3, pp. 963–65.
[35] Kerr, ed., *Fighting with Ross' Cavalry*, p. 166; Kilpatrick's report, September 13, 1864, U.S. War Department, *Official Records*, ser. 1, XXXVIII, pt. 2, pp. 858–59; Rose, *Ross' Texas Brigade*, p. 108.
[36] Minty's report, August 24, 1864, U.S. War Department, *Official Records*, ser. 1, XXXVIII, pt. 2, pp. 824–26; Barron, *Lone Star Defenders*, pp. 208–209; Kerr, ed., *Fighting with Ross' Cavalry*, p. 166.
[37] U.S. War Department, *Official Records*, ser. 1, XXXVIII, pt. 2, p. 826; Barron,

Fighting connected with the fall of Atlanta continued until September 3, although it was three days later before the brigade was officially released from its position on the railroad. Although there were more marches, countermarches, and alarms throughout September, the men of the brigade spent much of their time on picket duty near Newnan, Georgia. For some of the Texans it was their first real rest since the brigade entered the campaign three months before.[38]

For the first time, Ross found the morale, not the discipline, of his men demanding his attention. He recognized that the discontented rumblings in the brigade did not mean loss of the will to fight. Although brigade losses during the Atlanta campaign had reached 25 percent—the command entered Georgia with 1,009 men, but attrition had reduced this to just over 700—the Texans were not so disheartened that they would not "charge breastworks."[39] At the same time he realized his soldiers were dangerously discouraged regarding their field of operation.

Then, on September 6, 1864, he learned that former Texas governor Francis R. Lubbock was passing through Macon on his way to Richmond. Immediately Ross wrote Lubbock a long and confidential letter. Recalling Polk's April promise of a brigade-wide furlough, Ross reported that his men now "despaired of receiving furloughs." Also, Ross continued, he was convinced that most, if not all, of his men would go to the Trans-Mississippi Department "as soon as the enemy ceases to advance in Georgia." Ross therefore asked for all the help Lubbock could render in getting the Texas Brigade transferred to Mississippi. There a few men at a time could be furloughed, while the others could at least hear from their families. Ross stressed that he did not desire "a different field from the present" for himself, but was willing to have his command transferred without him in order to preserve "the brilliant, but hard-earned reputation" of the brigade.[40]

The fear that his brigade might desert en masse continued to

Lone Star Defenders, pp. 209–15. Barron mentions Ross's "laughable escape," but does not say how he accomplished it.

[38] Kerr, ed., *Fighting with Ross' Cavalry*, pp. 167, 170–72; Barron, *Lone Star Defenders*, pp. 228–30; Ross to D. A. Tinsley, September 14, 1864, Ross Family Papers, Baylor.

[39] U.S. War Department, *Official Records*, ser. 1, XXXIX, pt. 2, p. 881; Ross to D. A. Tinsley, September 14, 1864, Ross Family Papers, Baylor; John P. Dyer, *The Gallant Hood*, p. 274.

[40] U.S. War Department, *Official Records*, ser. 1, XXXVIII, pt. 5, pp. 1026–27.

plague the young commander. In a letter to his father-in-law Ross remarked that he would like to come home that winter, but knew if he left without the brigade the men would use his absence as an excuse to go without authority. By the end of October, the prospect of a general furlough for the Texans was more encouraging, but by then General John B. Hood's Army of Tennessee was moving north on the ill-fated Tennessee campaign.[41]

The disastrous Tennessee campaign of November–December, 1864, was the last of the active military operations in which Ross and his Texans took part. This series of skirmishes and pitched battles was also most illustrative of the skill and fighting qualities of commander and men, and can be viewed as a crowning achievement of Ross's active military career. By then the strength of Ross's brigade had declined to 686 men, but despite their small numbers, the Texans' fighting ability had not lessened.[42]

Hood's original intention had not been to cross the Tennessee River; rather, to assume the offensive, cut Sherman's line of communications, threaten Tennessee, and lure the Union general into giving battle on terrain favorable to the Confederates. At first this strategy succeeded; Sherman was forced to follow the rebel army northward. In a reversal of roles, his cavalry under Judson Kilpatrick battled Confederate horsemen intent on raiding the Union lifeline of the Western and Atlantic Railroad.[43]

Arriving at last in the northwest corner of the state where he had hoped to come to grips with Sherman, Hood found his army greatly outnumbered and his officers reluctant to fight the Federals at such odds. For two days he pondered the situation before determining to march into Tennessee.[44] It was a fateful decision for the Army of Tennessee as a unit and for the Confederacy as a whole. While Hood shattered the remnants of his army against the strength of Federal garrisons in Tennessee, Sherman was free to march to the sea.

With Frank Armstrong's brigade of Jackson's division, under For-

[41] Ross to D. A. Tinsley, September 14, 1864, and Ross to Mrs. Ross, October 23, 1864, both in Ross Family Papers, Baylor.
[42] U.S. War Department, *Official Records*, ser. 1, XXXV, pt. 1, p. 768.
[43] John Bell Hood, *Advance and Retreat: Personal Experiences in the United States and Confederate States Armies*, pp. 254, 264; Dyer, *The Gallant Hood*, p. 275; *New York Times*, October 8, 1864.
[44] Dyer, *The Gallant Hood*, pp. 281–83.

rest's cavalry command, Ross's Texans were given the honor of leading the Confederate advance into Tennessee. Some of the men, despairing now of ever returning to the Trans-Mississippi Department, deserted.[45] Although these men were considered unworthy skulkers by their comrades, it was an evil omen and one which accurately predicted the outcome of the campaign.

Hood hoped to isolate Union General John M. Schofield's twenty-three thousand troops then at Pulaski, Tennessee, from George H. Thomas's forces in Nashville. Accordingly, the gray-coated army hurried northward toward Columbia, in an attempt to reach and hold that strategic position. On the twenty-second of November, the probing Confederate cavalry advance attacked the enemy at Lawrenceburg, near Pulaski.[46]

Near Campbellsville the next day, Ross's brigade met and scattered an enemy division commanded by their old foe, Colonel Hatch. About eighty-four prisoners and four stands of colors were captured, but more important in the eyes of Ross's Texans were the beef cattle, coffee and other provisions, boots, overcoats, and blankets taken from the enemy. Two hundred horses plus a number of pack mules were an added bonus.[47]

Ross moved into position at Columbia the following day. But the trap Hood had planned failed to close, for the Federals at Pulaski had panicked and hurried to Columbia. Still the Texans were able to do good service until Hood's infantry reached the town on November 27.[48]

Released for cavalry service, the Texans pushed east on the Shelbyville Road. By then all of Forrest's troopers were moving in for another attempt at cutting Schofield off from Thomas. Near Rally Hill, Ross's Texans drove back a Union brigade, capturing an entire company of the Seventh Ohio Cavalry, three stands of colors, horses, arms, and wagons loaded with ordnance. Forrest then left Ross to follow James H. Wilson's Federal cavalry while he rode west toward Spring Hill. The Confederates were then between Schofield and Thomas, but

[45] Kerr, ed., *Fighting with Ross' Cavalry*, p. 188.

[46] John Bell Hood, "The Invasion of Tennessee," in *Battles and Leaders of the Civil War*, ed. Robert Underwood Johnson and Clarence Clough Buel, IV, 429; Kerr, ed., *Fighting with Ross' Cavalry*, p. 189.

[47] U.S. War Department, *Official Records*, ser. 1, XLV, pt. 1, p. 368, 768–69; Kerr, ed., *Fighting with Ross' Cavalry*, p. 190.

[48] Hood, "The Invasion of Tennessee," p. 429; U.S. War Department, *Official Records*, ser. 1, XLV, pt. 1, p. 769.

confusion of orders between Hood and one of his infantry corps commanders allowed the Federals to slip through.[49]

Meanwhile, Ross turned his brigade toward Thompson's Station,
where they destroyed an ordnance train and burned a railroad bridge,
before turning their attention to Schofield's wagon train, which was
passing on a nearby pike. A night raid on the train left thirty-nine
loaded wagons in the brigade's possession.[50] But while Ross's small brigade was an ideal size for raiding, he could do little to oppose the
Union march north and thus save the campaign from disaster.

After watching the Federal army "in full retreat" until daylight,
Ross marched his brigade toward Franklin, arriving there on November 30 just as Hood began his attack. While the desperate fighting of
the main battle raged on the outskirts of Franklin south of the Harpeth
River, Ross's Texans battled Yankee horsemen in a separate action on
the north bank. Finally the Confederates were forced back across the
river.[51]

It was late that evening before the firing in Franklin ceased.
About 3:00 A.M. Schofield's army withdrew and headed for Nashville.
The next morning Forrest's troopers galloped in pursuit. Ross and his
men reined up in front of Nashville on December 3, and again they
acted. With the approach of Hood's infantry, however, the cavalrymen
were allowed to fall back into the country, cook rations, and reshoe
their horses.[52]

Ross's Texans—indeed, Forrest's entire cavalry command—took
little part in the actual fighting around Nashville. Instead, the gray-
coated horsemen operated on the flanks of the Union army. Ross and
his Texans were near Murfreesboro on December 15 when Thomas initiated the battle at Nashville. While the battle raged, the Texans captured a freight train loaded with rations and other supplies. One hundred fifty bluecoats surrendered, but the ragged Confederates were
more interested in the goods on board the train than in the prisoners.
The next day, following Hood's demoralizing defeat, Ross's men fell

[49] Thomas Robson Hay, *Hood's Tennessee Campaign*, p. 106; U.S. War Department, *Official Records*, ser. 1, XLV, pt. 1, p. 769; Hood, "The Invasion of Tennessee,"
p. 431; Dyer, *The Gallant Hood*, pp. 286–88.

[50] U.S. War Department, *Official Records*, ser. 1, XLV, pt. 1, pp. 769–70; Kerr,
ed., *Fighting with Ross' Cavalry*, p. 191.

[51] U.S. War Department, *Official Records*, ser. 1, XLV, pt. 1, pp. 769–70.

[52] Hood, "The Invasion of Tennessee," p. 435; Kerr, ed., *Fighting with Ross' Cavalry*, p. 193.

back to Columbia. There they found the shattered remnants of Hood's army anxiously awaiting their arrival, for the reputation of Forrest's cavalry was the only deterrent to slashing attacks by Wilson's pursuing troopers.[53]

Hood organized a rear guard of Forrest's cavalry and several infantry regiments, which was left to hold off the menacing foe while the rest of the army fled south. At times Hood was only six or seven hours ahead of his pursuers, but the Federals could not break through the little rear guard. Meanwhile Ross's Texans proved their worth many times over. Alternating with Frank Armstrong's brigade as the last Confederate unit in the rear guard, the Texans bore the brunt of attacks by the pursuing Union troops for almost two weeks.[54]

Pursuit ended with the crossing of the Tennessee River on December 27. With the remnants of the once-proud Army of Tennessee, Forrest's troops moved into northeastern Mississippi. In January, at his headquarters in a private home in Corinth, Ross prepared his official report of the Tennessee campaign. The general noted that the entire Texan loss had been twelve men killed, seventy wounded, and five captured. In return the Texans had captured 550 prisoners, nine stands of colors, several hundred horses, and enough overcoats and blankets to supply their whole command. Although the horses were jaded by the strenuous campaigning, the brigade itself returned from Tennessee in no worse condition than when it started.[55]

[53] U.S. War Department, *Official Records*, ser. 1, XLV, pt. 1, pp. 770–71; W. A. Callaway, "Hard Times with Ross's Cavalry," *Confederate Veteran* 28 (December, 1920): 447; Kerr, ed., *Fighting with Ross' Cavalry*, pp. 195–96; Dyer, *The Gallant Hood*, p. 302.

[54] Hay, *Hood's Tennessee Campaign*, p. 175; U.S. War Department, *Official Records*, ser. 1, XLV, pt. 1, pp. 771–72; Dyer, *The Gallant Hood*, p. 302; French, *Two Wars*, p. 323; Robert A. Jarman, "A Mississippian at Nashville," *Civil War Times Illustrated* 12 (May, 1973): 15. One day during the retreat, while Ross was directing the rear guard, he came upon one of his men lying severely wounded on the roadside. Although enemy troops were approaching, the general dismounted beside the wounded enlisted man, examined his wounds, and then asked him if he thought he had strength to sit behind Ross on his horse. The soldier thought he was mortally wounded and told his commander he could do nothing to aid him. Ross then turned out his pockets in search of funds to give the wounded man so he would not be left penniless in enemy territory. The search produced only six dollars. Ross pressed the bills into the hands of his cavalryman, threw himself into his saddle, and galloped away as the Federals opened fire (John Henry Brown, *Indian Wars and Pioneers of Texas*, p. 318).

[55] U.S. War Department, *Official Records*, ser. 1, XLV, pt. 1, p. 772; Dyer, *The Gallant Hood*, p. 303.

The same day the Texan officer penned a private, and revealing, letter to Mrs. Ross. In it he reported that all the Confederate cavalry except his and Armstrong's men had been "badly scattered & demoralized" in Tennessee. A furlough had been promised his troops by February 1, but this had been done so many times without result that Ross saw little hope for fulfillment. By then the enemy would be moving, and "when there is an Emergency, the Texan Troops have a very slim chance to remain idle." Sandwiched among his opinions of the treatment of his command, Ross included an offhand statement that he had been so sick the past two or three days he had been unable to leave his room. Perhaps in this way he hoped to avoid alarming Lizzie, but the letter itself would have done so. Ross's handwriting had deteriorated so by that time that it looked like that of an old man.[56]

In late January, Ross's brigade received the assignment of picket duty in front of Vicksburg. Old friends in the Yazoo City area joyfully welcomed the Texans back and gave a round of parties and barbecues in their honor. While his men rode out on patrols or socialized with their Yazoo valley friends, their commander again directed his attention to the spirit of despair and dissension that was tearing his brigade apart. Morale had remained high on the march from Tennessee, as Hood had telegraphed Richmond asking for permission to furlough Ross's brigade. There was still no official word by late January, but ugly rumors abounded. It was reported that not only had the secretary of war refused to concur with Hood's request, but he had also recommended that the brigade be disbanded for a mere twenty days.[57]

Texan wrath was immediate. The more impatient or despairing soldiers among the brigade, some one hundred eighty strong, deserted. Neither their commander nor their comrades made an effort to stop them. Others, more loyal to their general and to the Confederacy, grimly determined to see the drama out, although not without protest. On January 28, 1865, there appeared in the *Meridian* (Mississippi) *Daily Clarion* a lengthy letter from a member of Ross's brigade who signed himself "Alamo," exposing the injustice inflicted on the Texans.[58]

---

[56] Ross to Mrs. Ross, January 12, 1865, Ross Family Papers, Baylor.

[57] Wooten, ed., *History of Texas*, p. 627; Lale and Key, eds., *Letters of David R. Garrett*, p. 90; Ross to Mrs. Ross, January 12, 1865, Ross Family Papers, Baylor; *Meridian* (Miss.) *Daily Clarion*, January 28, 1865.

[58] Barron, *Lone Star Defenders*, pp. 268–69; *Meridian* (Miss.) *Daily Clarion*, January 28, 1865. Typewritten copy of "Alamo" letter courtesy of Dr. Homer Kerr, Department of History, University of Texas at Arlington, Arlington, Texas.

It is not known whether the impassioned pleading of "Alamo," the confidential misgivings of Ross as expressed to Lubbock, or the realization by Richmond of a great wrong being perpetrated upon the brigade brought about a change in government policy, but in mid-February the long-desired furlough—for one-half the brigade—came through. On March 13, the general himself left for Texas on a ninety-day leave of absence.[59] His eagerness to see the young wife from whom he had been separated for two years, his failing health, and the hope of the Confederate high command that his reputation would enable him to recruit new troops probably contributed equally to his decision to return. He did not know that he had seen his men, as Confederate soldiers, for the last time.

The joyful reunion with wife and loved ones in Texas can only be imagined, but it probably occurred after the surrender of Robert E. Lee's Army of Northern Virginia. By then, or at least by the time of Johnston's surrender to Sherman on April 26, 1865, Ross doubtless knew that the Confederate cause was lost. His health was shattered, and it was more important for him to recover than to try to return to his brigade. So it was that Colonel Dudley M. Jones was in command of the Texas regiments at the time of their surrender at Jackson, Mississippi, on May 13, 1865.[60]

In retrospect, Ross can be considered an illustrious example of the American citizen-soldier who serves his country when needed and then returns to civilian life once the crisis is past. He had no vaunting military ambition, only a patriotic determination to serve his state and section and a young man's desire to win a name for himself. At the same time he rendered this service to the fullest extent of his ability and strength. A skillful officer on the regimental and brigade levels, Ross possibly could have developed into a fine division commander. As it was, he proved his ability and skill as a field and then as a general officer many times over.

Despite his ability and skill, it is doubtful that the Texan could have advanced by merit much above the rank of division commander. Although courageous and resourceful, he lacked both the formal mili-

[59] U.S. War Department, *Official Records*, ser. 1, XLVIII, pt. 1, pp. 1394–95; Lale and Key, eds., *Letters of David R. Garrett*, p. 90.

[60] Elizabeth Ross Clarke, "Life of Sul Ross," Ross Family Papers, Baylor, pp. 102–103; *Dallas Herald*, May 11, 1865; Wooten, ed., *History of Texas*, p. 627; Graves Diary, p. 41; A. W. Sparks, *The War Between the States as I Saw It: Reminiscences Historical and Personal*, pp. 116–17.

tary training and the natural brilliance necessary for a successful corps commander of cavalry. An excellent scout, raider, and battlefield tactician, it is unlikely he would have been able to formulate and direct strategy on a wide scale.

Although the political horizon looked dark at the end of the war, the people of Texas would not forget the soldier who had brought such glory to the Lone Star State. Before too many years had passed, Sul Ross would find that his experiences as a ranger and soldier had prepared him to serve as a statesman and educator whose influence would be felt beyond his lifetime.

☆ 9 ☆

Sword into Plowshare

UNFORTUNATELY for the historian, little is known about the activities of Lawrence Sullivan Ross during the period between the end of the war and his election in 1873 as McLennan County sheriff. Letters are few, newspaper accounts lacking, other records scarce. As far as Ross's life was concerned, it was a period of obscurity.

For many reasons obscurity surrounded—and probably suited—the young former general. It was a trying era of physical weakness, political disfranchisement, and economic recovery, which he experienced in common with other former Confederate Texans. But he endured and worked quietly to regain what had been lost in four years of war and later in eight years of Reconstruction.

With the surrender of the Texas Brigade in May, 1865, Sul Ross's active military career had ended. Probably his strong sense of duty and loyalty caused him to regret his absence from his command; at the same time, his poor health underscored the prudence of his decision to remain in Texas. His health was indeed precarious. Throughout his life he suffered from the wounds received in the Wichita village fight, but these injuries were aggravated from time to time by other physical distresses. Although never wounded during the war, Ross was plagued by debilitating illnesses. While at Corinth, Mississippi, in May, 1862, he had contracted a bad cold accompanied by a lingering fever, which he could not throw off for about eight weeks. Unhealthful conditions as well as strenuous skirmishing that required his active field command delayed his recovery. By the time he considered himself cured he had been reduced by illness to only 125 pounds and presented "quite a crane-like appearance."[1]

---

[1] *Waco Times-Herald*, January 4, 1898; Ross to Mrs. Ross, May 15, June 14, and June [July] 2, 1862, Ross Family Papers, Texas Collection, Baylor University, Waco, Texas (hereafter cited as Ross Family Papers, Baylor).

He recovered from the Corinth fever, but not without ill effects. Beginning September 26, 1863, he had attacks of fever and chills about every three days, which lasted until April, 1864—a classic case of recurring tertian malaria. Besides battling malaria, Ross suffered another bad cold while crossing arms over the Mississippi River in January, 1864, a cold that eventually settled in his lungs, causing chronic bronchitis.[2] If all this were not enough to bring about a physical breakdown, the overwork and strain of the rigorous Atlanta and Franklin-Nashville campaigns of middle and late 1864 further undermined his health. It would be months after his return to Texas before he regained his strength; years would pass before his health definitely improved. The rest of his life he would be susceptible to attacks of fever and bouts of respiratory ailments. Some of his bronchial trouble was so severe that in later years Ross feared the onset of tuberculosis.[3]

However, poor health was not his only problem, as Ross soon learned. As a Confederate army officer above the rank of colonel, the young Texan found himself in one of the fourteen classes of exemptions to President Andrew Johnson's amnesty proclamation of May 29, 1865. And although General Ross had avoided the humiliation of surrendering his command to the enemy, he had also missed obtaining a parole protecting him from arrest should the victorious Federals choose to jail him. In order to prevent arrest and confiscation of his property, regain his civil rights, and acquire political standing in his state, Ross had to apply for special pardon of what was now considered his treason against the United States. Accordingly, he applied for amnesty in Austin on August 4, 1865, thus proving his determination to abide by the decision of the battlefield.[4]

Such pardon would be two years in coming. Although his application with attached oath of future allegiance to the United States was delivered to Unionist former governor and family friend Elisha M.

[2] Ross to Mrs. Ross, April 26, 1864, Ross Family Papers, Baylor; Ross to Victor M. Rose, June 1, 1878, Lawrence Sullivan Ross Letters, Barker Texas History Center, University of Texas at Austin (hereafter cited as Ross Letters).

[3] Ross to Mrs. Ross, [August, 1870], Ross Family Papers, Baylor; Ross to Rose, June 1, 1878, Ross Letters. Sul and Lizzie's child conceived during this time of convalescence died of pneumonia in 1883 (*Waco Daily Examiner*, February 1, 1883; Elizabeth Williams Estes, June 26, 1979, personal communication).

[4] Jonathan Truman Dorris, *Pardon and Amnesty Under Lincoln and Johnson: The Restoration of the Confederates to Their Rights and Privileges, 1861–1898*, pp. 35, 111, 113, 117; Marcus J. Wright, *General Officers of the Confederate Army*, pp. 116–17.

Pease on September 2, 1865, two years passed before Ross secured a presidential pardon for his part in the rebellion. Eventually his application was recommended by leading Texas Unionists, including Provisional Governor Andrew J. Hamilton, James W. Throckmorton, and Judge I. A. Paschal. Hamilton and Paschal had been involved in state affairs while Ross was winning his reputation as an Indian fighter and ranger captain and were familiar with his service to the state. On the other hand, Throckmorton, a prewar Unionist later turned Confederate officer, had served with Ross in the Trans-Mississippi during the early years of the war. Johnson himself approved the Texan's application on October 22, 1866, but the wheels of bureaucracy turned so slowly that it was July the following year before Ross received his warrant of pardon and acknowledged his formal acceptance.[5]

In the meantime, the former soldier had to pick up the threads of his earlier life and adapt his adventurous spirit to peacetime. However, his battles were not over; the enemy had merely changed. Harder fighting, but of another kind, confronted him. As one of Ross's contemporaries remarked, it "required no less manhood to conquer the situation of peace which war had framed, than to battle with the armed foe."[6]

With his health somewhat better and amnesty at least actively sought, the twenty-six-year-old Ross turned his energies to the pressing problem of earning a living. At the close of the war, Texas, like her sister Confederate states, was economically exhausted, her trade at a standstill, her former bondsmen freed. Waco and McLennan County shared briefly in this exhaustion, which although shorter-lived than that of the South in general, was no less potent. When Sul Ross returned to Waco from the war his only substantial possession was land— 160 acres of rich bottomland on the South Bosque River west of Waco

---

[5] Adjutant General Papers, Reconstruction, Special Pardons, R—Miscellaneous, Texas State Archives, Austin, Texas; *Waco Tribune-Herald*, October 30, 1949. A member of the House of Representatives, Hamilton may have been familiar with a speech given by the Honorable John H. Reagan, also of Texas, mentioning Ross's involvement in the battle of Wichita village (*Dallas Herald*, April 6, 1859, and November 13, 1861). A careless clerk transcribed his name as "J. S. Rose" (U.S. Congress, House, *House Executive Documents*, 39th Cong., 2d sess., 1866, H. Doc. 31, vol. 7, p. 12; receipt of warrant of pardon, series Amnesty Oaths, Civil Archives Division, Department of State, National Archives, Washington, D.C.).

[6] L. E. Daniell, *Personnel of the Texas State Government, with Sketches of Distinguished Texans . . .* , p. 16.

and 5.41 acres in town—but with hard work the land could produce bountifully.[7]

Nor was he afraid of hard work, especially since his early training had been on the land. From long acquaintance he knew the cycles of the region's growing seasons, the rhythm of the farmer's working year. As a child and later as a youth he had had much practical experience in the methods and mechanics of plowing, sowing, cultivating, and harvesting. Farming was in his blood, as it had been in that of his forebears.

At the same time his early frontier training had taught him economy and "inculcated no very extravagant desires." A skilled hunter, he could provide his household with meat while other skills acquired in his youth could build the family shelter. Just what sort of dwelling, if any, was located on his Bosque farm is not known, but wood was plentiful and the other materials for building a cabin at hand. Like other parents, the senior Rosses and the Tinsleys probably contributed household goods and farm equipment to the young couple's first establishment. But whatever the arrangements, Sul and Lizzie soon settled down to farming and raising a family. Their second child, a son, Mervin, was born on January 2, 1866, and others soon followed in the accepted pattern of nineteenth-century family life.[8]

While his family was growing and his affairs were progressing, Ross found time to be moderately active in the civic and social life of his community. That he exercised some of his prerogatives as a citizen during 1866 and 1867 can be seen by his involvement in two civil suits, apparently over the question of land ownership. There were also social pleasures. In 1871 he served with Richard Coke, General Thomas Har-

[7] Charles William Ramsdell, *Reconstruction in Texas*, pp. 27–28; McLennan County Courthouse Deed Records, 1860–62, vol. J, pp. 164, 605, Waco, Texas (hereafter cited as McLennan County Deed Records).

[8] Ross to Rose, June 1, 1878, Ross Letters; *Dictionary of American Biography*, s.v. "Ross, Lawrence Sullivan"; Elizabeth Ross Clarke, "Life of Sul Ross," Ross Family Papers, Baylor, pp. 102–103. Sul and Lizzie's first child died, probably at birth, in the fall of 1863 while Ross was in Mississippi (Ross to Mrs. Ross, November 29, 1863, Ross Family Papers, Baylor). The other Ross children and their birth dates were Lawrence Sullivan, Jr., July 25, 1868; Florine, October 3, 1870; Harvey, March 5, 1873; Frank, April 27, 1875; Elizabeth, April 24, 1878; James Tinsley, December 30, 1880; and Neville P., March 23, 1882 (Ross family Bible, from private collection, Dr. and Mrs. Neville P. Clarke, Bryan, Texas; Ross to Rose, April 21, 1881, Ross Letters; various headstones, Ross family burial plot, Oakwood Cemetery, Waco, Texas).

rison, and others as senior managers of the Railroad Barbecue Ball celebrating the arrival of the Waco and Northwestern Railway.[9]

But these minor duties and pleasures were poor compensation for the loss of political privileges. Although Ross finally obtained a presidential pardon, the political situation in Texas during Reconstruction precluded any participation in government. At the time of the selection of delegates to the 1866 constitutional convention and the election of state officials that followed, he had not yet received pardon from Washington. Then Radical Republicans gained control of Congress and imposed their own reconstruction policies upon the South. In the process Ross was again disfranchised.

Records are sparse, but it seems that after a brief period of exercising his civil rights, Ross was again disqualified from voting or even serving as a juror. The First Reconstruction Act of March 2, 1867, following the guidelines of the Fourteenth Amendment, had disqualified all officers of the federal or state governments who had once taken an oath to uphold the Constitution of the United States and then had supported the rebellion. Fearing this disqualification was not broad enough to remove would-be Democratic voters from registration lists in the South, Congress passed the Supplementary Reconstruction Act twenty-one days later. This act simply disfranchised any person who had ever held any federal or state office and afterward supported the Confederacy. If the terms of the first act did not bar Sul from the ballot because of his prewar ranger commission, the second undoubtedly did so. Similarly, a state circular of April 27, 1867, promulgated by the authority of the military commander of Texas, General Charles Griffin, disqualified all those citizens from serving as jurors who could not swear the "Iron-clad" oath that they had never engaged in rebellion against the United States.[10]

These disqualifications stood until the Texas Radicals tried and failed to write the same restrictions into the state constitution of 1869. Thereafter disfranchisement was confined to that laid down in the Fourteenth Amendment. However, it is questionable how frequently Ross exercised his right to vote during a time when, as in 1871, the Democratic voters of McLennan County were forced to run the gaunt-

[9] McLennan County District Court Minutes, vol. D, pp. 435–36, vol. E, p. 76; Roger N. Conger, *Pictorial History of Waco*, p. 282.

[10] Ramsdell, *Reconstruction in Texas*, pp. 85, 146, 155–56, 234.

let between two lines of jeering, threatening state police and militia to reach the polling place.[11]

What he thought of the situation at the time is not known, for at no time in his career was Ross more reticent than during the Reconstruction era. Judging by his actions during this period, the young man who had spent so many of his early years serving Texas was content to avoid political involvement and enjoy the tranquillity of family and farm life.[12]

By the dedication, industry, and skill that had marked him as a soldier, Ross soon prospered in his farming and was able to purchase about 20 acres in town from his parents for $1,500. In May, 1869, he bought 40 acres of farmland downstream from Waco on the old Carlos O'Campo grant for an additional $400. A year later Lizzie's inheritance from the estate of her father, David A. Tinsley, added 186 acres of the old plantation on the Brazos south of town to the Ross holdings.[13]

Thereafter, Ross acquired land rapidly. Some property he procured individually, other parcels were bought in partnership, and still more acreage from the old Tinsley plantation was purchased from the estate of his brother-in-law. At an 1872 sheriff's sale he purchased three lots of ten acres each, which gave him land on the east bank of the Brazos upriver. Most city property was obtained with a view toward its eventual resale value, but he was always looking for parcels to add to his rural holdings. In this he was generally successful; by the end of the postwar decade, Ross owned about one thousand acres of farming land, much of it along the Brazos and adjoining his plantation about six miles downriver near Flat Creek.[14] He would continue to add to and sell from his varied holdings the rest of his life, but most of his purchases came during Reconstruction.

The questions arise why Ross prospered during this difficult economic period while so many of his contemporaries suffered losses, and where he obtained the capital necessary for his numerous ventures in real estate. Unfortunately, since most family records were lost in the

[11] Ibid., p. 254; William O. Wilkes, *History of the Waco Medical Association with Reminiscences and Irrelevant Comments*, p. 70.

[12] *Dictionary of American Biography*, s.v. "Ross, Lawrence Sullivan"; Clarke, "Life of Sul Ross," Ross Family Papers, Baylor, p. 103.

[13] McLennan County Deed Records, vol. M, pp. 124, 640, vol. N, p. 257.

[14] Ibid., vol. M, p. 465, vol. N, p. 598, vol. O, p. 699, vol. R, pp. 57, 210, and 496, vol. T, pp. 407 and 409–10; Dayton Kelley, ed., *The Handbook of Waco and McLennan County*, p. 233.

fire that destroyed the Ross home early in this century, the historian must use conjecture, rather than fact, to determine answers to these questions. However, several observations may be made from the few materials available from the Reconstruction era.

First, Waco's economy recovered quickly at the end of the war. By 1866 business was booming: the building trades were particularly busy, and a number of new manufacturers were operating.[15] Second, Ross was also fortunate to have a solid financial base among family and friends to draw on. To what extent he did so is not known, but this resource was presumably available. In addition to farming and horse racing, Shapley Ross had been for years a local entrepreneur, operating a store, a hotel, the first city water system, and the only ferry along the Middle Brazos. He was not poor by any standards and was better off than many of his planter neighbors at the end of the war because he had little capital tied up in slaves. Similarly Lizzie's parents were well-to-do, her father owning some four thousand acres of rich cropland in the Waco area. Although Dr. Tinsley lost considerable slave capital by emancipation, he was not beggared by the war. Sul also had a wealthy brother-in-law, George Barnard, whose economic gains came from banking and retail sales, and a number of financially able friends among the Gurley and Downs families of Waco.[16]

Finally, his farming ventures, in good years, made possible economic recovery. As the immediate postwar economic slump eased, Waco developed into a center for the production of three agricultural products much in demand in the marketplace then—cotton, wheat, and beef cattle. Cotton again became king, local growers shipping at times 33,000 bales a season. Like his neighbors, Ross at this time grew wheat (and probably cotton, since bottomland like his would produce more than a bale to the acre) and raised livestock, especially cattle. Apparently he entered the cattle business when there was money to be made trailing herds to eastern or northern rail centers. One of Sul's brothers, Pete, conducted trail drives to New Orleans during the early Reconstruction period. Since Ross himself claimed in later years to have been a cowboy, it is possible he accompanied Pete on these drives. Later, with the coming of the railroad, the demand for beef cattle continued, and stock from the Waco area was shipped to packing-

[15] Wilkes, *Waco Medical Association*, p. 20.
[16] *Waco Tribune-Herald*, October 30, 1949.

houses as far away as Chicago and Saint Louis. Ross's interest in fine beef cattle eventually led him to purchase, breed, and raise pedigreed Durham shorthorn stock. That he was able to do so by the mid-seventies again attests to his increasing prosperity.[17]

An astute husbandman, Ross plowed back most of his profits into his farming ventures. But despite buying more land, improving his stock, and helping tenants through bad years, he retained enough from his farm income to enable his family to live comfortably. Since there were no public schools in Waco at this time, he sent his children to private schools as they grew older. And sometime during this period, or at least before 1880, he was able to build a family home on some of his city property located on Austin Avenue.[18]

History records that Ross left his farm for only one extended period during Reconstruction. In August, 1870, he escorted his mother, Catherine Ross; Lizzie Ross, the white girl he rescued from the Comanches; and another woman and her baby from Waco to Los Angeles. According to local tradition, Sul's father, Shapley P. Ross, had run afoul of Union authorities in Waco during the period of military occupation that began in 1868. A man of fierce passions, Shapley Ross allegedly assaulted a Yankee soldier. Arrest followed, but use of the Masonic sign allowed the old frontiersman to escape. Thereupon Shapley deemed it prudent to travel (for his health, said friends) to California, where he was joined by his eldest son, Peter F. Ross. It was while he and Pete were living in southern California that Sul visited that state.[19]

Ever a home-loving man, Sul Ross returned to Waco after a stay in California of only a few weeks. At the request of his children Shapley

[17] John Sleeper and J. C. Hutchins, comps., *Waco and McLennan County, Texas: Containing a City Directory of Waco, Historical Sketches of the City and County; Biographical Sketches and Notices of a Few Prominent Citizens*, pp. 25–26, 28, 31; Kelley, ed., *Handbook of Waco and McLennan County*, p. 233; U.S. Department of Agriculture, Bureau of Animal Industry Special Bulletin, *Proceedings of an Interstate Convention of Cattlemen, Held at Fort Worth, Texas, Tuesday, Wednesday, and Thursday, March 11, 12, and 13, 1890*, p. 14; Ross to Mrs. Ross, September 7 and 13, 1875, Ross Family Papers, Baylor; *Waco Daily Examiner*, October 22, 1875.

[18] Ross to Mrs. Ross, September 7, 1875, Ross Family Papers, Baylor; Wilkes, *Waco Medical Association*, p. 36.

[19] Ross to Mrs. Ross, [August, 1870], and August 31, 1870, Ross Family Papers, Baylor; Julien Hyer, *The Land of Beginning Again: The Romance of the Brazos*, p. 227; John S. Ford, *Rip Ford's Texas*, p. 456; Kelley, ed., *Handbook of Waco and McLennan County*, p. 233. While in California, Lizzie Ross met and married a wealthy merchant living near Los Angeles (Ross to S. A. Cunningham, May 14, 1894, Ross Family Papers, Baylor).

Ross also returned to Waco in 1870, although Pete remained in the Los Angeles area for four years.[20]

Back home again and still engaged in farming, Ross was living quietly on his plantation with his wife and children in 1873 when his fellow citizens again appealed to him for assistance, this time in cleaning out the desperadoes infesting McLennan County.[21] The years of obscurity were at an end: Sul Ross was again to enter the service of his state, this time as a sheriff.

[20] Kelley, ed., *Handbook of Waco and McLennan County*, p. 233.
[21] *El Paso Times*, August 28, 1886; *Waco Tribune-Herald*, October 30, 1949.

10

Lawman and Lawmaker

BY early 1873, Reconstruction was all but over in Texas. The general election of the preceding November had succeeded both in carrying Democrats into Congress and in securing the party a substantial majority in the state legislature. True, the hated Radical Republican E. J. Davis would remain as governor for another year, but with a Democratic majority in Austin his policies would be hamstrung if not completely disabled.[1]

But although Reconstruction was nearing an end, the problems growing out of eight years of political and social revolution were only beginning to be solved. Texas law and order were in chaos, for the state police under Davis had been despotic, arbitrary, and the haven of desperadoes.[2] Law-abiding citizens suffered harassment, loss of property, and bodily harm without recourse while the ever-growing criminal element murdered and plundered almost unopposed. In the words of one contemporary, during Reconstruction "many of the most desperate and abandoned characters in the whole country had fled into Texas, and many sections of the State were almost given over to the terrorism created by these miscreants."[3]

Although McLennan County was in the process of changing from a largely stock-raising economy to a diversified agricultural, manufacturing, and merchandising community by the end of the decade following Appomattox, Waco was still a frontier town. The city on the Brazos had never been particularly tame, but since 1868 cattle herds

---

[1] Charles William Ramsdell, *Reconstruction in Texas*, p. 313.

[2] Ibid., p. 302. Northerners had an opposite view (see Edward King and J. Wells Champney, *Texas: 1874. An Eyewitness Account of Conditions in Post-Reconstruction Texas*, p. 60).

[3] James T. DeShields, *They Sat in High Place: The Presidents and Governors of Texas*, p. 337.

from south and central Texas bound for Dodge City and other railhead towns in Kansas had passed through Waco. The rapidly growing city of over five thousand soon experienced all the liveliness and lawlessness associated with a trail town. In 1871 the railroad arrived, making Waco a railhead in its own right, and with the railroad came the multitudinous saloons, gambling halls, and bordellos that grew up in such an area.[4]

In this environment the difficulties of law enforcement were great. Because of the extreme turmoil of the Reconstruction era, law was either in the hands of the corrupt state police and political sheriffs or left to the responsibility of the individual. In either case enforcement was generally by fist, knife, or firearm. Since armed ruffians walked the streets, citizens were forced to arm themselves, with bloodshed often the result. Therefore, it is not surprising that during this time Waco gained an unsavory reputation as "Six-shooter Depot." Indeed, the story is told that upon arrival by train at Waco, dudes expected to witness a killing while they paused for lunch.[5]

These general problems of law enforcement were compounded by the proximity of the Tomás de la Vega eleven-league grant. By 1873 the ownership of this land across the Brazos from Waco, more than sixty thousand acres, had been in litigation for twenty-two years. Legally a no-man's land, the grant became a haven for squatters and other troublemakers and, far worse, a hideout for criminals of every type. Many of the squatters were men of evil repute who stole timber, rustled livestock, and harbored criminals worse than themselves. "All the bad men who came to our county gravitated to them," recalled one resident. These malefactors "pursued their dark and fraudulent plots and schemes with impunity," for the law was powerless. Arrests, if made, proved worthless, because the outlaws, or "Modocs," as they were called, intimidated or suborned witnesses or simply broke their cohorts out of jail.[6]

[4] Roger N. Conger, *Pictorial History of Waco*, pp. 9, 12–13; *Austin Daily Democratic Statesman*, March 27, 1875; King and Champney, *Texas: 1874*, p. 50.

[5] Conger, *Pictorial History of Waco*, p. 13; Julien Hyer, *The Land of Beginning Again: The Romance of the Brazos*, p. 260.

[6] Roger N. Conger, "The Tomás de la Vega Eleven-League Grant on the Brazos," *Southwestern Historical Quarterly* 61 (January, 1958): 379; John Sleeper and J. C. Hutchins, comps., *Waco and McLennan County, Texas: Containing a City Directory of Waco, Historical Sketches of the City and County; Biographical Sketches and Notices of a Few Prominent Citizens*, p. 35. Journalist Edward King noted the boldness exhibited by outlaws in effecting a rescue of their friends (King and Champney, *Texas: 1874*, p. 45).

One particularly noxious band lurking on the de la Vega grant was a gang of horse thieves, who stole animals from McLennan and surrounding counties, hid them on the grant, and then drove them as far east as Alabama before selling them. This proved quite lucrative for the perpetrators, but the citizens demanded it be stopped.[7]

Meanwhile, the election of 1873 approached. Until January of that year, the sheriff of McLennan County had been William H. Morris, a man hand-in-glove with Judge John W. Oliver, Waco's own militant radical carpetbagger. Morris had apparently helped himself to county funds and had embittered many citizens by his support of Judge Oliver, who was teetering on the brink of insanity. At the same time he had done little to end the reign of lawlessness sweeping the county. Morris eventually was succeeded by P. McClelland, but local citizens were far from happy with the change.[8] The position called for a man of courage, but one in whom they had confidence. Finally, his fellow citizens turned to Lawrence Sullivan Ross.

In obedience to their urgent pleas for help, Ross agreed to leave the tranquillity of his plantation and buckle on his revolvers for yet another campaign, this time against outlaws and desperadoes. Without campaigning or other solicitation, he was elected sheriff in December, 1873. Transference of power from McClelland to Ross went smoothly—much more smoothly than that of officials on the state level. Sheriff McClelland was commended for his determination to vacate his office on January 12, while citizens hoped that the change from Davis's Republicans to the incoming Democratic regime of Waco's Richard Coke would go as well.[9]

Once in office, Ross set about restoring law and order with characteristic courage, integrity, and skill. Assisted by his brother Peter F. Ross and other deputies, the former general began cleaning the Modocs out of the de la Vega grant. In less than two years the Ross brothers had arrested more than seven hundred outlaws, and by 1876 the de la Vega grant was reported purged of their presence.[10]

[7] Myrtle Whiteside, "The Life of Lawrence Sullivan Ross" (M.A. thesis, Barker Texas History Center, University of Texas at Austin), p. 59.

[8] Tony E. Duty, "The Home Front: McLennan County in the Civil War," *Texana* 12, no. 3 (1974): 226, 233, 234.

[9] Texas, Department of State, Register of State and County Officers, Election Register, 1870–74, Texas State Archives, Austin, Texas, p. 423; *Waco Daily Examiner*, March 30, 1886, and January 4, 1874.

[10] *Waco Tribune-Herald*, October 30, 1949; Sleeper and Hutchins, comps., *Waco*

But Ross was not only concerned with the de la Vega grant: in March, 1874, he arrested murderer William Elgin. By August, the *Waco Daily Examiner* was warning would-be thieves that the sheriff was "esteemed a dead shot" and that it was unusual for him to miss his mark. "Thieves should therefore, be more guarded in making their depredations in daylight, especially, for they will not always get off with a whole hide."[11]

November of that same year saw the inauguration of the new county jail, built to be "absolutely impervious to saws, picks, acids, and other means of egress." Ross supervised the removal of forty-two prisoners from the old to the new building;[12] during the December court term, Waco sent "nine disciples of crime" to the penitentiary. Once Ross arrested two desperadoes single-handedly and without weapons. At other times, he used deputies and even a posse of the Waco Grays, the local militia company, to assist him in his duties.[13]

The fame of most of the outlaws arrested by Sheriff Ross has proved ephemeral, disappearing along with their names. However, he did arrest one desperado of lasting reputation: the infamous Belle Starr, the "Bandit Queen." In the early 1870s, when Indian Territory and Missouri were too hot to hold her, Belle came to Texas with the outlaw Jim Reed, whom she had supposedly married on horseback. Settling in the Dallas area, Belle and Jim opened a livery stable, which they used as a cover for selling stolen horses. In those days Dallas was a wide-open, booming railroad town and Belle made the most of the situation, dressing like an actress, riding blooded horses, drinking in the local saloons, playing poker with other gamblers, and, when the mood struck her, shooting up the town.[14]

Usually Dallas law officials left her alone, but sometime during

---

and McLennan County, p. 35. In the term immediately preceding September, 1875, the district court of McLennan County had 455 criminal cases on its docket (*Journal of the Constitutional Convention Begun and Held in Austin, September 6, 1875*, p. 131).

   [11] *Waco Daily Examiner*, August 4, 1874.

   [12] *Austin Daily Democratic Statesman*, November 24, 1874. According to Edward King, only one-fifth of the county jails in Texas were secure (King and Champney, *Texas: 1874*, pp. 45–46).

   [13] *Austin Daily Democratic Statesman*, December 19, 1874; Elizabeth Ross Clarke, "Life of Sul Ross," Ross Family Papers, Texas Collection, Baylor University, Waco, Texas (hereafter cited as Ross Family Papers, Baylor), p. 104; *Waco Weekly Examiner and Patron*, August 13, 1875.

   [14] Edwin P. Hicks, *Belle Starr and Her Pearl*, pp. 26–28; Burton Rascoe, *Belle Starr: "The Bandit Queen,"* p. 284.

this period the Bandit Queen decided it would be better to leave Dallas, at least temporarily. Accordingly, she and Reed went to Calvert, a little town in Robertson County some fifty miles down the Brazos from Waco. Here she repeated the success of the Dallas venture by operating a livery stable. In 1874 Belle and Jim came to the Waco area and purchased a farm on Cook Creek in Bosque County. When Reed was killed, Belle returned to Dallas, where she stayed until 1875. Then, with a man named McManus, she returned to the Waco area. While en route to her farm where Reed's share of robbery loot was concealed, she and McManus were arrested by Sheriff Sul Ross on a Dallas telegraphic warrant for horse stealing. Eventually Ross returned her to that city to face charges.[15]

While in the Waco jail McManus told one of the guards the reason for their visit and sought to enlist his assistance in recovering the booty, but the guard refused to be tempted. In 1880, after serving his time, McManus looked up the guard and showed him greenbacks and gold pieces supposedly recovered from the Reed farm. Whether Belle received her share is not known, for she never returned to Waco again.[16]

Although Ross was of great value to his fellow citizens in arresting desperadoes infesting central Texas, his term as sheriff was important in other ways. His fearless, honest performance "delighted good citizens and renewed in their minds an abiding feeling of respect for and confidence in the law and its executors."[17]

Not content to merely serve the citizens of his county, Ross also improved the status of his fellow sheriffs. In 1874 he was instrumental in the establishment of the Sheriff's Association of Texas, an organization that still exists today. Although organization records do not go back to Ross's time, his role as originator and coordinator can be traced in the newspapers of the day.[18]

In August of that year, sheriffs and their representatives from sixty-five Texas counties met at the courthouse in Corsicana in response to a call published in various state newspapers. General Ross

[15] *Waco Tribune-Herald*, October 30, 1949; *Fort Worth Gazette*, February 6, 1889; *Austin Daily Statesman*, February 7, 1889.

[16] *Austin Daily Statesman*, February 7, 1889.

[17] *Galveston Daily News*, May 15, 1886.

[18] Gordon Johnson, Sheriffs' Association of Texas, February 26, 1980, personal communication; *Austin Daily Democratic Statesman*, August 26, 1874; *Waco Daily Examiner*, August 18, 1874.

called the meeting to order, but he soon vacated the chair in favor of J. E. Barkley of Dallas, who was elected permanent chairman. As the meeting continued, a committee of three, including Ross, set about drafting resolutions expressing the reason for the convention. This meeting, as expressed in a preamble and ten resolutions, was not political, but instead for the purpose of "more successfully aiding each other as officers" and for the "further and better protection of the citizens of our respective counties and of the State at large."[19]

After stating the reason for the convention, the committee then proceeded to list its resolutions. Most of these dealt with requests for greater compensation for sheriffs under certain circumstances, but three resolutions in particular stand out. Of these, the first condemned "the spirit of mob law" prevalent in various parts of the state and pledged all sheriffs as officers and as individuals to enforce the laws and "make them honored, respected, and obeyed." At the same time the committee asked the help and willing cooperation of all good citizens and promised assistance to law officers coming into their respective counties "so that the aforesaid combinations may be destroyed and the pre-eminence of rightful authority fully vindicated, and peace, law, order and good government restored."[20]

In order to carry out this program, the second resolution requested that the legislature modify existing laws so that arresting officers "may use such force as may be necessary to compel the criminal to obey the mandates of the law." Along those same lines, the committee then entreated Governor Richard Coke to pardon Mat Caldwell, a sheriff who, in 1869, killed a man in the line of duty, but was sentenced to the penitentiary for five years. Thirdly, before adjourning to meet again in December, another committee including Ross resolved to correspond with the officers of the various railroads in Texas regarding transportation of prisoners. It was a satisfactory organizational meeting, one that would continue to bear fruit in following years. Amid praise for the groundwork he had laid, Ross returned from Corsicana to Waco, where he continued to help his brother officers.[21]

When it appeared that the people of Waco would elect him as one of three delegates from their senatorial district to the Constitutional Convention of 1875, Ross made known his determination to resign as

[19] *Austin Daily Democratic Statesman*, August 26, 1874.
[20] Ibid.
[21] Ibid.; *Waco Daily Examiner*, August 18, 1874.

sheriff. Although deploring his decision, the *Waco Weekly Examiner and Patron* evaluated the former general's accomplishments and concluded that "no county in Texas can show a better record in criminal matters" than McLennan since Ross had been in office.[22]

Other observers praised Ross as the "Model Sheriff of Texas" and noted his efficiency as well as his bravery. To the *Austin Daily Democratic Statesman* he was that "excellent gentleman and sheriff." To those who followed him in the office, among them his brother Peter, he set a standard that they strove to uphold. Thereafter Waco had a reputation for law and order—a dramatic change from the days when Ross first entered office.[23] Meanwhile, Ross was elected to the constitutional convention. Leaving behind the office of lawman, he was to take on the function of lawmaker.

With the ouster of the hated Republican majority from the state legislature in 1872, there arose public agitation to rid the state of the 1869 Republican constitution forced upon Texas by Reconstruction. This agitation grew stronger as more and more public offices fell into the hands of Democrats. During the precinct, county, and district conventions leading up to the congressional campaign of 1874, citizens were given the opportunity to express their wishes on the subject. Although these generally favored a new constitution, it was not until August, 1875, that this question went to the voters. Nevertheless, newspapers continued to agitate on the subject. One, the *Austin Daily Democratic Statesman*, urged haste in calling a convention, warning that the federal government under President Grant would intervene to prolong Reconstruction by preventing the people from forming their own government.[24]

Despite these fears, Governor Coke and the legislature delayed calling a convention until 1875. Finally, the Texas House and Senate passed a joint resolution requiring that an election be held the first Monday in August. At that time voters could approve or reject such a

[22] *Waco Weekly Examiner and Patron*, July 30, 1874.

[23] Victor M. Rose, *Ross' Texas Brigade: Being a Narrative of Events Connected with Its Service in the Late War Between the States*, pp. 170–71; *Austin Daily Democratic Statesman*, December 10, 1875; *Waco Tribune-Herald*, October 30, 1949; Dayton Kelley, ed., *The Handbook of Waco and McLennan County*, p. 33.

[24] Seth Shepard McKay, *Seven Decades of the Texas Constitution of 1876*, pp. 47, 59; *Austin Daily Democratic Statesman*, February 10, 1875. The Northern opinion as expressed by King was that the 1869 constitution had been salutary (King and Champney, *Texas: 1874*, p. 61).

convention and vote for ninety delegates, three from each senatorial district. Should the electorate approve the calling of a convention, it would meet in Austin the first Monday in September.

August 2, the day of the election, dawned warm and sultry. As the day went on, fewer than one-half of the registered voters bothered to turn out. Nevertheless, those votes cast approved the call for a convention by a majority of 29,034.[25]

As soon as the joint resolution to call a convention was made public, the voters in the various senatorial districts began considering candidates. Sul Ross's record as sheriff early gained him the nomination for a delegate's seat; in fact, the *Waco Weekly Examiner and Patron* considered it a "foregone conclusion" that he would be "triumphantly elected" to the convention. Ross's willingness to serve can be seen by his determination to resign the office of sheriff.[26]

Other candidates from the Nineteenth Senatorial District were George B. Erath, B. F. Fleming, and a man named Graves. In the election held August 2, Ross proved to be the most popular of the four candidates. In Waco alone he polled some 523 votes to Fleming's 490, Graves's 292, and Erath's 224. In the rest of the district he held his lead, although Erath eventually displaced Graves as the third of the district's representatives.[27]

When the convention met for the first time at noon on September 6, Ross saw more than one familiar face. Among the delegates were John Henry Brown, fellow Indian fighter John S. ("Rip") Ford, and his former brigade commander, General John W. Whitfield. Around him in the Hall of Representatives were seventy-four other Democrats and fifteen Republicans. Of the latter, six were black. Besides Ross there were forty other farmers, twenty-eight lawyers, three physicians, three editors, two merchants, one printer, one ranchero, and twelve delegates whose occupations were not listed. Although Ross was not a member of the Texas branch of the Patrons of Husbandry, at least half of his fellow delegates were Grangers. This issue would have considerable importance as the convention proceeded.[28]

As the work progressed, Ross had many opportunities to observe his fellow delegates. Later he noted that the farmers and "anti-

[25] McKay, *Seven Decades*, pp. 67, 74.

[26] *Waco Weekly Examiner and Patron*, July 30, 1875.

[27] *Austin Daily Democratic Stateman*, August 5 and 20, 1875; *Journal of the Constitutional Convention*, p. 4; *Waco Weekly Examiner and Patron*, August 6, 1875.

[28] Ross to Mrs. Ross, September 7, 1875, Ross Family Papers, Baylor; Seth Shepard

politicians" were in the majority. As far as he could judge these were
men of "pretty fair ability," although some were considered extreme.
Of the Republicans, one resigned, but the others gave "an earnest of a
true desire to act honestly and work fairly for the good of the State."[29]

After presenting his credentials, Ross took with the other delegates the prescribed oath of office, in which he promised to support
the Constitution of the United States and "faithfully discharge the duties of a delegate" to the best of his ability. Almost immediately he was
appointed as one of a committee of three to wait upon convention Pres-
ident-elect E. B. Pickett and conduct him to the chair. After Pickett's
welcoming address, the convention then voted for secretary and
sergeant-at-arms. This balloting completed, it was resolved that the
president appoint a committee of fifteen to ascertain what other officers
and employees were needed by the convention and rate of per diem
and mileage allowed the delegates. Ross was one of those given this
task.[30]

Other appointments followed. On September 8, he was made part
of the Standing Committee on the Legislative Department. Later he
appeared as a member of the Committee on Revenue and Taxation, as
well as of the Committee on Apportionment. Out of deference to his
experience as an Indian fighter, Ross was named a member of the Select Committee on Frontier Affairs and as such helped draft a resolution to be sent to the president and Congress of the United States asking for help in the undeclared border war with Mexico. Foreshadowing
his future position as president of the Texas Agricultural and Mechanical College, Ross also served on the Select Committee on Education
and a special committee concerning public schools.[31]

When the first committee assignments were made, Ross wrote
home optimistically that the convention would probably be in session
about forty days. However, after a week, he had extended his estimate
to sixty days. At the thought of being away from home for two months
or more his old homesickness returned, and he confided to Lizzie that
he was already weary of it and "anxious to get through here & return

McKay, *Making the Texas Constitution of 1876*, pp. 74, 75; *Austin Daily Democratic Statesman*, August 20, 1875. Ross said three ministers were among the delegates (*Waco Weekly Examiner and Patron*, September 24, 1875).
[29] *Waco Weekly Examiner and Patron*, September 24, 1875.
[30] *Journal of the Constitutional Convention*, pp. 3–4, 8.
[31] Ibid., pp. 15, 35, 228, 339, 395, 404, 802–807.

home." He longed to see her and the children, he added, and was concerned about the farm. But despite his feelings, duty bound him to the convention, for he believed he would be able to do "much good for our section of the Country."[32]

That Ross took his constitution making seriously was evidenced by his record: he missed only five days of the sixty-eight the convention was in session. During these five days he traveled home for the Second Annual Exhibition of the Texas Agricultural and Industrial Association of Waco, where he spoke, saw his Durham cattle exhibited, and attended the association organizational meeting and reunion of his old brigade.[33]

On the sixty-three days he attended, Ross voted 343 times, missing or abstaining from voting only 66. In his voting he sided with the majority 252 times and with the minority 91 times. Although he supported much major legislation such as free public schools, it was in the role of a representative of the minority opinion that Ross did his best, if unsuccessful, service to his state.

This service began early. On the fourth day of the convention, Ross offered a resolution that would have taxed all land in the county in which it was situated. This was an especially important measure because under existing laws, Texas land owned by absentee nonresident landlords was not taxable. When the convention considered the article, however, the majority view prevailed. With the legislature's permission, the taxes on such property could be paid also at the state comptroller's office in Austin or in the county where the owner lived. Ross and eight other members of the Committee on Revenue and Taxation replied to this argument with a minority report that dealt with the "enormous wrongs" perpetrated by this method of taxation. Commenting that "all other subjects of retrenchment and reform sink into comparative insignificance when compared to this," the committee pointed out that some thirty-five million acres of land in Texas had thus far completely escaped taxation. Taxation, the committee concluded, should be "equal and uniform" and "no man or set of men should have exclusive privileges."[34]

[32] Ross to Mrs. Ross, September 7 and 13, 1875, Ross Family Papers, Baylor. In his letter of September 13, Ross urged Lizzie to "write me frequently as I am very desirous to know how things are going on at Home."

[33] *Waco Daily Examiner*, October 22, 23, and 24, 1875.

[34] *Journal of the Constitutional Convention*, pp. 31, 404–405. Later estimates

Ross's interest in equitable taxation of the privately owned land in Texas soon led him into related interests in the public lands of the state. As the session continued, he unsuccessfully opposed carving up the public lands into grants to corporations. He also opposed additional grants to railroads, particularly to the Texas and Pacific, which had forfeited its earlier grants for failure to complete its service. Joining with other sympathetic delegates, Ross wished the convention to assign these forfeited acres to the permanent school fund. When the convention passed the article awarding the grant to the Texas and Pacific over its opponents' protests, Ross joined twenty-three others in strongly censuring the action. Had the minority view carried, it would have added nine million acres—land valued within a decade at $50 million—to the school fund. [35]

In much the same way Ross showed financial farsightedness in arranging for the sale of the three million acres to be set aside to build the new capitol. With Judge W. H. Stewart of Galveston, he opposed a change in the original resolution that would make a sale possible at the legislature's whim, instead of at the end of ten years. As land values increased, the possible revenue for the state from these millions of acres would also be enhanced if they were not prematurely sold. [36]

Another unsuccessful battle Ross waged in the convention was an attempt to have payment of a poll tax made a prerequisite to voting in Texas. This measure was voted down by the Grangers and the Republicans, but others took notice and approved his stand. "General Ross'

---

placed the value of back taxes due the state from this acreage at $6 million, then enough to pay the state debt (*Waco Daily Examiner*, March 30, 1875).

[35] *Journal of the Constitutional Convention*, pp. 265, 751; McKay, *Making the Texas Constitution*, pp. 114; *Waco Daily Examiner*, March 30, 1875. Another delegate, Elijah Sterling Clack Robertson of Salado, viewed the growing power of railroads with alarm. "The contest is on us between capital and laborer, between a monied oligarchy and a Republic of the people—both are dangerous to happiness—the people may run into communism, and the money power into the tyranny of a king. . . . The first shock will be terrible while it lasts, but is bound to terminate in a military despotism. Grant will be the next and last president of the United States" (E. S. C. Robertson to Mrs. Robertson, November 12, 1875, T. S. Sutherland Collection, Robertson Colony Collection, courtesy of Dr. Malcolm D. McLean, University of Texas at Arlington, Arlington, Texas [hereafter cited as Robertson Colony Collection]).

[36] *Austin Daily Democratic Statesman*, November 12, 1875. The *Waco Daily Examiner*, March 30, 1886, estimated a loss of over $7 million to the state by such a premature sale.

head is wholly level," commented the *Austin Daily Democratic States-man* of September 21.[37]

Not all of the former general's legislative battles were in vain. Before the convention met he had expressed a desire for laws to protect Texas cities from unfair railroad rates. Although this stand was ridiculed by critics who believed competition would prevent excesses, the convention did pass laws providing for future regulation of railroads within the state.[38]

Ross's work was generally done in committee; he rarely took the floor except to offer an occasional resolution or move for adjournment. There was, however, one notable exception. Although a Jeffersonian Democrat in politics and somewhat of a conservative in nature, Ross nevertheless resisted some of the measures of economy and retrenchment introduced by other delegates.[39] He combated emphatically the proposal to reduce the salaries of district and supreme court judges, breaking his usual silence to rise and deliver a lengthy speech against a cheap judiciary.

In this speech, which was prompted by a proposal to reduce the salaries of supreme court judges from $4,000 to $3,500 per year, Ross reminded his colleagues that he desired "retrenchment and reform in governmental expenses" as much as any delegate present. However, he went on, he was unwilling to cross the lines that "separate a wise and commendable economy from a niggardly parsimony." Demonstrating that at most the state could be saved $57,000 a year by the proposed reduction, he then pointed out that it was the "vicious criminal system of Texas" that was "burdening the State and bankrupting the counties." Here, he said, "the pruning knife should be vigorously applied." Quoting costs and expenditures for the year ending August 31, the former sheriff showed that it cost the state about one thousand dollars apiece to send 972 men to the penitentiary. From experience he estimated that such cost could be reduced by one-third should the convention really desire to do so, and he reminded his colleagues that the people of Texas who were seeking economy "did not desire that effi-

[37] *Journal of the Constitutional Convention*, pp. 308–11; McKay, *Making the Texas Constitution*, pp. 97–99.
[38] *Austin Daily Democratic Statesman*, July 25, 1875; McKay, *Making the Texas Constitution*, p. 114.
[39] *Journal of the Constitutional Convention*, p. 296.

ciency . . . shall be sacrificed to a mistaken idea of economy, which saves a dime on one hand and squanders thousands of dollars on the other."[40]

Ross went on to warn the assembled delegates that they could construct the best constitution ever devised by men, but unless they had men of "brain, integrity, and patriotism" to carry it out, it would fail. Therefore, it was the duty of the state to attract and honor only the best and most capable men. It would be the "most profuse extravagance and the most puerile statesmanship for any people to lower the standard of their government."[41]

In such a case, he asked if the delegates thought they could secure men of high character by the "illiberal salary" thus proposed. No man with a family could live decently on the proposed salary; did the delegates wish to compel judges to "labor for the public good for about half what it costs them to live"? In his opinion, the amount saved the state by such reduction was too small to "justify the risk of the occupation of the bench by incompetent men." It seemed to him, he said in closing, most economical to provide "such salaries as justify the most intelligent men to seek the positions." But economy was the watchword of the hour, and his plea was ignored.[42]

As the convention dragged on, Ross found ways to relieve the weariness of legislating. Having received a standing invitation from Mrs. Coke to ride with her in her buggy every evening, he went as often as possible. At other times he wrote home and incorporated within his letters inclusions for his children, repeating for Mervin's benefit a salutary story about a little Austin boy who played hooky and subsequently smothered in a large pile of cottonseed.[43]

In November, during a fair held at Austin, Ross, along with former Confederate General John W. Whitfield and former Union General E. O. C. Ord, served on a committee to judge a drill team competi-

---

[40] Seth Shepard McKay, ed., *Debates in the Texas Constitutional Convention of 1875*, pp. 425–30. The *Austin Daily Democratic Statesman*, November 12, 1875, praised Ross's "able and eloquent address." Ross's criticism was valid, as later events proved. Censure of the judiciary article continued, especially after it was put into practice (Alwyn Barr, *Reconstruction to Reform: Texas Politics, 1876–1906*, p. 25).

[41] McKay, ed., *Debates in the Convention*, pp. 425–30; *Austin Daily Democratic Statesman*, November 12, 1875; Barr, *Reconstruction to Reform*, p. 25.

[42] McKay, ed., *Debates in the Convention*, pp. 425–30; *Austin Daily Democratic Statesman*, November 12, 1875; Barr, *Reconstruction to Reform*, p. 25.

[43] Ross to Mrs. Ross, September 7 and 13, 1875, Ross Family Papers, Baylor.

tion. According to one observer, while Ross and Whitfield were "distinguished fighters in the late war," they "had but little experience in infantry drill."[44]

In addition to his convention work and extramural activities such as drill team judging, Ross soon found his name before the public again. This publicity concerned a controversy over the Granger membership of the convention that threatened, for a few days at least, to disrupt the progress of the sessions. John Johnson, a Granger delegate from Collin County, happened to make an unwise jesting remark to S. H. Russell, one of the Republicans, in the presence of a number of the delegates, including Sul Ross. When the Grangers and the Republicans defeated the poll tax requirement, this joke was remembered and interpreted by many to mean that these two groups had agreed to join forces to control the convention. Rumors flew thick and fast, growing as always in the telling. The *Austin Daily Democratic Statesman* then entered the fray, charging that the two groups had formed a "holy alliance" to defeat certain measures in the convention and gain legislation favorable to their interest groups. Soon the resultant uproar was great enough to cause the convention concern and mandate an investigation.[45]

During the earlier course of the inquiry, Ross stated what he knew about the controversy. He probably did this because he was rumored to be one of the sources of the story, and the *Statesman* was calling upon him to tell what he knew. The same day of the *Statesman's* appeal, Ross explained briefly what he knew of the matter. He had paid little attention to it, but thought the remarks were "thoughtless and inconsiderate" and calculated "to do great injustice" to the Grangers, whom he considered worthy men. Immediately after the exchange he had "called attention to it, and advised the gentlemen to correct the impression, as it would probably be used against him [*sic*] to manufacture capital." Ross closed his explanation with a denunciation of the *Statesman*, saying it had "exceeded its mission."[46]

After disrupting the work of the convention for several days, the alliance uproar began to die down. Eventually a committee investi-

[44] Robertson to Mrs. Robertson, November 12, 1875, Robertson Colony Collection.

[45] McKay, *Making the Texas Constitution*, pp. 131–33; *Austin Daily Democratic Statesman*, October 9 and 10, 1875.

[46] *Journal of the Constitutional Convention*, p. 809; McKay, ed., *Debates in the Convention*, pp. 204–205, 206; *Austin Daily Democratic Statesman*, October 9, 1875.

gated the charges, but it either could not or would not make any definite pronouncements on the case.[47]

Meanwhile, as the convention was ending, President Pickett placed Ross on a committee of twelve to prepare an address to the people of Texas "setting forth the leading principles of the new constitution, the reforms provided by it, and its claims to the approbation of the freemen of Texas."[48] When the convention ended on November 24, the members of the committee charged with preparing the address remained in Austin to complete their work. In the finished address the framers discussed the inadequacies of the Constitution of 1869, briefly touched on the history of the present convention, and then proceeded to the accomplishments of the body just adjourned. Economies were praised and various articles, such as those on suffrage, education, railroads, and the judiciary, considered. In conclusion the committee noted that they made "no pretense to perfection" or even to unanimity on the subject of the constitution; however, all agreed that it was much better than the present one and would "bring great relief to the people." Therefore, they called on the voters to ratify the document at the election to be held in early February, 1876.[49]

Although newspaper and citizen debate on the constitution would continue until its adoption, Sul Ross's part in the document was over. Despite his early optimism that "nearly if not all the measures I am interested in will be incorporated in the Constitution," he had failed to secure a poll tax or prevent the legislature from recklessly squandering valuable public lands.[50] He had also met defeat in his attempt to provide a strong judicial system for Texas.

Still, his labors had not been wasted, for he had helped write the document that (with amendments) governs Texas today. Equally important, he had participated in the parliamentary process and worked with men from all backgrounds and of all shades of political persuasion. Although not trained in law or experienced in statecraft, Ross had held

[47] *Journal of the Constitutional Convention*, pp. 808–809. After an "exhaustive investigation of the entire matter," Seth Shepard McKay came to the conclusion "that no compact with a serious purpose was entered into by members of the convention" (*Making the Texas Constitution*, p. 137).

[48] *Journal of the Constitutional Convention*, p. 500.

[49] (Austin) *State Gazette*, November 25, 1875; *Galveston News*, November 28, 1875; *Houston Telegraph*, November 30, 1875. A résumé of the address appears in McKay, *Seven Decades*, pp. 136–43.

[50] Ross to Mrs. Ross, September 13, 1875, Ross Family Papers, Baylor.

his own among those more expert than he. At the same time he had formed political friendships that would be useful later.

At that time, however, Ross apparently had no further political ambitions. From all indications he was glad the session was over so he could return to his family and farm. But at least one other delegate thought he detected the fervor of political ambition within Ross and predicted the former general would probably be a candidate for the Texas Senate the next session.[51]

It was 1880 before Ross would take a seat in the senate—again at the request of his friends and neighbors—but the experience gained in the constitutional convention would be invaluable in pursuing his later political career.

[51] Ross's fellow delegate, Elijah Sterling Clack Robertson, observed from Waco: "Genl Sul Ross will probably be a Candidate for the Senate in this seat—I think that he is looking forward to going to Congress after a while—but if he really wants to go there, he had better keep out of the Texas Senate the next session. . . . He is a good fighter, but no statesman" (Robertson to Mrs. Robertson, December 3, 1875, Robertson Colony Collection).

11

Two Years as State Senator

HAVING completed his term of service in the Constitutional Convention of 1875, Lawrence Sullivan Ross returned to the life he loved—the private life of a successful farmer. During the next four years he exhibited little interest in politics. More important to him then were his growing family, his prospering plantation, and his surviving comrades.[1]

Although friends frequently nudged him in the direction of a political office, Ross resisted. During the summer of 1878, Victor M. Rose, formerly a cavalryman under Ross, now editor of the *Victoria Advocate*, and one of those determined to place his former commander in office, tried to force the issue. When Ross read the letter published by Rose pointing out his suitability for high office, he thanked the editor but reminded him that he had "never aspired to positions of public trust." Besides, Ross said, the positions of prominence in Texas "are mortgaged & usually fall to those who ardently seek them early & late," something he was not willing to do.[2]

Instead, like most former Confederates of his generation, Ross showed increasing interest in maintaining an organization of his old comrades and in preparing a brigade history as war memories began to fade. He wished to honor the memory of the dead, organize frequent reunions of the living, and convey to posterity a record of what his men had accomplished. Therefore, when Rose announced his purpose of writing a history of the brigade, Ross hastened to convey his approval of this "commendable" plan. Although Ross admitted that his memory

---

[1] Ross to Victor M. Rose, June 1 and 8, 1878, Lawrence Sullivan Ross Letters, Barker Texas History Center, University of Texas at Austin (hereafter cited as Ross Letters).
[2] Ross to Rose, June 8, 1878, Ross Letters.

was "too defective to be relied upon at this day for much valuable information," he promised and delivered all assistance within his power, including financial aid.[3]

Meanwhile, Ross's friends and comrades continued to put his name forward as a possible candidate for high state office. In June, 1878, he was heralded as an ideal candidate for lieutenant governor on a ticket with U.S. Congressman Roger Q. Mills of Corsicana; by early 1880, his supporters talked of making him the next governor.[4]

Evidently Victor M. Rose was again a leading figure behind this boom, for Ross asked him to take no steps to bring his name "before the people as one seeking or desiring the nomination." Even if the nomination were offered him spontaneously by the people, Ross reasoned, it would be beyond his power to canvass the state as the Democratic party would demand. He also believed the influential *Galveston News* would oppose him because of its "implacable hatred" of Governor Coke, from Waco as well. Although Ross did not think the *News* would justify its opposition in a personal attack, he shrank from "that most potent of all weapons—ridicule," which would be used to make him appear as the chief "of the large number of aspiring mediocrity in our State." Assuring Rose that he wanted to please his old comrades, even by sacrificing his own desires for theirs, he was "fully persuaded that nothing but defeat would follow any effort to secure the nomination" at that time.[5]

Ross's emphatic refusal to run for governor in the spring of 1880 notwithstanding, by fall he had agreed to run for state senator for the Twenty-second District. This change in thinking came about by actions of his friends and neighbors. When the nominating convention met to choose between two candidates for the state senatorial race in that district, neither man could win the necessary two-thirds majority vote. For several days the warring factions remained deadlocked. Then

[3] Ross to Rose, June 1, 1878, September 23 and October 5, 1880, April 21, June 21, and July 9, 1881, Ross Letters. Victor M. Rose's book, *Ross' Texas Brigade: Being a Narrative of Events Connected with Its Service in the Late War Between the States*, was finally published in 1881.

[4] *Fort Worth Daily Democrat*, June 7, 1878; John H. Broocks to Victor M. Rose, February 20, 1880, Victor M. Rose Papers, Kathryn Stoner O'Connor Collection, from private collection, Dr. and Mrs. Malcolm D. McLean, Arlington, Texas; Rose, *Ross' Texas Brigade*, pp. 171–72.

[5] Ross to Rose, February 15, 1880, Ross Letters.

someone proposed Sul Ross as an acceptable compromise candidate. Triumphantly, the now-united convention nominated him—without waiting to secure his consent—and then adjourned.

Although Ross had not sought the nomination and did not want it, he consented to run. His refusal, he explained later to a friend, would have meant burdening his fellow citizens with the trouble and expense of another convention. Therefore, as he had done at the beginning of the war, he agreed to see the race through.[6]

In spite of his modest nature, once Ross entered the political arena he did not depreciate the value of his previous service to Texas. He wrote his friend Victor Rose that since he was a candidate for the state senate, "it will be *fashionable* & quite customary for the papers to give the *Pedigree* of the running Horses." Therefore, Ross continued, there was no impropriety in Rose's "afflicting the public attention at that time with any notice you may choose to make of my life & previous history & exploits."[7]

Rose responded with an appropriate biographical sketch, which Ross corrected and returned. "I am satisfied the publication of this sketch would swell my vote greatly," he said, and then added that he was leaving it to Rose to determine the best time for publication.[8]

Despite the comparative strengths of the Republican and Greenback parties in Texas at that time, a place on the Democratic party ticket in most districts ensured election. This proved true in the election of 1880, but Sul Ross surprised the politicians, and probably himself, by proving so popular with a majority of the electorate that he swept to victory several thousand votes ahead of the other party candidates.[9]

His election was equally popular with observers outside the district. After the returns were in, the *Austin Daily Statesman* noted approvingly that "Gen. L. S. Ross of Waco will be one of the ablest senators in the Seventeenth Legislature" and added that Ross had been elected by a large majority. Joining him as newcomers to the senate

[6] Norman G. Kittrell, *Some Governors Who Have Been and Other Public Men of Texas*, p. 97.

[7] Ross to Rose, September 23, 1880, Ross Letters.

[8] Ross to Rose, October 5, 1880, Ross Letters.

[9] Texas, secretary of state, Election Returns, 1880, McLennan County, Texas State Archives, Austin, Texas.

were Marion Martin, W. J. Swain, and A. W. Terrell, all soon to compete with Ross for the governor's chair.[10]

During the early days of the session Ross, now balding and forty-two, showed disinclination to put himself forward. As he found his footing, however, he began to enter more actively into lawmaking. Nevertheless, the freshman senator's first session was not to be a happy one. Hardly had he received his committee assignments and settled down to the everyday work of legislating when a frantic telegram arrived from Lizzie, announcing the serious illness of their month-old son. Immediately he wrote home, saying that it appeared impossible for him to leave Austin then. Expressing sorrow that he had ever engaged in the business of lawmaking, Ross said the duties of the position were upon him and he could not escape. The only hope he could offer Lizzie was that if the illness proved more dangerous he could possibly come home.[11]

With great anxiety he watched for further dispatches from home, his mind too full of domestic troubles to be of much use in the legislature. Fortunately, the next day was Sunday, but the day brought tragic news—his youngest son was dead. Asking to be excused from his duties indefinitely, Ross returned to Waco, where another son lay close to death. It was a week before he returned.[12]

After returning from Waco, Ross threw himself into his work, serving on the Committees on Educational Affairs, Internal Improvements, Finance, Penitentiaries, Military Affairs (as chairman), State Affairs, Contingent Expenses, Stock and Stock Raising, Agricultural Affairs, and Enrolled Bills. With Senators Duncan and Rainey he also served as a teller. Later in the session Ross was added to the Commit-

[10] *Austin Daily Statesman*, November 6, 1880, January 9, 1881. The Seventeenth Legislature was the last to meet in the old capitol.

[11] Ross to Mrs. Ross, February 5, 1881, Ross Family Papers, Laura Clarke Mittel Collection, now in private collection of Dr. and Mrs. Neville P. Clarke, Bryan, Texas (hereafter cited as Ross Family Papers, Mittel Collection). An engraved portrait of Ross at this period of his life serves as the frontispiece of *Ross' Texas Brigade.*

[12] Ross to Mrs. Ross, February 5, 1881, Ross Family Papers, Mittel Collection; Ross to Rose, April 21, 1881, Ross Letters; *Austin Daily Statesman*, February 8 and 13, 1881. Ross was in Austin two years later when he was called home because of the serious illness of his eldest son; Mervin contracted pneumonia when he braved a blizzard to fetch a doctor for his aunt, who was in labor. He died January 31 (*Austin Daily Statesman*, January 20 and 21, 1883; *Waco Daily Examiner*, January 25 and February 1, 1883; Elizabeth Williams Estes, June 26, 1979, personal communication).

tee on Industries, Public Health, and History of Texas and to that on Senatorial and Representative Districts.[13]

Still he was concerned about personal matters, for Lizzie's health had broken under the strain of nursing and bereavement, heightened by the loss of her mother. Until the session ended he was pulled two ways by family and duty, but duty won and he remained at his post.[14]

During the rest of the session he introduced bills dealing with agricultural and judicial affairs, voted unsuccessfully for J. W. Throckmorton to succeed S. B. Maxey as U.S. senator, and presented three petitions. The first was from a disabled veteran of the Texas War for Independence asking for a double pension; a second, from the citizens of Young County, asking relief for a group of Tonkawa Indians, survivors of the old Brazos Reserve; and, more importantly for further developments in Texas, a third, signed by five hundred citizens of McLennan County, asked that a prohibition amendment be placed on the ballot at the next statewide election.[15]

The introduction of the prohibition issue sparked considerable interest the remainder of the session. Eventually the senate provided for just such an amendment, to be presented to the voters at a general election in September. Acting jointly with the house, it also passed an act regulating the sale of "spirituous, vinous or malt liquors or medicated bitters" and fixing the rate of an occupation tax on liquor salesmen.[16]

In keeping with the actions of the senator responsible for introducing the issue, Ross supported the various prohibition measures brought before the senate. When one of his colleagues suggested providing local option exemption from prohibition, Ross joined with a majority of other senators in voting it down.[17]

Although he supported such measures as prohibition and the establishment of the University of Texas at Austin, Ross opposed reduction of the ad valorem tax and separation of the medical school from the University of Texas proper. He also opposed what he considered un-

[13]*Journal of The Senate of Texas: Being the First Session of the Seventeenth Legislature, Begun and Held at the City of Austin, January 11, 1881*, pp. 79, 104. It was during this session that government offices in Austin were provided with telephones (*Journal of the First Session*, p. 149).

[14]Ross to Rose, April 21, 1881, Ross Letters.

[15]*Journal of the First Session*, pp. 20, 38, 64, 98, 100, 129.

[16]Ibid., pp. 158, 173–74, 229.

[17]Ibid., pp. 158, 174.

necessary government spending, voting against appropriating $15,000 for a state exhibit at the World's Fair, against commissioning portraits of deceased presidents and governors of Texas, and against paying a $45,000 claim arising out of the Texas Revolution. With other senators he defeated a proposal that would have allowed county tax collectors a commission of 5 percent on the first $20,000 collected and 4 percent on sums over $20,000. Another time, Ross, with W. H. Burgess, protested fixing the rate of a tax in the constitution; the two senators maintained that "representatives fresh from the people" were the "best qualified to say what taxes are needed and what taxes the people can afford to pay." He and Burgess went on record as considering it "a dangerous departure from principle to take this power from the Legislature."[18]

Having established himself as a fiscal conservative, Sul Ross found his views in harmony with most of his colleagues. Since his early struggles with mathematics, he had developed considerable skill with figures. Added to this was his business acumen, which had brought prosperity to his farming ventures. A valuable addition to the Committee on Finance, he was appointed chairman of that committee when the legislature met again.

In the meantime, as the end of the session drew near, the legislature still had not passed the appropriations bill for the operation of the state government over the next two years. As a member of the Finance Committee and later as part of the senate and house conference committee to consider disagreements over the appropriations bill, Ross was offended by the petty politicking of some of his colleagues. These men, he wrote Lizzie scornfully, refused to pass bills crucial to the government because they were afraid the legislature would adjourn before they could pass "their pet measures."[19]

With only three days to spare, the two chambers came at last to an agreement. When the legislature finally adjourned at the end of March, Ross returned home to put his affairs in order before taking Lizzie to a resort where she could regain her health and spirits.[20] Then it was back to his beloved plantation until the legislature met again. By law it would have been another two years before the legislature again

[18] Ibid., pp. 21, 51–52, 72, 137, 161, 191–92, 276, 308.
[19] Ibid., p. 265; Ross to Mrs. Ross, March 15, 1881, Ross Family Papers, Mittel Collection.
[20] Ross to Rose, April 21, 1881, Ross Letters.

convened. However, the fire that destroyed the old capitol early in November, 1881, made necessary a special session, which met the first week in April, 1882.

This session, which lasted until May 5, handled considerable business regarding the temporary housing of state offices. Early in the session the senate voted to provide rooms for the state supreme court, court of appeals, commission of appeals, and the state law library. Later a joint committee from the house and the senate investigated suitable buildings for the legislature and comptroller's and treasurer's offices. Toward the end of the session the senate further empowered the Capitol Board, established by the Sixteenth Legislature, to provide for the construction of a new capitol. The board was granted the necessary authority and $50,000 to prepare buildings for the use of state departments and agencies until the new capitol was ready.[21]

This called session also dealt with matters other than the urgent one of providing temporary quarters for state agencies. "Grave irregularities" at the Blind Asylum, a burned building at the Lunatic Asylum, extensive storm damage at the Prairie View Normal School, and better treatment of convicts drew the legislators' attention, as did the question over the boundary line between Texas and Indian Territory.[22]

During this session, Senator Ross opposed further land grants to railroads, asked for a reduction of the poll tax (which legislators had found they needed after all), approved extending the time limit for citizens to redeem land sold for taxes, moved to destroy certain unused engraved state bonds, and served as chairman of the Finance Committee.[23]

Ross showed considerably more legislative expertise during this session. More at ease with parliamentary procedure, he was noticeably active on the floor of the senate. This time there were no distractions from home. Lizzie was in good health and spirits, the older children were doing well in school, and the prospects for his farm crops were good. Although interested in affairs at home—in one letter he hoped

[21] *Journal of The Senate of Texas: Being a Special Session of the Seventeenth Legislature*, pp. 16, 18, 52–54.

[22] Ibid., pp. 15, 18, 34, 35.

[23] Ibid., pp. 17–19, 33, 43, 45, 47, 52, 71, 77, 84. According to the *Waco Daily Examiner*, March 30, 1886, Ross became "a faithful friend and ally of Governor Roberts, in his financial policy, and . . . contributed materially to the success of that commendable policy which reduced our state taxes from fifty cents to thirty cents on the hundred dollars, and still filled the treasury to overflowing."

for rain and told Frank to keep off the railroad tracks—he was more relaxed than he had been the year before.[24]

At the same time a style of personal statesmanship had developed. Characteristically reluctant to leave home at the start of the session, Ross wrote Lizzie upon his arrival in Austin that he hoped the session would not last more than thirty days, since he was "certain this venture will satisfy me."[25] But despite his initial reluctance to leave home, Ross knew what was due his constituents and the people of Texas as a whole. Generally he stood for simple, basic legislation: a survey of Ross's voting patterns during this session shows that he tended to support basic bills but voted against most amendments. Similarly, he almost always voted against postponing consideration of a piece of legislation. Rarely did early adjournment win his support, apparently because he did not wish to extend unduly the length of the session. As the session ended, Ross could point to solid achievement on his part.

This achievement should have continued when the legislature met again in January, 1883. However, two days before the special session ended, the senate passed a reapportionment bill, which reduced Ross's four-year senate term to only two years. As he had no real liking for politics, he declined to run for a second term.[26]

Those two years in the Texas Senate were by no means wasted. During that time Ross had polished the legislative skills learned at the constitutional convention and had furthered his political friendships. He had also gained considerable insight into the political process, but had found personal politicking distasteful. This, however, was no disadvantage, for at the same time he had earned a reputation as a hardworking, honest statesman untainted by the cruder forms of politics. Such a reputation would make him extremely popular with his fellow citizens in years to come. Moreover, he had worked on a daily basis with his future political rivals, feeling them out and noting their strengths and weaknesses. Without knowing it Ross had prepared for his gubernatorial career, which would begin shortly in response to demands by the people of Texas for his leadership.

[24] Ross to Mrs. Ross, April 10, 1882, Ross Family Papers, Texas Collection, Baylor University, Waco, Texas.

[25] Ross to Mrs. Ross, April 7, 1882, Ross Family Papers, Mrs. Paul Mason Collection, College Station, Texas.

[26] Constitution of Texas, 1875, art. 3, secs. 3 and 28; H. P. N. Gammel, comp., *The Laws of Texas, 1822–1897*, IX, 269; Kittrell, *Governors Who Have Been*, p. 97.

12

From Senate to Statehouse

GIVEN the family background, leadership ability, practical experience, and legislative training of Lawrence Sullivan Ross, it is not surprising that he should have decided to run for governor. What is surprising is that although not a politician himself and certainly not fond of politics, he was able to enter the political arena and win largely, upon his first attempt.[1]

More surprising than Ross's victory to those loyal friends and supporters who had dreamed of high office for him since 1875 was his reluctance to actively seek the governor's office. A modest, reticent, and sensitive man, Ross shrank from having to employ what he considered questionable political methods in order to achieve office. In 1878, 1880, and again in 1882 he had declined to interest himself in Texas gubernatorial politics. During the campaign of 1880 he had been emphatic in his denial and had asked particularly vocal supporters such as Victor M. Rose of Victoria not to bring his name before the people.[2]

Two years later Ross had not changed his mind, although his supporters were as eager as always to bring him to high political office. According to George Clark of Waco, who later served as the former senator's campaign manager, Ross's friends desired to enter him in the governor's race against John Ireland. The general himself demurred, and when the state Democratic convention met at Galveston, Ross asked Clark to attend the meetings and prevent him from being named

---

[1] Norman G. Kittrell, *Some Governors Who Have Been and Other Public Men of Texas*, p. 97. In Ross's two victories, the elections of 1886 and 1888, he polled the largest majorities until that time and the third largest victory before 1900 (*Texas Almanac and State Industrial Guide, 1978–1979*, p. 530).

[2] *Waco Weekly Examiner and Patron*, July 30, 1875; Ross to Victor M. Rose, February 15, 1880, Lawrence Sullivan Ross Letters, Barker Texas History Center, University of Texas at Austin (hereafter cited as Ross Letters).

a candidate. Clark agreed but found the assignment difficult, since a large number of the general's friends had determined to nominate him over his protests. At last only written authorization from Ross through Clark convinced them of the futility of continuing to seek the nomination.[3]

With the early political stirrings of the 1884 election year, Ross's supporters began to try to put their man in the governor's chair. Again Victor M. Rose, editor of the *Victoria Advocate*, went to work, and in February a letter from Rose discussing Ross's popularity and praising the former general's honesty, competence, and "sterling probity" appeared in the press.[4] The day after this effusion was published, Ross wrote his friend and comrade. Much as he had done in 1880, Ross stressed that the mention of his name in connection with his supposed candidacy for governor had not come about by any efforts on his part. Although admitting that he was neither indifferent to his neighbors' good opinion nor lacking in ambition, he stated that he had long since decided nominations in Texas were manipulated by "combinations or personal associations of limited membership." Therefore, Ross concluded, "the man who will not resort to questionable methods for the election of either self or friend can hardly be considered in the line of probable promotion."[5]

After considering the impossibility of his candidacy, Ross discussed at length the tensions between ranchers and farmers and the lawlessness resulting from fence cutting and land grabbing in the various counties where farm met frontier. "We have attained prosperity & must preserve its fruits, & our people should not be left to settle in blood the controversy between them," he told Rose. Noting that circumstances demanded bold actions and words, he went on to remind his friend that "the country wants something more substantial than the mere personal glory or success of this or that individual before the next Democratic nominating convention."[6]

From being concerned with state affairs to being willing to do

[3] George Clark, *A Glance Backward or Some Events in the Past History of My Life*, p. 86.

[4] *Galveston Daily News*, February 26, 1884.

[5] Ross to Rose, February 27, 1884, Ross Letters.

[6] Ibid. According to one source, Ross's supporters refused to oppose Governor Ireland in the 1884 election in an attempt to win his backing for their candidate in the next gubernatorial race (Alwyn Barr, *Reconstruction to Reform: Texas Politics, 1876–1906*, p. 73).

something about them was not a long step. This time Ross was not long in taking it; by late 1885 he had decided at last to run for governor.[7]

Although Ross did not announce his candidacy until late February, soon after the first of the year newspapers began to give his campaign serious consideration. Generally this coverage was favorable, although State Comptroller William J. Swain had already entered the race, captured most of the large daily papers, and enlisted them on his side. Of those papers supporting a Ross campaign, the *Waco Daily Examiner* was the most vocal and vehement.[8]

After a delay of some weeks, Ross formally announced his candidacy in an extensive interview conducted February 25 by a reporter from the *Galveston Daily News*. This interview, which covered a variety of topics with the candidate's stand on each, was reprinted in various papers around the state and did much to further the former general's chances of election. According to the reporter, Ross gave "frank, manly, concise and straightforward" answers to questions on land sale and lease laws, the state penitentiary and convict labor, the Agricultural and Mechanical College, prohibition, libel laws, railroads, the Knights of Labor, and the Farmers' Alliance. Of these, his views on public school lands, prohibition, railroads, the Knights of Labor, and the Farmers' Alliance were the most important, reflecting the issues of the day.[9]

On the question of the public school lands then being leased or sold by the state Land Board, Ross opposed the board and favored the sale of the school lands to actual settlers over a long period and at a low interest rate. He pointed out that investment of the proceeds in "safe, interest-bearing securities" would net the state ten cents interest on every acre as opposed to only five cents per acre from leasing. At the same time, reorganization of the state's land policy would put the

---

[7] Ross to N. H. Woodale, December 4, 1885, Lawrence Sullivan Ross Vertical File, Barker Texas History Center Library, University of Texas at Austin (hereafter cited as Ross Vertical File).

[8] *Galveston Daily News*, January 10 and 18, 1886; *Waco Daily Examiner*, January 12 and 23, and February 9 and 10, 1886; Ross to Woodale, December 4, 1885, Ross Vertical File. Ross later repudiated the "indiscreet utterances" of the *Examiner*, but the paper continued its ardent support of Waco's favorite son (Ross to H. M. Holmes, April 22, 1886, Lawrence Sullivan Ross Papers, Texas A&M University Archives, College Station, Texas [hereafter cited as Ross Papers, Texas A&M Archives]). See also *Waco Daily Examiner*, May 9, 1886.

[9] *Galveston Daily News*, February 25, 1886.

small-scale farmer and stockraiser on equal footing in their communities with wealthier cattlemen and corporations.[10]

Concerning regulation of the sale of intoxicating beverages, Ross opposed statewide prohibition—a reversal of his earlier views. Since local option laws were already part of the organic law of Texas, he saw no reason why the question should be brought up again. It was, in his opinion, a local instead of a statewide political issue and should be treated as such.[11]

When asked about the railroad question, Ross answered that he thought they should be encouraged and investments in them protected. At the same time, he cautioned, the public should be protected against arbitrary action on the part of the railroads. Deviating slightly from an earlier stand, he considered that competition between the various lines would eventually solve the railroad problem, but in the meantime the railroads should not be allowed to combine "against the public interest."[12]

Regarding the Farmers' Alliance and the Knights of Labor, the candidate admitted that he knew little of the purposes or aims of these organizations. However, as a farmer (although not a member of the Alliance), he believed that the farmers were only demanding "fair legislation and impartial administration." As for the Knights of Labor, who were to strike the Texas and Pacific soon after this interview, Ross said he could not withhold his sympathy for these men as they struggled to better themselves, but he most certainly deplored the lawlessness of their means. "Arbitrary and high-handed methods on the part of organized capital . . . should be corrected by peaceful and lawful methods," instead of by a "summary stoppage of industries, a paralysis of commerce and trade, and the closing of avenues of employment, all of which entail ruin upon the community and serious losses to innocent parties." The state, Ross concluded, should provide some tribunal to arbitrate differences between capital and labor.[13]

In an editorial published the next day, the *News* commented on the soundness of Ross's platform and noted that the general was

[10] Ibid.

[11] Ibid. After considerable thought, Ross had concluded that statewide prohibition would destroy individual liberty (see *Austin Daily Statesman*, May 3, 1887, for a detailed statement on the question).

[12] *Galveston Daily News*, February 25, 1886.

[13] Ibid.

squarely against Swain on many points. "As the campaign looks now, it is bound to be interesting and, perhaps, exciting," the editorial predicted. As foretold, the heated campaign leading up to the state Democratic convention generated much interest as well as excitement. Despite a flare-up of his old bronchial trouble and a bad throat, Ross toured north and central Texas for two months beginning in May, addressing cheering crowds in Sulphur Springs, Greenville, Paris, Cameron, Dublin, and Mount Calm.[14]

This is not to say he was unopposed. Early opponents were Comptroller William J. Swain and former Lieutenant Governor Marion Martin, nicknamed the "Swamp Fox of Navarro" and now the darling of the Knights, the Alliance, and the Prohibitionists. Both men had been in the legislature with Ross. Later John T. Brackenridge, a banker from San Antonio, and D. C. Giddings, a Brenham banker and former congressman, entered the field against Ross, who was being called variously the "little cavalryman" (although the diminutive was a misnomer) and the "war horse." Ross's earliest and most formidable opponent in the contest was Swain. Although he also debated Martin, his contacts with Giddings and Brackenridge were minimal throughout the campaign.[15]

In spite of his two years in the legislature, Ross did not think of himself as a politician, nor did other politicians consider him one of them. Therefore, they resented his "poaching" in what they considered their preserves. To the people, however, Ross's lack of political involvement was a recommendation and ensured a hard, bitter battle ahead.[16]

As might be expected, the campaign was not without its share of shenanigans and nineteenth-century political dirty tricks. These included talk of a Ross-Ireland combination, Ross allegedly agreeing to back Ireland's bid for U.S. senator in return for Ireland's support for Ross's campaign; rumors that Ross was a man of such little intellect and learning that he could not write or speak on his own; and a false report leaked to the *Austin Daily Statesman* and reprinted in the *Houston Daily Post, Galveston Daily News,* and *Fort Worth Gazette* early in the

[14] Ibid., February 26, May 9, June 28, and July 3, 1886; *Waco Daily Examiner,* April 21, May 11 and 13, June 6, and August 6, 1886.

[15] *Waco Daily Examiner,* March 17, June 2, and July 6 and 29, 1886; Clark, *A Glance Backward,* pp. 86–87; Barr, *Reconstruction to Reform,* pp. 96–97.

[16] *Galveston Daily News,* May 18, 1886; *Pittsburg* (Tex.) *Gazette,* in *Waco Daily Examiner,* March 7, 1886.

campaign that Ross's friends were about to withdraw him from the contest.[17]

In the end these tactics failed in their objective, rebounding most upon Swain, whose political skirts were later shown to be far from clean. Although he had correctly accused Ross of changing sides on the prohibition question, Swain himself was ambivalent on the subject. At the same time many Texans resented Swain's support of a scheme to substitute Indiana limestone for Texas granite in constructing the new capitol. Finally, reports of nepotism, fictitious names on the state payroll, and a treasury deficiency of $80,000, in addition to Swain's rash statements about bypassing civil authorities and sending rangers to quell land-lease disturbances, tarnished his image.[18]

Although a man of great physical and moral courage, Ross was timid when it came to politics. According to his campaign manager George Clark, twice during the campaign he became discouraged and wanted to withdraw. "There was nothing the matter with his candidacy and everything was progressing beautifully," Clark recalled. When Ross came to his office to declare his abandonment of the campaign, Clark "only laughed at him for his timidity."[19] In reality Ross's campaign was progressing better than the candidate thought. Even before the county conventions, Swain's strength had ebbed. Marion Martin, with his backing of the Farmers' Alliance, the Knights of Labor, and the Prohibitionists, then appeared to be his greatest threat. However, as the county Democratic conventions began meeting in July, the strength of the "little cavalryman" became apparent as convention after convention declared for him.[20]

[17] *Galveston Daily News*, February 26 and May 13, 1886; *Waco Daily Examiner*, February 12, 13, 14, and 19, March 23, April 9, 23, and 29, and August 6, 1886. The alleged understanding between Ross and Ireland proved the hardest rumor to squelch, even though Ross indignantly denied it as early as February (*Galveston Daily News*, February 25, 1886). The friends of Ireland repudiated it in March (*Waco Daily Examiner*, March 23, 1886). Ireland did not become senator.

[18] *Waco Daily Examiner*, January 3 and 16, 1886; *Galveston Daily News*, May 15, 1886; *Dallas Daily News*, May 28, 1886. During the campaign, someone tried to connect Swain with a woman killed in Austin in December, 1885. Although the comptroller's supporters attributed this to Ross partisans, they were able to prove nothing. Some voters simply wrote the incident off as more Swain dirty tricks (see "Campaign Tricks," in *Waco Daily Examiner*, March 7, 1886).

[19] Clark, *A Glance Backward*, p. 87. Clark recalled that Ross spent no money for his campaign beyond his traveling expenses.

[20] *Waco Daily Examiner*, July 11, 14, 15, 16, 17, 18, 25, and 30, 1886. Ross enjoyed tremendous support among Texas Confederate veterans and also among the non-Alliance farmers (*Waco Daily Examiner*, March 17 and June 2, 1886).

When the delegates gathered in a Galveston skating rink with poor acoustics for the state Democratic convention beginning August 10, the size and enthusiasm of the Ross caucus indicated the direction the nomination would take. Next day, in an attempt to halt the Ross momentum, the supporters of the other four candidates pooled their votes to elect an anti-Ross man temporary chairman of the convention. Although it was conceded that the Ross backers lost this first round, they soon bounced back with all the élan the general himself had shown on the battlefield and captured the position of permanent chairman.[21]

The second day of the convention, the candidates presented themselves and their platforms to the delegates. Although suffering one of his periodic bouts of illness, Ross spoke modestly for twenty-five minutes. He was followed by Giddings, whose speech was also moderate; by Martin, whose statements were more self-centered; by Swain, who had by this time adopted many of Ross's views; and finally by Brackenridge, who admitted his inexperience, but said he was willing to take advice.[22]

A critical reporter for the *Galveston Daily News* found fault with the way Ross entered the hall, noted his poor health, and thought he ferreted out a Ross claque. His description of the scene continued:

> General Ross is a good-looking man. He has a frank, open face that always wears a kindly expression. It is no wonder that he has so many personal friends. His face tells the nature of the man, which is that he would stick to his friends to the death. He stands as straight as an arrow, and is not far from six feet high. Why he was named the "little" cavalryman is one of the freaks of the campaign. . . . He would attract attention in any crowd. He was nervous, his face was flushed and his eyes devoid of their customary luster. He was not in good voice. . . . General Ross is no orator. He is not even an ordinarily good speaker. He has a camp meeting drawl, and the intonations of his voice sound unpleasantly. . . . His speech was a disappointment to his friends.[23]

Despite such criticism by the press, Ross led as the first balloting got under way. Soon he had 433 votes to Swain's 99, Giddings's 97, and Martin's 67. Before the roll call of counties was completed, the chairman of the Fayette County delegation rose and informed the chair that his group wished to cast their entire vote for Ross. This led to other

[21] Ibid., August 10 and 11, 1886; *Galveston Daily News*, August 11, 1886.

[22] *Waco Daily Examiner*, August 11, 1886.

[23] *Galveston Daily News*, August 12, 1886.

vote changes, which gave the general the necessary two-thirds vote. Amid pandemonium his opponents withdrew from the race, leaving the field open for his nomination by acclamation.[24]

Ross was not present at the actual moment of victory, but he was soon informed of his nomination and carried back into the convention hall on the shoulders of his friends. Pale, but "cool and collected," Ross stepped forward to accept the nomination in a speech that was judged "well timed and sensible." An impromptu reception followed, the candidate and his campaign manager receiving the congratulations of the crowd.[25]

Although Ross had received the votes of the Knights of Labor and the Farmers' Alliance delegates who switched to his side after a complimentary vote for Martin, the Prohibitionists were dissatisfied by his nomination and stated their intention to form their own ticket. Castigating Ross as the weakest of all the candidates, a man of mediocre brain who would be "entirely an unpresentative [*sic*] governor," the leader of the Prohibitionist element called the general's nomination an "unpardonable affront."[26]

This was a minority opinion, however. The once hostile *Galveston Daily News* maintained that there had never been a candidate "presented to the people by a convention that was nominated more fairly" than Ross. Although the *News* writer believed a political machine had been responsible for Ross's nomination, he admitted that perhaps such support was not the nominee's fault. "The managers of the machine, the practical politicians and the time servers know they must do a popular thing occasionally in order to maintain themselves." Fearing the general's popularity, the reporter concluded, the politicians adopted him for their own purposes.[27]

The remaining days of the convention were spent in nominating the rest of the ticket—Judge Thomas B. Wheeler, lieutenant governor; James S. Hogg, attorney general; John S. McCall, comptroller; Francis R. Lubbock, treasurer; Richard M. Hall, commissioner of the

[24] Dudley G. Wooten, ed., *A Comprehensive History of Texas, 1685–1897*, II, 265–66; *Galveston Daily News*, August 13, 1886.

[25] *Galveston Daily News*, August 13, 1886.

[26] Ibid., August 11 and 13, 1886. A hostile correspondent for the *Corpus Christi Caller*, August 22, 1886, criticized Ross because of the former general's war record.

[27] *Galveston Daily News*, August 13, 1886. Kittrell said "no man could have defeated 'Sul' Ross in that convention" (*Governors Who Have Been*, p. 95).

General Land Office; Oscar H. Cooper, superintendent of public instruction; and R. R. Gaines, state supreme court—and in preparing a party platform. This document reflected Ross's campaign platform and a good many of his earlier views, such as economy in state fiscal affairs, reform of the weak judiciary article of the constitution, and stricter control of railroads within the state.[28]

Although the news of Ross's nomination had been received in Waco by wild excitement (the citizens blew steam whistles, fired anvils, pealed church bells, and thronged the streets to the sounds of band music and musket salutes by the local militia company), this celebration paled in comparison to that welcoming the hero's return. Long before the nominee's train pulled in from Galveston, the streets of Waco were hung with bunting and Chinese lanterns and decorated with transparencies and memorials in preparation for the victory parade, to be held that evening. Upon Ross's arrival he was ensconced in an open carriage pulled by four white horses and then escorted by five hundred horsemen (many old brigade veterans among them), the Waco Light Infantry, the Firemen's and African bands, the fire department, and numerous private carriages to his home. En route the procession halted at the home of Sul's sister, Kate Padgitt, long enough for the candidate to greet his parents, who were staying there, and to allow the elder Rosses to receive the congratulations of the crowd. The aged frontiersman was overcome with emotion as he greeted his returning son; Mrs. Ross was equally proud. When she heard of her son's nomination, she exclaimed, "Sul will do right wherever they put him."[29]

Then it was on to the Sul Ross residence at Eleventh and Austin, where Lizzie and their six surviving children waited to extend their welcome. A throng of well-wishers had gathered there also, bursting into a frenzy of cheering; when Ross had finally recovered from his confusion, the crowd then demanded speeches from the former general and his friends. Despite his obvious weariness, Ross took time to thank his friends and neighbors for their demonstration and to speak to the crowd. He was, he said, going into office prepared to serve all Texans regardless of their party affiliation, race, or color. Speaker followed speaker, but at last the satiated crowd was content to depart and leave the nominee with his family. It was a day few Waco residents forgot.

[28] Ernest William Winkler, ed., *Platforms of Political Parties in Texas, 1846–1916*, pp. 237–40.
[29] *Galveston Daily News*, August 14, 1886, January 21, 1887.

"The Grandest Day This City Ever Added to Its Annals," exulted the *Waco Daily Examiner*.[30]

In the general election held November 2, the once-reluctant candidate proved as popular with the electorate of Texas as he had with his fellow Democrats, polling the "largest majority of popular votes to that time." When all the votes were tabulated, he had received 228,776 votes to his Republican opponent's 65,236 and the Prohibitionist candidate's showing of 19,186. It was a noteworthy victory for the Waco resident, tainted only by the knowledge that his seventy-four-year-old mother had not lived to see it.[31]

When the time came for the new governor to take up his duties, his campaign manager, George Clark, preceded him to Austin. Ross was expected to arrive on January 16 with an escort of the Waco Light Infantry and a large following of Waco's prominent citizens.[32] Even though the Missouri Pacific train scheduled to transport the governor-elect and his party to Austin arrived some five hours late, a large crowd was present to welcome him. Later, with friends and family around him, Ross held a friendly reception, prompting one reporter to write that if first impressions counted for anything, Ross had "already planted himself in the hearts of his people."[33]

At last the day of the inaugural dawned, bright and beautiful for mid-January. About noon the governor-elect with his lieutenant governor was conducted ceremoniously to the house of representatives. After a brief farewell address by Governor Ireland, Ross took the oath of office and then read his hour-long inaugural address. It was a detailed document, stressing the grave responsibilities facing the legislature and touching on such matters as careful fiscal policy, need for a reformed judiciary, education of delinquents, judicious control of railroads, and reformation of present land policy. His speech was pronounced an able one by those attending.[34]

[30] Elizabeth Ross Clarke, "Life of Sul Ross," Ross Family Papers, Texas Collection, Baylor University, Waco, Texas, pp. 108–11; *Waco Daily Examiner*, August 15, 1886. The *Examiner* noted that all criticism to the contrary, Ross was a good speaker.

[31] L. E. Daniell, comp., *Personnel of the Texas State Government, With Sketches of Distinguished Texans* . . . , p. 16; Wooten, ed., *Comprehensive History of Texas*, II, 266; *Galveston Daily News*, September 23, 1886.

[32] *Austin Daily Statesman*, January 9, 11, and 18, 1887; *Galveston Daily News*, January 18, 1887.

[33] *Austin Daily Statesman*, January 18, 1887.

[34] *Galveston Daily News*, January 19, 1887. An editorial in the *Austin Daily States-*

Arrangements had been made to hold the inaugural ball in the recently completed, richly appointed Driskill Hotel, thus initiating a practice that became traditional in Texas political circles. After an elaborate banquet, served in shifts to about one thousand guests, the incoming and outgoing officials and their wives and families held a reception. Among the prominent women that gala evening were Lizzie, elegant in a beaded black silk dress with train; the governor's eldest daughter; a sister; a sister-in-law; and a niece. In another room the musicians struck up a tune for those inclined to dance, although the floor was soon so thronged as to render dancing out of the question until a later hour.[35]

During the course of the evening, an incident occurred involving the new governor's spry seventy-six-year-old father. No intoxicating beverages were served at the banquet, and Shapley Ross preferred to celebrate his illustrious son's accession with something stronger than coffee or ice water. Throughout the day Shapley had made the rounds of the local bars, so that he was in fine fettle by the time he returned to the ball. When an officious doorkeeper asked to see his invitation, the old frontiersman ripped out an oath and roared, "If I don't get in there, I'll call my boy, Sul, out, and we'll take this place apart!" He was admitted.[36]

On January 20, Governor Ross sent to the legislature his list of appointments and his first message.[37] His first administration as chief executive of his state had begun. During the next four years Ross would serve the people of Texas well, giving leadership and direction to vari-

---

man, January 19, 1887, proclaimed, "Rarely has it been granted to any audience to listen to a state paper equal in merit of every kind to the inaugural address of Gov. Ross."

[35] Mary Starr Barkley, *History of Travis County and Austin*, p. 126; Joe B. Frantz, *The Driskill Hotel*, p. 32; *Austin Daily Statesman*, January 19, 1887; *Galveston Daily News*, January 19, 1887. A copy of the menu, found in Ross Family Papers, Neville P. Clarke Collection, Bryan, Texas, listed the following courses: raw oysters, consomme a la cohort, spiced salmon, roast turkey, ham, roast chicken, beef tongue, corned beef, lamb tongue, escalloped oysters, fried oysters, chicken salad, lobster salad, boned turkey in jelly, lemon ice cream, vanilla ice cream, assorted cakes, confectionery, compotes of fruits, nuts and raisins, and coffee.

[36] Rosalind Langton, "Life of Colonel R. T. Milner," *Southwestern Historical Quarterly* 44 (April, 1941): 439. There are several versions of this incident. The first, somewhat different, appeared in the *Galveston Daily News*, January 21, 1887. The one given was from notes of an interview with Sul's grandson by R. Henderson Shuffler, in Ross Papers, Texas A&M Archives.

[37] *Galveston Daily News*, January 20, 1887.

ous affairs of the state. His two mildly progressive terms would see the completion and dedication of the new capitol; the attainment of new heights of industrial, agricultural, and commercial growth; and the strengthening of state eleemosynary and educational institutions. His time in office would later be considered one of exceptional good will and harmony.

☆ 13 ☆

Issues and Events of the
Ross Administration

Two days after taking office, Governor Lawrence Sullivan Ross sent his first message to the Twentieth Legislature. Like his inaugural address, this message expressed the executive's views on taxation, public lands, prohibition, and the railroads. It was customary for the governor at this time to recommend legislation he wished passed, and Ross followed executive tradition. His detailed recommendations concerned property evaluation and taxation, disbursements and collections, aid for drought victims, revisions of land use and land sale laws, and making penitentiaries self-supporting. Enactment of a livestock quarantine law and extension of the state's statistical services, investigation of the weaknesses of the judiciary system, and formulation of laws preventing railroad discrimination and combinations also claimed his attention. During the session the legislature passed much of what he had recommended.[1]

According to the Constitution of 1876, the governor had prescribed powers that enabled him to serve as commander-in-chief, convene the legislature, give messages, account for moneys, present estimates, act as executor of the laws and direct trade with other states, grant pardons and paroles, fill vacancies in some states and district offices, and exercise the veto. He also had implied powers to perform ceremonial functions and act as head of his party within the state.

Compared to the powers of the chief executives of other states, the position of governor of Texas was "relatively weak." At the same

---

[1]Texas Governors, Executive Series, *Governor's Messages, Coke to Ross (Inclusive) 1874–1891*, pp. 574–95, 599–600. The *Austin Daily Statesman*, January 21, 1887, noted the favorable comments on the new governor's first message, adding that it showed "strength of mind, independent thought, fervid patriotism, and a power to express clearly and forcibly his views and convictions."

time, the powers of the executive under the 1876 constitution were limited compared with those of previous Texas constitutions. Still smarting from the ills of too powerful an executive during Reconstruction, the framers of the Constitution of 1876 sharply reduced gubernatorial powers, especially those dealing with the militia, appointments, and fiscal matters.[2]

During his four years as chief executive of Texas, Sul Ross faced issues and events that would test his skills of statesmanship and challenge anew his position of party leadership. He recommended legislation and initiated reform, united his party in time of crisis, supervised the construction and dedication of the new capitol, curtailed fence cutting and mob rule, and evoked interest in Texas tourism and investment. Using both the prescribed and the implied powers of his office, he brought about what would later be described as the "era of good feeling" in Texas politics.[3]

When Lawrence Sullivan Ross became the fourteenth governor of Texas, he found himself in the midst of a transition. In 1887 Texas was both frontier and modern and was experiencing the problems inherent in both worlds. Upon his accession, Ross found problems relating to the frontier still demanding executive attention; at the same time, the state was rapidly entering the modern age, with its impetus to reform. A hallmark of his four years as governor was his ability to strike a balance between these often conflicting ways of life and provide effective leadership in dealing with their problems.

Although Texans occasionally suffered raids by Mexican bandits, outbreaks of mob violence, threats of Indian uprisings, and lapses of law enforcement just as in the old days, by the late 1800s the most serious of the state's frontier dilemmas stemmed from disagreements between ranchers and farmers over land. Mishandling of Texas' public domain, especially since 1876, had produced speculation, fraud, and conflict, with little gain to the state. Although the establishment of a Land Board in 1883 alleviated some problems, laws regulating the leasing of public lands and battles between farmers and ranchers, especially over water rights and fence cutting, continued to disrupt the peace.[4]

[2] Fred Gantt, Jr., *The Chief Executive in Texas: A Study in Gubernatorial Leadership*, pp. 33, 35, 333–34.

[3] Paul Bolton, *Governors of Texas*.

[4] *Austin Daily Statesman*, October 8, 16, and 27 and November 4, 1887, March 7

Ross, who had campaigned on land use reform, considered the problem at length in his first inaugural address, suggesting a four-point program for dealing wisely with land policy. First, the state should precisely classify its public lands in order to know their value and insure title and true boundaries. Second, the acreage should be sold at low interest over a long period. Next, the power of the commissioner of the Land Office should be restored so that the public lands could be controlled by a single authority. And fourth, the new governor suggested stringent measures to deal with all persons occupying and using state lands illegally. At the time of his first message to the Twentieth Legislature, the governor reiterated these same basic recommendations. During the course of the session, the legislature enacted all these recommendations into law.[5]

When the Twenty-first Legislature met in 1889, Ross declared that under land policy reforms made by the Twentieth Legislature, the state would be able to profitably dispose of its public school lands without retarding settlement. His only additional recommendation was that compliance in good faith by the purchasers under the 1883 laws should grant valid title to the lands purchased. Again the legislature responded by further amending the land sale and lease laws to conform to the governor's suggestion.[6]

By the end of his four years in office, Ross believed that the policies enacted by his legislatures had resulted in "great good." Although the present laws would possibly require future amendments, he enjoined the legislators to avoid serious modification of the successful features of the laws.[7]

Besides land sale and lease laws, one of the first problems facing the new Ross administration was a severe drought, affecting twenty-one central, north-central, and southwestern counties. In some areas rain had not fallen since the previous spring; partial crop failures were general, and many sections had suffered a total crop failure. Despite

---

and December 18, 1888, September 7, 1889, and December 19 and 23, 1890; Alwyn Barr, *Reconstruction to Reform: Texas Politics, 1876–1906*, pp. 81–82; Wayne Gard, "The Fence-Cutters," *Southwestern Historical Quarterly* 51 (July, 1947): 1–15.

[5]Texas Governors, *Governor's Messages*, pp. 565–69, 583–84; H. P. N. Gammel, comp., *The Laws of Texas, 1822–1897*, IX, 805, 881–89.

[6]Texas Governors, *Governor's Messages*, pp. 629–32; Gammel, comp., *The Laws of Texas*, IX, 1078–81.

[7]Texas Governors, *Governor's Messages*, pp. 688–89.

assistance from the private sector, relief was needed for about thirty thousand Texans.[8]

It was an era when government paternalism was infrequent and meager. Therefore, most citizens tried to help themselves before finally seeking state and federal aid. Mason County, one of those hardest hit by the drought, resisted asking for aid until May, 1887, when assistance was requested for sixty families.[9]

In his first message to the Twentieth Legislature, Ross acknowledged the need for government aid to protect these citizens from starvation. He suggested that the unfortunate citizens of the stricken counties should have "some measure of consideration and relief" and that they should "not be permitted to suffer the pangs of hunger and destitution" because of crop failures "no human precaution could have guarded against." Thus exhorted to action, the legislature responded quickly, establishing a special relief committee and appropriating $100,000 for aid and the purchase of corn, flour, or meal for distribution to the sufferers.[10]

Although Governor Ross had met the worst of the state's economic problems squarely, offering solutions his legislatures were willing (and sometimes unwilling) to adopt, the tide of reform was rising in Texas, as it was elsewhere in the United States. Growing farmer discontent as voiced by the Farmers' Alliance had played a part in his election. Founded in the mid-seventies as a farmer protection organization, the Alliance quickly enveloped the Grange; by 1886, the Alliance boasted about fifty thousand members in Texas.[11]

More politically minded and vocal than the Grangers had been, Alliance members soon made their presence felt on the Texas political scene. The week before the Democratic state convention of 1886, Alliance delegates met in Cleburne and drew up a platform listing sixteen demands. Among these were legal recognition of trade unions and cooperative stores, sale of public lands in small blocks to settlers only

[8]*Austin Daily Statesman*, January 8 and 11, 1887.

[9]Stella Gibson Polk, *Mason and Mason County: A History*, p. 70.

[10]Texas Governors, *Governor's Messages*, pp. 581–82; Gammel, comp., *The Laws of Texas*, IX, 800–802. Ross called it an "extraordinary appropriation." The amount was generous compared with a $10,000 appropriation passed by the U.S. Congress but vetoed by President Cleveland (Barr, *Reconstruction to Reform*, p. 103).

[11]John Stricklin Spratt, *The Road to Spindletop: Economic Change in Texas, 1875–1901*, pp. 186–88.

on easy terms, prohibition of alien ownership of U.S. land, removal of illegal fences, rigid enforcement of state tax laws concerning corporations, full assessment of railroad property, free coinage of gold and silver, and passage of an interstate commerce law. These demands were bolstered two years later by requests for additional railroad legislation and by a law prohibiting the formation of trusts and combinations.[12]

These political aims of the Alliance influenced Democratic party platforms; the articles on land, railroads, and convict leasing appeared in the 1886 platform. In 1888 the Democrats again borrowed from the Alliance platform, putting forth their own planks favoring further railroad regulation and antitrust measures. This borrowing would continue until the Alliance members had all but captured the Democratic party and gained their most desired objective—the creation of a railroad regulatory commission during the administration of Ross's successor, James S. Hogg.[13]

That was still several years off, however, and at the 1886 convention Ross gained enough Alliance votes to assure his nomination. Soon another problem that could have seriously challenged Democratic party unity became important in the Texas political life. This was the issue of prohibition, which again surfaced soon after the Waco governor's inauguration.

Prohibitionists had played a minor if vocal role in the election of 1886, but the issue continued to gain momentum. When the Twentieth Legislature met, it passed a number of Prohibitionist laws, including a constitutional amendment to be presented to the voters. With vehement supporters on either side of the issue, battle was soon joined. In March the supporters of the amendment met in Waco to map their strategy for victory when the question came up for approval in August. Two months later the anti-Prohibitionists gathered in Dallas, among them George Clark, the new governor's campaign manager. During their convention opponents of the measure prepared a nine-plank platform against the amendment.[14]

[12] Ernest William Winkler, ed., *Platforms of Political Parties in Texas, 1846–1916*, pp. 234–36, 268–71.

[13] Ibid., pp. 238–39, 258–59; Spratt, *The Road to Spindletop*, pp. 211, 214–15. Although of growing importance in Texas politics during this period, the Knights of Labor had less influence than the Farmers' Alliance. Both groups worked for railroad regulation (Barr, *Reconstruction to Reform*, pp. 96–99).

[14] Gammel, comp., *The Laws of Texas*, IX, 856–58, 868–69, 930; Winkler, ed., *Platforms of Political Parties*, pp. 247–51.

Following an appeal to join the Dallas convention, Governor Ross wrote a vigorous letter condemning the amendment as "impolitic, unwise and against the genius of our free institutions." A search of the Scriptures, he pointed out, revealed no intolerance of the use of wine. He continued, "No government ever succeeded in changing the moral convictions of its subjects by force." Finally, as the leader of the Democratic party in Texas, Ross commented on the destructiveness of the division of the party over prohibition. Although he had faith in the "honest instincts and just intentions, the desire to do right of the great mass of the people," he was afraid that the roar of the high tide of feeling on the subject would forever drown out the voice of reason.[15]

Despite a bitter campaign, in which Ross was lampooned in a cartoon as a groveling subject of King Beer, the prohibition amendment was defeated by over ninety thousand votes. The issue would not be viable again until after the turn of the century.[16]

Although Ross was not to go down in history as a crusading executive, he did have lasting influence upon the safe construction of the capitol dome. When he took office early in 1887, the builders of the new red granite capitol were preparing to erect the dome, slated to rise 260 feet above the rotunda—some 7 feet higher than that of the national capitol. That April, Abner Taylor, general contractor responsible for the construction of the mammoth structure, suggested revision of the dome plans, indicating that greater stability was needed in its supports.

As a member of the Capitol Board, charged with overseeing the building's construction and ensuring its acceptance by the state, Governor Ross approved this change at the builder's expense, but Attorney General Hogg, also on the board, protested changing the contract under any circumstances. He implied that deviousness of some sort on Taylor's part was the reason for the proposed change.[17]

There the matter stood through the summer of 1887, as the superstructure of the dome began to rise over the shoulders of the building itself. Then W. C. Walsh, a former Capitol Board member who was following the construction process carefully, happened to compute the weight of the specified brick dome. He found to his horror that the

[15] *Austin Daily Statesman*, May 3, 1887.
[16] Ibid., June 30 and August 5, 1887; Barr, *Reconstruction to Reform*, pp. 89–91.
[17] Robert C. Cotner, ed., *The Texas State Capitol*, pp. 63–64; *Galveston Daily News*, April 28, 1887.

"weight shown not only wiped out the 'factor of safety' but exceeded the theoretical resistance of the foundation." A rechecking of his estimated figures by a colleague showed them to be correct, and Walsh hastened to consult with Gus Wilke, the subcontractor. When Wilke admitted his own fears for the safety of the dome, Walsh took the problem to the new governor, Sul Ross.[18]

After other consultations, Ross formed a board of three prominent architects from New Orleans, Houston, and Galveston and placed the problem in their hands. Eventually they came to the same conclusion as Walsh and Wilke—that the dome as planned was dangerously heavy—and recommended that iron plates be substituted for the proposed brick lining. This was done, and the construction proceeded.[19]

While the contractors labored to complete the capitol, Sul Ross became the first and only governor of Texas to call a special session of the legislature (April–May, 1888) to deal with a surplus in the treasury. Revenue reforms suggested by Ross and enacted by the regular session of the Twentieth Legislature, plus an indemnity claim paid by the federal government, filled the treasury to overflowing. Praising the legislators for the wise reform measures passed during the last session, the governor in his welcoming address repeated his earlier recommendations on just and equal assessment, taxation of attached property, and taxation of property belonging to individuals or corporations outside Texas.

In dealing with the surplus, Ross, a fiscal conservative, believed the money was better left in the treasury than squandered. He had, however, several suggestions to submit. Although revenue collection had greatly increased, it was still far from regular, the bulk of collections reaching the treasury in December and January. Therefore, Ross reasoned, enough money should be set aside to cover government expenses during the months when little came into the treasury. Of the remainder, one-third could be remitted to the taxpayer. But, he cautioned, the tax rate should be left alone to avoid later financial embar-

[18]*Austin Daily Statesman*, July 22 and November 6, 1887; Charles W. Ramsdell, Jr., ed., "Memories of a Texas Land Commissioner, W. C. Walsh," *Southwestern Historical Quarterly* 44 (April, 1941): 493–94.

[19]Cotner, ed., *The Texas State Capitol*, pp. 22–24. Walsh theorized the reason for this error was that the brick dome had been proposed as if the supporting walls were solid when in reality they were arched (Ramsdell, ed., "Memories of a Texas Land Commissioner," pp. 494–95). Galvanized iron had already been substituted for cast iron in the shell around the brickwork (*Austin Daily Statesman*, August 23 and 24, 1887).

rassment. With what remained the governor suggested the state pay deficiencies, adjust the state debt to the university, expand the capacities of the asylums, put the new reformatory into operation, provide for a geologic survey of the state, furnish the new capitol, bolster the state militia, erect a memorial to Texas veterans, and increase the pay of public school teachers.[20]

Although the legislators followed most of the governor's suggestions on spending the surplus, they ignored his admonition to retain the present rate for the ad valorem tax; as a result, collections again fell behind expenditures. Meanwhile the date set for the dedication of the capitol approached. Despite other differences between the contractors and the Capitol Board, especially over the building's copper roof and some of its fittings, the edifice was considered all but completed on May 8, 1888.[21]

Planning for the week-long dedication celebration to be held May 14 through 19, 1888, had begun shortly after the first of the year. By late February actual preparations were in progress, with plans to erect grandstands, sell vendor privileges, and hold an interstate drill team competition concurrently with the dedication. Also scheduled for that week were fireworks displays and a showing of the famous Battle of Gettysburg Cyclorama. A dress ball would complete the festivities. Shortly thereafter, elaborate full-color gilded invitations depicting the capitol, famous Texans, and features of Texas life were sent to President Grover Cleveland and his cabinet, to U.S. senators and representatives, to other governors, to the president of the Republic of Mexico, and to many other prominent Texans.[22]

Early in April concession privileges went on auction. These included all kinds of alcoholic and nonalcoholic beverages, barbecue, chili, tamales, Mexican candy and other confectionery, ice cream, peanuts, popcorn, fruit, flowers, cigars and tobacco, newspapers and books, stationery, fans, umbrellas, and souvenirs. The beer concession alone sold for over $5,000 on the assumption that the 50,000 to 100,000 peo-

[20]Texas Governors, *Governor's Messages*, pp. 605–608. This thorough survey, begun in 1888, was still not complete when Ross left office in 1891 (see Walter Keene Ferguson, *Geology and Politics in Frontier Texas, 1845–1909*, pp. 76–93).

[21]Gammel, comp., *The Laws of Texas*, IX, 1008–12; Cotner, ed., *The Texas State Capitol*, pp. 24–25.

[22]*Austin Daily Statesman*, February 29, 1888; Mary Starr Barkley, *History of Travis County and Austin*, p. 206.

ple expected to attend the dedication would spend $500,000 during the five-day celebration.[23]

Although the ceremonies were to begin at 8:30 the morning of the dedication, thousands of spectators arrived before seven. Soon an estimated eight thousand people crowded into the capitol and its grounds, with thousands more lined along Congress Avenue. Still others thronged the hillsides to the east and west of the capitol. About nine o'clock the parade from the drill grounds to the capitol began, featuring over forty military and musical groups. Near the capitol the parade was joined by members of the Masonic Grand Commandery and the Grand Lodge of Masons of Texas, who were to perform Masonic dedication ceremonies during the day. Spectators thought it a grand scene as the military procession passed up Congress Avenue to the "flourish of trumpets, beat of drum and blast of bugle" and entered the capitol grounds.[24]

It was eleven o'clock before Governor Ross and his state officials and distinguished guests took their places beneath the triumphal arch spanning the south entrance of the capitol. With the executive were Alexander Watkins Terrell, Oran M. Roberts, Temple Houston, and other celebrities, including a large delegation of Mexican civil and military notables. On the platform and in the vestibule were members of the Texas Veterans Association. Prayer by the Reverend J. C. Wootan, chaplain of the association, and speeches by Ross, Terrell, and Abner Taylor followed, with solemn Masonic ceremonies completing the dedication. There was only one disappointment. At one point during Ross's speech a shower fell, making it obvious to the governor and those around him that the roof of the yet-to-be-occupied building leaked.[25]

Intermittent rain continued to dampen the rest of the week's outdoor festivities, but despite a leaking roof, showers did not hinder the Dedication Ball, held the night of May 18. The ball was opened by grand marches from the senate chamber and the house of representatives, one led by the governor and first lady and the other by Colonel and Mrs. S. B. M. Young. While six bands alternately played, several hundred luminaries participated in the "Most Brilliant Assemblage Ever Gathered in the Lone Star State." It was an occasion to remem-

[23] *Austin Daily Statesman*, April 3, 1888.
[24] *Austin Daily Statesman*, May 17, 1888.
[25] Ibid.; Cotner, ed., *The Texas State Capitol*, p. 25.

ber, one of the highlights of the century, and certainly the apex of Ross's first term.[26]

That year of the dedication, 1888, was also an election year. Ross's popularity with his party and with the majority of his fellow Texans meant he would have no opposition within his party and little within the state when he stood for reelection. "Governor Ross . . . has filled his high office with signal ability and with genuine and complete satisfaction to the state," wrote the *Austin Daily Statesman* before going on to list the accomplishments of the governor's first term. Praise came even from the Republican State Convention, which met in April and again in August and ended by refusing to try to oppose Ross in the fall election.[27]

Adoption by the Democrats of many Farmers' Alliance demands undercut much of the Alliance's potential opposition to Ross. By midsummer it appeared that the only true resistance to a Ross victory in November would come from a coalition party made up of Prohibitionists, Knights of Labor, and the more radical farmers. This fusion party eventually fielded Ross's earlier opponent, Marion Martin, for governor, but with little success. Despite attempts by the Prohibitionists and their cohorts to break the monolithic character of the Democratic party and split the party vote, Ross won easily, polling the largest number of votes to date and defeating Martin by a majority of 151,891 votes.[28]

As the 1888 election campaigns ended, the governor as executor of the laws faced a new problem—the rash of fence-cutting incidents plaguing the state. The practice of fence cutting was a natural outgrowth of the increased use of barbed wire in Texas after 1875. Fence cutting was most common in counties where the farm met the frontier and farmers and ranchers competed for grazing land, water, and rights of way.

Despite a variety of circumstances, the problem was epidemic; by 1883 one-half of the state's organized counties had suffered incidents of fence cutting. In some areas the practice was so general it constituted a war between the fencers and the cutters. Estimates of damages soared

[26]*Austin Daily Statesman*, May 19, 1888.

[27]Ibid., March 31, May 23, and July 25, 1888; Winkler, ed., *Platforms of Political Parties*, pp. 253, 272–73.

[28]Winkler, ed., *Platforms of Political Parties*, pp. 254–57, 260–62; *Texas Almanac and State Industrial Guide, 1978–1979*, p. 530.

to $20 million; at times, tensions resulting from fence cutting led to bloodshed. A special session of the legislature met in 1884 to deal specifically with the problem, making both fence cutting and illegal enclosure of land felonies. Those building fences were required to place gates at three-mile intervals. Although these laws reduced the incidents, it was not until the local citizens cooperated with Texas Rangers and other law enforcement agents that the custom died out.[29]

Like other governors of this period, Ross offered rewards for the apprehension of fence cutters, but he also became personally involved late in his first term. In mid-1888 a fence-cutting war broke out around Corsicana, in Navarro County. An open clash between the cutters and the fencers seemed likely, and at last the sheriff and a county judge appealed to the governor's office for help. Ross responded by assigning to the mission two young rangers, Sergeant Ira Aten and Jim King. Aten had had considerable experience in dealing with fence cutters in Brown County, but this time the cutters at first proved too clever for the rangers.

After much cogitation, the sergeant hit upon an ingenious scheme. Since state law did not prohibit the protection of property by use of dynamite or shotguns, Aten devised a booby trap using both and proposed to "dynamite boom" a few recently built and therefore still intact fences in Navarro County. He also took the time to teach the owners of the fences how to construct the "booms."[30]

When news of this proposal got back to the governor, Ross called the young ranger in and gave him a dressing down Aten never forgot. Ross became so angry that his bald head "got redder and redder," or so Ira recalled. Although accounts differ as to whether the dynamite traps were used in Navarro County, it is certain that fence cutting in that area decreased drastically following Aten's invention. By the end of the decade the practice had all but ended elsewhere in the state.[31]

Ross's second inauguration, held January 15, 1889, was the first to be celebrated in the new capitol. Despite the unfinished state of the "handsome and complete furnishing" of the building, the ceremony in

[29] San Antonio Light, June 27, 1968.

[30] Harold Preece, Lone Star Man: Ira Aten, Last of the Old Texas Rangers, pp. 161–65.

[31] Walter Prescott Webb, The Texas Rangers: A Century of Frontier Defense, pp. 436–37; Preece, Lone Star Man, pp. 161–65.

the house of representatives hall was imposing and worthy of the magnificent new building. The governor delivered a forceful inaugural speech to a large audience crowding the chamber floor and packing its galleries.[32]

Traditionally, no inaugural ball was held for a second term, and this quieter entrance into the new term foreshadowed the quieter, less hectic pace of Ross's last two years in office. Although much was accomplished by the governor, it was done without the statewide celebrations of the first term. There was, however, one serious exception to the general peacefulness of this period.

Although outbreaks of lawlessness and violence occasionally plagued the Ross administration, the most serious incident occurred in the late summer of 1889, during what has been called the Jaybird-Woodpecker War. Trouble had been brewing in Fort Bend County since Reconstruction days. Supported by a group of whites (the Woodpeckers), blacks had retained political power in the county long after white supremacy had asserted itself elsewhere in Texas. The white supremist Democrats (the Jaybirds) sought time after time to oust the Woodpecker-black faction from power, but the combination proved too powerful. Social and personal hostilities helped to keep the antagonisms going and growing.[33]

Ross's predecessor had been called on to deal with an outbreak of mob lawlessness in Richmond in 1886, but the real battle did not begin until the political campaign of 1888. Then the murder of one prominent Jaybird in August and the attempted assassination of another in September kept tempers inflamed, since blacks were implicated in both cases. In the assassination case, the suspected blacks were ordered out of the county while a Jaybird mob formed to ensure that they departed. Soon rumors were rife that the blacks were arming for insurrection rather than running. The situation eventually became so tense that Sheriff Jim Garvey telegraphed the governor's office for assistance.[34]

Using his constitutional powers as commander-in-chief, Ross called

---

[32] *Austin Daily Statesman*, January 9 and 16, 1889.

[33] Charles Leland Sonnichsen, *I'll Die Before I Run: The Story of the Great Feuds of Texas*, pp. 186–90; Gilbert Cuthbertson, "The Jaybird-Woodpecker War," *Texana* 10, no. 4 (1972): 300–301.

[34] Cuthbertson, "The Jaybird-Woodpecker War," pp. 301, 303; Sonnichsen, *I'll Die Before I Run*, pp. 195, 198–99; *Houston Post*, September 8, 1888.

out two militia companies. Eventually Adjutant General King arrived, and after some difficulty arising from county resentment of outside interference, an uneasy peace was restored. It lasted four months.[35]

Early in 1889, violence flared again when Kyle Terry, a Woodpecker, killed Ned Gibson, a Jaybird. Day by day the tension grew. Hoping to prevent further bloodshed, Ross sent in Sergeant Ira Aten and three other rangers. Despite Aten's attempts at peacemaking, the long-expected showdown between the Woodpeckers and the Jaybirds came on August 16.[36]

In the ensuing exchange of gunfire on the streets of Richmond, four people (two Woodpeckers, one Jaybird, and one black girl) were killed and six (including one ranger) wounded. This time Aten and County Judge Weston wired the governor for troops. The Houston Light Guard reached the town about one o'clock the morning of the seventeenth and instituted martial law: at seven o'clock that evening Ross himself arrived, accompanied by Assistant Attorney General R. H. Harrison and another militia company, the Brenham Grays.[37]

Once in Richmond, Ross set up headquarters in the National Hotel, where he ordered all civil officials relieved of their duties. Expecting indictments, Harrison requested the impaneling of a special grand jury.[38]

Sunday morning the governor met with a committee of citizens claiming to be law abiding. Ross, in reply, pointed out that their section had an "ugly reputation" for lawlessness and that relief from factionalism within the county must come by enforcement of the law. It would not be democratic, he lectured, to dispossess the present officers by the military. Instead, a sheriff acceptable to both parties should be selected to fill the place of Garvey, who had died in a gun battle two days ago. He would, he told them, use his influence to select a disinterested party from out of the county. But despite Ross's attempts at reconciliation, the committee jibbed at accepting this solution, some of the citizens preferring to maintain martial law. This Ross did not favor. He then suggested the desperate and unpopular mea-

---

[35] Sonnichsen, *I'll Die Before I Run*, p. 200.

[36] Ibid., pp. 204–205; Preece, *Lone Star Man*, pp. 187, 189.

[37] *Austin Daily Statesman*, August 18, 1889; Sonnichsen, *I'll Die Before I Run*, pp. 214–15; Preece, *Lone Star Man*, p. 196.

[38] Sonnichsen, *I'll Die Before I Run*, p. 215; Preece, *Lone Star Man*, p. 196.

sure of disorganizing the county. Still neither side would give way, and that day's conference ended with little accomplished.[39]

At the next day's meeting Ross held to his original proposal, even suggesting Sergeant Aten of the rangers as the compromise candidate for sheriff. This was acceptable to the Jaybirds, and after another day of bickering the Woodpeckers agreed. Six days after the battle, Ira Aten became the new sheriff of Fort Bend County.[40]

Eventually many former Woodpeckers left the county, leaving the Jaybirds in strong political control, which was not shaken until the mid-twentieth century. Ross returned to Austin from Richmond on August 22, rightly confident that Aten had the ability and courage to bring order to the Fort Bend country.[41]

Throughout most of his two terms, Ross had wished to persuade President Grover Cleveland to visit Texas. In August, 1887, Ross had written Cleveland, extending an invitation to visit the state during the Texas State Fair and Exposition to be held at Dallas in October that year. The president, however, did not accept.[42]

The invitation to the nation's first Democratic president since the antebellum era was extended again when the new capitol was dedicated, but still without result. Nevertheless, Ross did not abandon his plan. Then, in March, 1890, Ross discovered that through Congress, the U.S. attorney general had launched a suit in the Supreme Court against the state of Texas. The purpose was to determine the ownership of the disputed territory of Greer County.[43]

In an attempt to save these valuable 1,511,576 acres north of Red River, Ross determined early in May to travel to Washington for a per-

[39] *Austin Daily Statesman*, August 20, 1889.

[40] Sonnichsen, *I'll Die Before I Run*, pp. 216–17.

[41] Ibid., p. 217; Cuthbertson, "The Jaybird-Woodpecker War," p. 307; *Austin Daily Statesman*, August 22, 1889. The feud did not end until Volney Gibson avenged his brother's death by killing Kyle Terry in January, 1890 (Cuthbertson, "The Jaybird-Woodpecker War," p. 305). The governor had not heard the last of the affair. In September, two of the blacks forced out of the county the year before sued forty-three prominent Jaybirds in the federal court at Galveston. The matter was eventually settled out of court and to the satisfaction of the government of Texas (see Sonnichsen, *I'll Die Before I Run*, pp. 218–20; and *Austin Daily Statesman*, December 28, 1889).

[42] Lawrence Sullivan Ross to Grover Cleveland, August 9, 1887, Grover Cleveland Papers, Library of Congress, Washington, D.C. (hereafter cited as Cleveland Papers); Cleveland to Ross, September 7, 1887, Cleveland Papers.

[43] Texas Governors, *Governor's Messages*, pp. 692–93.

sonal interview with the attorney general. Accordingly the Texas delegation, including the governor and Mrs. Ross and Colonel A. H. Belo, publisher of the *Galveston Daily News*, left for Dallas on May 13. There the party was joined by Mayor W. C. Connor, who helped persuade Ross to extend his trip to New York in order to invite former president Cleveland to visit the state fair that fall. Traveling on a special boudoir car, Ross and his party journeyed to the capital city via New Orleans and Saint Louis.[44]

Arriving in Washington, the Texas delegation visited President Benjamin Harrison at the White House, where Ross had the pleasure of renewing the acquaintance of an old soldier who had met him as a curly-haired youth during the Wichita village campaign. In a meeting with the attorney general, the governor also arranged to have former attorney general Garland, former congressman John Hancock, and the Honorable George Clark represent Texas interests in the Greer County case before the Supreme Court. During his brief stay in Washington, Ross also met national political figures like Chauncey Depew, Daniel W. Voorhees, John G. Carlisle, and Abram S. Hewitt.[45]

From Washington the party proceeded to New York, where the Texans met Mr. and Mrs. Cleveland and again extended an invitation for them to visit the Lone Star State. Financial advisers called upon the governor to discuss investments, while newspaper reporters, learning of his adventurous youth spent on the Texas frontier, swarmed around him. One newspaperman, a reporter for the *New York Herald*, conducted a lengthy interview of Ross that described his Indian-fighting career in detail. Calling Ross a "Texan of the Texans," the reporter noted that the governor had "played a conspicuous part in the exciting scenes of pioneer life on the Texas frontier," holding his own against the Comanches since early youth. "The heroism and romance of war have been personal experiences with him," the reporter concluded.[46]

Other newsmen were as enthusiastic, and the governor received good press coverage wherever he went. Noted the *Austin Daily Statesman* on his return:

[44] W. C. Connor, Mayor of Dallas, to Lawrence Sullivan Ross, May 9, 1890, Ross Family Papers, Neville P. Clarke Collection, Bryan, Texas (hereafter cited as Ross Family Papers, Clarke Collection); *Austin Daily Statesman*, May 13, 15, and 18, 1890; *Washington Post*, May 21, 1890.

[45] *Washington Post*, May 21, 1890; *Austin Daily Statesman*, May 28, 1890.

[46] *New York Herald*, May 25, 1890.

There has been more learned of Texas in the North since Ross has been governor than was ever known of it before. The enforcement of the laws, the happiness and prosperity of the people, the protection given property and life have been recognized and the State is in a better condition in every way now than it has ever been in its history. He is recognized in the North as a remarkable man. His life is known, and he is considered a marvel in having succeeded in developing from a ranger boy into a governor. . . . The ranger is, of course, considered . . . as a man who has more fight than polish, more bravery than education. So when they have seen the governor their wonder is great.[47]

Although the Clevelands expressed great interest in visiting Texas, they did not do so while Ross was in office. Nevertheless, the governor's trip was successful in that he excited much interest in Texas among easterners, an interest that would eventually bear fruit in increased investment, tourism, and immigration.[48]

As the election of 1890 approached, Ross's friends and supporters began talking of a then-unprecedented third term for the governor. Ross himself was adamantly opposed to the idea and wrote to a Texas editor that he had not "formed so high an opinion of himself as to suppose the people of Texas are going to abrogate a settled line of policy for his special benefit."[49]

Since his lieutenant governor, Thomas B. Wheeler, and Attorney General James S. Hogg were both pursuing the governorship, Ross chose to stay in the background during the campaign. The rambunctious, crusading Hogg favored creation of a strong commission to regulate the state's railroads, while other prominent Texas politicians such as George Clark, Ross's campaign manager in 1886 and 1888, opposed it.[50]

Although Ross actively sought legislation regulating the railroads, he did not favor creation of a state railroad commission. He feared such an agency would prove a "costly and useless luxury" incapable of correcting abuses or bringing permanent relief. It is not known to what extent, if any, the governor was influenced by the views of Clark, who was a railroad attorney, but Lieutenant Governor Wheeler and the

---

[47] *Austin Daily Statesman*, May 25, 1890.

[48] Ross was not successful in saving Greer County for Texas. In 1895 the U.S. Supreme Court awarded the disputed acreage to Oklahoma (Robert C. Cotner, *James Stephen Hogg: A Biography*, p. 456).

[49] *Austin Daily Statesman*, September 11, 1889, and February 2, 1890.

[50] Barr, *Reconstruction to Reform*, pp. 118–19; Cotner, *James Stephen Hogg*, pp. 189–90.

other anticommission candidates apparently had his tacit support in this campaign.[51]

The governor's disapproval of a commission plank in the party platform stemmed partly from his belief that an amendment creating the commission would be adopted by the Twenty-second Legislature. He also opposed bringing it to the front as a distinctive party measure, since every Democrat "should be left free to vote his convictions." Finally, he opposed inclusion of the issue because he feared many Democrats would be "forced to invite the accusation of treason against the party rather than outrage their conscientious convictions of duty to their state."[52]

As it was, the Hogg faction carried the summer conventions as well as the state in November. When the thirty-nine-year-old progressive Hogg acceded to office on January 20, 1891, his inaugural marked the beginning of a new political era. It also established a precedent for succession to the governorship by the attorney general. This pattern continued throughout the nineties until it was upset in 1898 by political manipulator Colonel Edward M. House, who later directed the career of Woodrow Wilson.[53]

The old era just past was certainly not without value, however. During his years as governor Lawrence Sullivan Ross had brought strength, character, honesty, and dignity to the office—qualities not forgotten by the people he had served.

[51] Texas Governors, *Governor's Messages*, pp. 594–95.

[52] Notations on questions about the railroad commission by Lawrence Sullivan Ross, July 22, 1890, in Ross Family Papers, Clarke Collection.

[53] *Austin Daily Statesman*, January 21, 1891; Arthur Douglas Howden Smith, *The Real Colonel House*, p. 60.

☆ 14 ☆

Ross as Governor

A veteran of many different campaigns and situations, Governor Lawrence Sullivan Ross took up his duties with ease, self-assurance, and style. Whether it was entertaining visitors at the capitol, attending drill team competitions and seasonal festivals, addressing fair crowds and university commencements, or visiting sites of new state institutions, he was gracious, friendly, and popular.[1]

A true democrat, Ross was readily accessible to the people he governed. Before the completion of the new capitol he could be seen sitting many evenings in front of the temporary seat of government, surrounded by common citizens "discussing current events, or indulging in anecdotes, or in other words passing the time like any other crowd of respectable men." Plain in dress, manner, and action, he was nevertheless "entirely free from any semblance of demagoguery."[2]

In many ways Ross represented what Fred Gantt, Jr., has called the "Composite Texas Governor." According to Gantt's statistics, the typical governor of Texas was a native son who entered office at about forty-eight. Usually he was a lawyer with experience in state government, particularly in the legislature, and had held a law enforcement position of some kind. This typical governor, Gantt found, was college educated, married, and the father of several children. He was either a Methodist or a Baptist, a Mason, and an enthusiastic supporter of a veteran's organization. Elected from central or eastern Texas, the typical governor served four years and then retired to a public service of-

---

[1]*Austin Daily Statesman*, February 11, April 20, June 16 and 24, and October 5 and 21, 1887. Ross's visitors ranged from railroad entrepreneur Jay Gould to Mexican military commissioners to a two-year-old boy who strayed from his parents and wandered into the governor's office, where Ross entertained him until his parents arrived (*Austin Daily Statesman*, May 23, 1888, and January 11 and April 8, 1890).

[2]*Henderson* (Tex.) *Times*, May 5, 1888.

fice. From that position he continued to exert considerable influence over public affairs in Texas until his death.[3]

Ross, who served as president of Texas A&M College while still a leader of his party, failed to meet the norms in only two respects: he was not a native son, having been born in Iowa Territory, and he neither trained for nor obtained a position as a lawyer. Otherwise, he qualifies as an outstanding example of Gantt's typical governor.[4]

Philosophically Ross, like many statesmen of his day, was a Jeffersonian Democrat, believing that the best government was one that governed least. In his second inaugural address, given January 15, 1889, he told the assembled legislators and guests that he considered "a plain, simple government, with severe limitations upon delegated powers, honestly and frugally administered, as the noblest and truest outgrowth of the wisdom taught by its founders." This same government, Ross said, working through local agencies, should limit its authority to the preservation of public order and the administration of justice, leaving all else to the self-reliant, conscientious, and intelligent citizen. In his opinion, a serious threat to the integrity of the American form of government lurked in the growing tendency of the people "to underestimate their duty and power and to call upon Hercules for aid, when their own shoulders are ample to move the wheels if applied with vigor and energy."[5]

Stressing self-reliance and self-maintenance as well as individual over corporate enterprise, Ross called upon the people of Texas to apply this vigor and energy to solve the state's problems. Thus he was a conservative when conservatism was considered a virtue. At the same time, he was "sufficiently progressive to be up with the urgent need of the times."[6] This blend of reasonable conservatism and careful progressivism was to ensure his general success as governor.

In his handling of various issues and events throughout his four years in office, Ross used his gubernatorial powers skillfully. When it came to use of the veto, however, he exercised it sparingly, less than ten times in four years, the least of any Texas governor other than

[3] Fred Gantt, Jr., *The Chief Executive in Texas: A Study in Gubernatorial Leadership*, pp. 69–70.

[4] Ibid.

[5] Texas Governors, Executive Series, *Governor's Messages, Coke to Ross (Inclusive) 1874–1891*, p. 650.

[6] Ibid.; *Austin Daily Statesman*, January 21, 1887.

Richard B. Hubbard (a predecessor) and Ross Sterling (a successor). When he used the veto, Ross did so reluctantly, since he disliked dissenting from the conclusions of the legislators unless absolutely necessary.[7]

Under the Constitution of 1876, the governor had ten days (excepting Sundays) to veto a bill by returning it to the house of origin with a statement of his objections. By a vote of two-thirds of the present members of both houses, the legislation could be passed over the veto. If the legislature was not in session, the governor had twenty days after adjournment to file his objections with the secretary of state and to give notice of his action by public proclamation. Although he could item veto appropriation bills, the Texas governor lacked the power of a pocket veto.[8]

Ross's opposition to a bill usually centered on its unconstitutionality or the legislators' "extravagant expenditure." Once, however, Ross vetoed a bill suspending the forced collection of taxes. The legislators, eager to cut taxes, promptly passed the tax bill over the governor's objection. An experienced general, the governor knew when to abandon a lost cause. At least, he noted, the people would be pleased by the action of the legislature.[9]

Besides the veto, another constitutional power granted the chief executive in Texas was clemency, by which he could pardon, grant reprieves, remit fines, and commute sentences. Until 1893, when a Board of Pardon Advisors was established, this was a power belonging to the executive alone. Under the Constitution of 1876, the governor was often besieged with applications for pardons. Ross noted that applications by mail and personal appeals would have consumed all his time if he had not subordinated "this character of business to that of more general concern."[10]

Nevertheless, in cases of special merit, Ross was willing to consider clemency. During his four years in office he granted 861 full pardons. One man was pardoned because of feeble health, sixteen others

[7] Gantt, *The Chief Executive in Texas*, pp. 178, 180, 190–91; Texas Governors, *Governor's Messages*, pp. 597–98.

[8] Constitution of Texas, 1875, 4, sec. 14.

[9] Texas Governors, *Governor's Messages*, pp. 597–98, 604, 619.

[10] *Austin Daily Statesman*, February 1 and 21, 1888. In 1960 Governor Price Daniel handled over nine thousand clemency actions (Gantt, *The Chief Executive in Texas*, p. 154).

because of incurable disease. Three pardons were granted with the understanding the recipients would leave the state and never return. The governor also twice revoked a pardon already granted.[11]

Governor Ross also used his powers of clemency to commute various prison sentences and remit fines and imprisonment. In 195 instances he reduced sentences; in 8, he commuted the death penalty to life imprisonment. Other clemency actions included remission of imprisonment, reduction of fines, and freeing of prisoners.[12]

In all, Ross used his powers of clemency judiciously. Compared to the number of pardons issued after the establishment of the Board of Pardon Advisors, Ross's total, 844, is small indeed. For example, during two years Governor James E. Ferguson issued 2,253 pardons; in more than three years Governor William P. Hobby granted 1,518; and Miriam A. Ferguson granted 1,161 pardons in two years.[13]

But although Ross was willing to consider cases on their own merits, he also refused to interfere routinely in the process of law. Such was the case with James McCoy, scheduled for execution in July, 1889, for murdering the sheriff of La Salle County. Although numerous citizens in the prisoner's home county signed a petition for commutation of the death penalty to life imprisonment, the governor refused to grant clemency. Ross examined the case, looked into the legal aspects of the trial, and weighed the evidence before deciding that the only sure means of "preserving both public and private security, as well as social order and domestic happiness" and of preventing crime was to adhere to certain inflexible procedures. Denouncing the mawkish sentiment that, he said, "too frequently interposes between the outraged laws and their violators," he ordered that the "extreme penalties of the law be executed in cases like this."[14]

Not only did Ross believe in exacting the death penalty when the

[11]*Austin Daily Statesman*, March 18, 1887; Governor's Papers, executive record book, pardons and remissions, 1886–89, Texas State Archives, Austin, Texas (hereafter cited as Governor's Papers).

[12]Executive record book, Governor's Papers.

[13]Gantt, *The Chief Executive in Texas*, pp. 151, 152.

[14]*Austin Daily Statesman*, July 25, 1889. One prisoner, an aged Mexican sentenced to life imprisonment for murder, made elaborate identical tables for Mrs. Ross and Mrs. Cleveland in hopes of securing clemency. The one given Lizzie was made of fourteen different kinds of wood in 74,000 pieces. Although it is not known whether the man's appeal bore fruit, the table today is owned by Ross descendant Neville P. Clarke, Bryan, Texas (see "If This Table Could Talk," in *Waco Tribune-Herald*, September 22, 1957).

enormity of the crime demanded it, but he also took a consistently strong position on law and order. In June, 1887, the governor issued a proclamation decrying the lawlessness then prevalent in Texas and promising to harness the "whole civil machinery" of the state to assist the sheriffs. He exhorted each individual to "set his face against crime and criminals" and to make the "murderer, the assassin and the thief odious, instead of sympathizing with and signing petitions for their pardon."[15]

As governor, Ross also had the authority to post rewards for wanted criminals. It was a power he used only occasionally; he believed the fundamental diligence of state law enforcement officers was not dependent upon rewards but rather upon the faithful performance of their sworn duties. In the words of one observer:

> Just in this desire and craving for extra compensation . . . is found one of the greatest evils clinging to the means used for the detection of crimes and deciding their punishment. And if Governor Ross . . . can bring this matter pointedly and convincingly home to all the officials of the state, he will have inaugurated a reform that will distinguish his administration for years to come.

In the same way, Ross bitingly condemned the outbreak of lynch law in Madison, Wharton, and Panola counties that, in his opinion, maligned the state and its communities and served to "baptize our people anew in a perfect stream of calumny."[16]

Ross reacted similarly in the case of vigilantes near Waco who flogged a man for immorality, boasting that they took up preservation of the law where the statutes left off. In a letter to the McLennan County attorney, Ross stated that Texas did not need a "lawless body of this character as an agency to right the wrongs, real or imaginary, of its citizens." Furthermore, he continued, "Whenever any organization, on any pretext whatever, takes into its own hands the punishment of supposed offenses, government, in a proper sense, ceases to exist." Therefore, he requested an investigation of the matter with prosecution of the guilty parties.[17]

In late August, 1890, an incident occurred that, like the mob violence in Fort Bend County, challenged the peacekeeping authority of the executive. At that time authorities in Temple applied to Governor

---

[15] *Austin Daily Statesman*, June 22, 1887.
[16] Ibid., October 8, 1887, and March 9, 1888.
[17] Ibid., December 18, 1888.

Ross for permission to establish a quarantine against Waco because of an alleged case of smallpox originating in that city. Ross sent the state health officer, Dr. Robert Rutherford, to Temple to look into the matter.[18]

After due investigation, Dr. Rutherford pronounced it needless to institute a quarantine against Waco, and Ross issued a proclamation to that effect. However, at nearby Marlin, the city fathers determined to ignore the proclamation and institute their own quarantine against Waco. At their direction, the city marshal began enforcing a strict quarantine against travelers coming into the city from Waco.[19]

This challenge to executive authority gave Ross a chance to show his wartime mettle. In a telegram to John Ward, the sheriff of Falls County, Ross directed that officer to arrest the city marshal of Marlin. This was done, but Ross learned on September 4 that the Marlin city fathers were still trying to enforce their quarantine without the marshal's aid. He then fired off another telegram to Ward, inquiring about compliance with the laws, and ordered S. E. Harland, county attorney, to deal with those defying the sheriff's authority. Under such pressure from the executive, the Marlin authorities capitulated. As the "supremacy of executive authority" had been finally recognized, Ross did not desire to prosecute the matter further and ordered the release of the marshal.[20]

Commented the *Austin Daily Statesman* about the incident:

Governor Ross has had a remarkably quiet and peaceful administration. He has had but few opportunities to show that his back bone still retained the rigidity for which it is proverbial. But now just as he is about to retire to private life, he comes across a snag in the shape of little Marlin—and he at once sets about pulling it up, root and branch. . . . It strikes us with the force of added certainty that Sul. Ross is the governor of Texas.[21]

Having proved himself a conservative regarding the maintenance of law and order, Governor Lawrence Sullivan Ross also established himself as a moderate fiscal conservative. Although he did not favor a

---

[18] Ibid., August 30, 1890.

[19] Ibid., August 31, 1890. The cotton buyers of Marlin were blamed for most of the imbroglio. According to one source, Marlin cotton buyers were sending out printed circulars warning farmers not to take their cotton into pest-ridden Waco and persuading them to sell it in pest-free Marlin (*Austin Daily Statesman*, September 2, 1890).

[20] Ibid., September 2, 4, 5, 6, and 11, 1890.

[21] Ibid., September 6, 1890.

"sacrifice of efficiency to a false idea of economy," neither did he believe in reckless disbursement of public funds. Ross was willing to consider needed fiscal reforms, for despite his policy of economic vigilance and reduced spending, and even with a treasury surplus in 1888, finances were a perennial problem.[22]

As Ross pointed out in his first message to the Twentieth Legislature, serious deficiencies undermined the handling of state taxation and revenues. Of these the most serious was inequality of assessment. Also, the taxpayer was called upon to assess his own property, and some citizens were removing personal property from the counties of assessment without paying taxes. Lack of confidence in tax sales caused further problems. At the same time the mechanics of tax collection were faulty and irregular, and the actual handling of the funds open to irregularities.[23]

In order to strengthen the state's fiscal system, the executive recommended an extensive system of reform laws in order to provide for just assessments of property. He also recommended certain constitutional amendments to restore confidence in tax sale titles and enforce prompt and sure collection of taxes. More laws would be needed to regulate the flow of revenue into and out of the treasury. His final, perhaps most farsighted, recommendation was that tax collectors "report collections and pay the same into the treasury on the first of each month commencing with a specified month in each fiscal year."[24]

Evidently the legislature concurred at least in part with the governor's assessment of the problem, for during that 1887 session and the special session of 1888 the Texas House and Senate passed laws dealing with most of these problems. Nevertheless, the legislators did not heed Ross's request to retain the present rate for the ad valorem tax at the time of a treasury surplus.[25]

The question was still at issue when the Twenty-first Legislature met in regular session. At that time Ross chided the lawmakers for their failure, which had again thrown the treasury into difficulties, and pleaded with them to restore the former tax rate. In the meantime he suggested that all expenditures be scrutinized carefully, appropriations

[22] Texas Governors, *Governor's Messages*, p. 559.

[23] Ibid., pp. 575–79.

[24] Ibid.

[25] H. P. N. Gammel, comp., *The Laws of Texas, 1822–1897*, IX, 925–26, 950–52, 967, 1001–1002, 1008–12; Texas Governors, *Governor's Messages*, pp. 605–608.

be reduced, and a special sinking fund be created to pay maturing state bonds.[26]

In his farewell address of January 13, 1891, Ross reviewed the many financial accomplishments of his two terms. He then turned his attention to recommending policies he hoped the legislature would enact under his successor. Among more general reforms, these included issuance of manuscript bonds and a plea that the sinking fund be maintained. The legislature responded by passing more tax reforms, but the lawmakers refused to pass those concerning the bonded debt and the sinking fund.[27]

In all, Governor Ross's leadership had fostered economic growth, fiscal prudence, and financial stability. During his administration taxes had been reduced, revenues increased, and, as will be seen, the state's support of educational and charitable projects increased. Despite Ross's fiscal conservatism, his four years in office had been important for Texas' future economic growth.

Ross's philosophical conservatism was reflected in his actions to perpetuate the memory of the valiant Texas soldiers of the Confederacy, although he refused to dwell on the past. During the summer of 1887, an incident illustrated his opinion of those harboring rancor from the war years. Governor Ross had been in office about five months when he received a message from the Adjutant General's Office, U.S. War Department, offering to turn over to him the battle flags captured from Texas Confederates during the war. The department had been prompted in this move by an executive order of President Grover Cleveland.[28]

Ross gave his hearty approval to the scheme, suggesting that the return be made at the Confederate veteran reunion to be held in Dallas later that summer. Expressing his regret that he could not reciprocate the "tokening of peace" by returning the Northern standards captured by his brigade, Ross explained that the captured colors had been destroyed with his baggage at the close of the war.[29]

But even while plans proceeded in the South to receive the returned flags, fanatical opposition by members of the Grand Army of

[26]Texas Governors, *Governor's Messages*, pp. 620–25.
[27]Ibid., pp. 659–62; Gammel, comp., *The Laws of Texas*, X, 41, 53, 86, 137, 172–73, 189.
[28]*Austin Daily Statesman*, June 14 and 17, 1887.
[29]Ibid., June 15, 1887.

the Republic forced Cleveland to rescind his order. Ross was disappointed, but he commented on the fiasco in a speech given before the survivors of Hood's brigade in late June.

"It is a remarkable fact that those who bore the brunt of the battle were the first to forget old animosities," he observed, and noted that these same men were the first to "consign to oblivion obsolete issues." In his estimation, "Those whose hatred had remained implacable through all these years of peace, are men who . . . seek to make amends for their lack of deeds of valor by preaching a crusade of bitterness." Acclaimed by those who had worn the gray, his statement was publicized even in the North.[30]

Lawrence Sullivan Ross was the last governor of Texas to have served in the war; later executives were sons and grandsons of Confederate soldiers. As a former Confederate, Ross was interested in Southern veteran organizations and in the support of a state home for indigent and disabled Texas veterans. Because of this interest, it is appropriate that the Confederate home in Austin was formally dedicated during Ross's first term.[31]

Within two years, however, the earlier accommodations proved inadequate, and Governor Ross agreed to serve as chairman of a committee to finance the relocation of the home into larger quarters. Funds flowed in from various sources throughout the state, including the governor's own pocket, and by August, 1890, enough had been collected to move the home to roomier premises.[32]

In his final message to the Twenty-second Legislature in January, 1891, Ross recommended enacting a provision to buy or lease a suitable site for a permanent home for Confederate veterans and to ensure adequate appropriations for its support. As he saw it, neither the language nor the meaning of the Constitution inhibited or restricted repayment of the debt Texas owed to her soldiers. Neither were the people of Texas "guilty of the folly of authorizing ample provisions to be made for erecting monuments over dead soldiers, and for purchasing and collecting all accessible data as to their deeds of heroism, while carefully inhibiting any provision for them while alive and in destitution." Reminding the legislators that despite the federal pension paid

[30] Ibid., June 17 and 22, 1887. The *Statesman*, July 23, 1887, quotes Ross's speech from the *Toledo* (Ohio) *Bee*, July 6, 1887.

[31] *Austin Daily Statesman*, March 15, 1887.

[32] Ibid., July 23 and August 4, 1889, and August 12, 1890.

Union veterans, state aid was necessary for their support, Ross added: "Surely Texas ought to afford one home for her defenders. . . . If this duty is neglected the State's prosperity will only make more glaring her ingratitude."[33]

Although Governor Ross proved to be a reasonable conservative in his use of clemency and the veto, in his administration of fiscal affairs of law and order, and in his preservation of Texas' Confederate heritage, he was also a careful progressive. His philosophy of reform was that "we should not continue to tolerate evils which have become almost insupportable, simply to avoid a change or interfere with the designs of those for whom we have a profound reverence."[34]

One of the reasons for need of increased state revenue early in Ross's first term had been the financial demands of its penal and charitable institutions and educational facilities. In the interview announcing his campaign, Ross had expressed hopes that the state's prisons could be made self-supporting. As governor he fostered skilled-labor prison industries that yielded financial returns. At the same time, he maintained that short-term and unskilled convicts should be employed on state prison farms.[35]

As interested as he was in saving taxpayers' money by careful management of state prisons, Governor Ross believed money was needed to institute reforms in the handling of juvenile offenders. He considered this problem in his first inaugural address, citing neglect of reform efforts in the state and comparing the hearts and minds of delinquent children to a part of the state's productive capital. Noting that generally crime was the result of "neglected and miseducated children," he charged citizens with evasion of duty unless they established industrial or reform schools.[36]

Ross repeated this recommendation in his first message to the Twentieth Legislature, urging the prompt establishment of an industrial school for youthful criminals. The legislature responded willingly with funds for an open farm reformatory. Eventually the state obtained 696 acres of land near Gatesville in Coryell County at a cost of $10,000

[33] Texas Governors, *Governor's Messages*, pp. 694–95.

[34] Ibid., p. 588; Gammel, comp., *The Laws of Texas*, IX, 1106.

[35] *Galveston Daily News*, February 25, 1886; Texas Governors, *Governor's Messages*, pp. 677–79.

[36] Texas Governors, *Governor's Messages*, pp. 561–62.

and spent another $62,117 to erect buildings and fences and to equip the institution. The reformatory opened before Ross left office.[37]

When Ross became governor, the state boasted only four public charitable institutions—two insane asylums, a blind institute, and a deaf and dumb institute. During his four years in office, these public institutions increased by one-third. In 1887 a state orphans home was established at Corsicana, followed later that year by a state institute for deaf, dumb, and blind black children. By 1891 the deaf and dumb institute had been expanded, the plant of the blind institute improved, and a branch asylum for the insane planned for San Antonio.[38]

Besides his interest in expanding charitable services, Governor Ross wished to improve the quality of public education in Texas. When he became governor, Texas was in the "anomalous position of having the best school fund and the poorest school system in the United States." Defects in the system were many: Superintendent of Public Instruction O. H. Cooper reported grave inequalities among the state's school districts. Other weaknesses included absence of local taxation and lack of protection of appropriated state funds; also, young Texans spent an average of eight years in school as compared with twelve years in most other states.[39]

It was this report that the governor brought before the special session of the legislature in 1888, recommending laws to ensure better control over the school funds and, something far less popular, to require local taxation to support the public schools. The legislature gave Ross his first request, but denied the second. The Twenty-first Legislature proved more amenable to the governor's pleas, although their laws still did not completely rectify the problem.[40]

In his farewell address of 1891, Ross again reminded Texas legislators that available school funds provided only half the revenue needed to educate the state's increasing student population. Another concur-

[37] Ibid., pp. 582, 632–35; Gammel, comp., *The Laws of Texas*, IX, 862–64; *Austin Daily Statesman*, August 22, 1887.

[38] Texas Governors, *Governor's Messages*, pp. 616, 635–36, 673–75, 679–82; Gammel, comp., *The Laws of Texas*, IX, 948–49, 1107.

[39] *Encyclopaedia Britannica*, article quoted in Frederick Eby, comp., *Education in Texas Source Materials*, University of Texas Bulletin no. 1824, Education Series no. 2, pp. 817, 831–34.

[40] Texas Governors, *Governor's Messages*, pp. 610–13; Gammel, comp., *The Laws of Texas*, IX, 1003–1004, 1043–44, 1156–57.

rent problem was the lack of control over county-level disbursement of school funds. Also, the school term was still too short. But one of the greatest problems plaguing public education in Texas was furnishing textbooks. Ross suggested that either the state publish the texts and sell them to the students at low cost, or that the state purchase the books for the students' free use. Although farsighted in this matter, he could not persuade his legislators to pass the required bills, and these educational reforms would have to wait until the twentieth century before acceptance.[41]

From the earliest days of his first campaign, Ross had expressed interest in the University of Texas and in the Agricultural and Mechanical College. The university, he knew, suffered from poor use and development of its landed endowment, and he urged the Twenty-first Legislature to pass laws properly using these resources. The legislature was dilatory, however, and when he left office, Ross was still unhappily harping on the same theme.[42]

Concerning other needed reforms, Sul Ross exhibited more progressive ideas than his legislatures. Toward the end of his tenure, the governor recognized the need to reform the state's election laws. In order to do this, the first step was to determine who had the right to vote; the second, dependent upon the first, was to prevent corruption in elections.[43] In this, as in other reforms, the governor proved more amenable to change than his legislators. Election reform, like changes in public education, had to wait until after the turn of the century.

Ever since his service at the Constitutional Convention of 1875, Sul Ross had considered the judiciary article of the constitution weak and ineffective. During his two terms in office he was able to see the judicial system of Texas somewhat strengthened, although many weaknesses remained. In his first inaugural address Ross touched on the need for reform, noting that it was quite possible to have a "wise system of legislation, and at the same time, such defective organization for enforcement . . . that the laws will be either too lax or too tardy in

[41] Texas Governors, *Governor's Messages*, pp. 663–68. Ross was also proud of what had been done in the field of black education in Texas (see Lawrence Sullivan Ross, *Education of the Colored Race*, pp. 1–3).

[42] *Galveston Daily News*, February 25, 1886; Texas Governors, *Governor's Messages*, pp. 638–39, 668.

[43] Texas Governors, *Governor's Messages*, pp. 695–96.

their operation." Appeal should be both sure and swift; judges should be both able and independent.[44]

In order to effect this change, the governor suggested in his first message to the Twentieth Legislature that the state's lower courts be reorganized. He also recommended that the legislators consider a plan for system-wide reorganization prepared by the State Bar Association of Texas.[45]

Despite the governor's strong feelings on this subject, the legislators passed only limited judicial reforms during the Ross administration. However, the foundation for judicial reform had been prepared, although it was left to the Twenty-second Legislature in 1891 to complete the actual revision of the judiciary article of the constitution.[46]

Aside from his interest in general reforms, Ross mainly concerned himself with specific policies to benefit Texas' developing economy. One of these policies concerned the development and protection of the faltering livestock industry.

While addressing the Twentieth Legislature, Ross again stressed the importance of the livestock industry and recommended passing laws to favor and protect the stock raiser. Although the governor rightly condemned the "many serious embarrassments and depressing agencies" that combined with "merciless moneyed syndicates" to prevent the sale of livestock at a profit, he also recognized the importance of modern animal health and quarantine laws. Citing a recent worldwide outbreak of bovine pleuropneumonia, he noted that the disease had caused the loss of over $500 million worth of cattle in the British Empire alone.[47]

It would be difficult, Governor Ross pointed out, to compute the terrible losses that would result from an outbreak of the plague in Texas. The world's markets would be closed to Texas stock raisers and bankruptcy and ruin would follow. Therefore, he invited the legislature to consider enacting a "proper and wise" quarantine law to protect the people of Texas from the introduction of infected cattle.[48]

---

[44] Gammel, comp., *The Laws of Texas*, IX, 444–46; Texas Governors, *Governor's Messages*, p. 560.

[45] Texas Governors, *Governor's Messages*, pp. 588–89.

[46] Gammel, comp., *The Laws of Texas*, IX, 444–46; Constitution, art. 5, sec. 1.

[47] Texas Governors, *Governor's Messages*, pp. 585–86.

[48] Ibid.

But although the legislators were willing to allow state quarantine of humans during outbreaks of yellow fever or other contagious diseases, they were not sufficiently indoctrinated in animal health to pass the necessary laws requested by the executive.

At the same time, the governor was interested in passing laws to protect the Texas stockman–meat producer from the growing power of monopolies and trusts. When the Kansas legislature suggested in early 1889 that its sister body in Texas join a campaign against trusts and combinations regulating the beef and pork industries, Ross passed the appeal along, requesting solidarity with the efforts to enact laws that would "impair the power of these combinations to rob our people of the fruits of their honest labor and capital."[49]

In March the next year, during an interstate convention of cattlemen held at Fort Worth, Ross sent a message to the convention expressing again his strong feelings in the case. Reminding his listeners of his own "long and faithful apprenticeship as a cowboy," Ross praised the stockmen of his state as the "avant couriers" of civilization. He stressed again the importance of lasting actions against the syndicates, suggesting that Texas cattlemen look across the Atlantic for their markets. "You cannot hope to reap the full benefit of your great industry until your beef goes from your own slaughterhouses to the markets of the world," he pointed out, adding that the law of supply and demand would have to reestablish a vigorous competition in order to reap the benefits of setting cattle prices.[50]

Even so, the governor was farsighted enough to realize that change was underway and that stockmen would soon have to use scientific methods. Large ranches would have to yield eventually to the small stock farmer, just as the feral cattle of the open ranges would give place to "better and more carefully nurtured stock."[51]

The legislators, however, continued to move slowly. In his farewell message Ross again brought the question of quarantine—this time against the equine disease glanders—before the legislators. He also stressed the importance of eradicating the disease within the state. Through a campaign conducted by private organizations, federal agen-

[49] Ibid., pp. 655–56.
[50] U.S. Department of Agriculture, Bureau of Animal Industry Special Bulletin, *Proceedings of an Interstate Convention of Cattlemen, Held at Fort Worth, Texas, Tuesday, Wednesday, and Thursday, March 11, 12, and 13, 1890*, pp. 14–16.
[51] Ibid.

cies, and U.S. Army veterinarians, the disease was being controlled in Texas. Nevertheless, Ross believed that quarantine laws should be passed to prevent livestock from being imported from other states. His request, however, was in vain.[52]

In dealing with two of the reform movements of his administration, antitrust legislation and railroad regulation, Governor Ross was both conservative and progressive. His moderate stand, however, has robbed him of much of the credit for accomplishments in both areas.

During the two decades following the war, Texas had undergone an industrial metamorphosis, changing from a localized agricultural economy to one of limited manufacturing. This new economy used an increasing variety of local farm products and a growing number of the state's natural resources. It was also a time of farmer and laborer unrest; both the producer of raw materials and the factory worker sought a larger share of industrialization profits. Similarly, it was a time of resentment against trusts, monopolies, and combinations of all kinds denying the producer and the laborer their desired profits, often in defiance of state laws.[53]

Governor Ross unquestionably recognized the nature of the enemy. In his first inaugural address, Sul dealt at length with the problems of irresponsible corporations in Texas. Noting that if their powers were not curtailed "the great body of citizens will have fastened upon them a bondage, compared with which the bondage of Israel in Egypt was tender mercy," he reminded the legislature that these artificial bodies were created by the people as the "instruments of their convenience . . . designed for their service and not their subjection." Therefore, he urged quick and effective action by the state to control the corporations.[54]

Ross denounced railroad combinations in his first message to the Twentieth Legislature in January, 1887, and at the same time condemned the stranglehold of monopolies within the livestock industry. While asking the legislators to pass new laws for better control of trusts and monopolies, Ross unleashed Attorney General James S. Hogg upon the worst offenders. How much Hogg undertook on his own ini-

[52] Texas Governors, *Governor's Messages*, p. 690.
[53] Alwyn Barr, *Reconstruction to Reform: Texas Politics, 1876–1906*, pp. 111–24; John Stricklin Spratt, *The Road to Spindletop: Economic Change in Texas, 1875–1901*, pp. 210–11.
[54] Texas Governors, *Governor's Messages*, pp. 563–64.

tiative and how much he was spurred by the governor is unclear, but during Ross's administration Hogg attacked various illegal monopolistic and discriminatory practices.[55]

Meanwhile the cry for regulation from Texans grew louder, while Congress and other state legislatures experienced similar agitation. By the beginning of his second term in office Ross was condemning the privileges of limited liability enjoyed by corporations, questioning "the character of justice that exempts the corporation under these privileges from the same care and liability that is exacted from the individual." He suggested, therefore, curtailing the privileges of corporations instead of extending them.[56]

This time the executive had a legislature willing to carry out his suggestions: almost immediately, four different antitrust bills were introduced into the Texas legislative mill. These were later combined by Attorney General Hogg into a compromise bill that passed the house in February and the senate in March. Thus it preceded the federal Sherman Antitrust Act, which was not enacted until 1890. Although it exempted farmer and labor organizations, the Texas law of March 30, 1889, prohibited practices that prevented competition, controlled prices, restrained trade, or fixed rates.[57]

Because he had helped consolidate and rewrite the antitrust bills and had guided their way through the legislature, Hogg received a large share of credit for the bill's eventual passage. It is inconceivable, however, that he could have accomplished this without the knowledge, approval, and support of the executive. Similarly, Ross's balance between progressivism and conservatism has created an apparent ambivalence regarding railroad regulation; this has robbed the governor of much of the deserved credit concerning this reform.

The 1870s and 1880s had seen tremendous growth of railroad mileage throughout Texas. Before 1882, legislators had voted liberal

[55] Robert C. Cotner, ed., *Addresses and State Papers of James Stephen Hogg*, pp. 12, 34. Although the governor occasionally called his attorney general "bull-headed," Hogg's zealousness apparently did not cause any major clashes. The pair did have a minor disagreement over the acceptance of the capitol (see *Austin Daily Statesman*, October 19, 1889; and *Galveston Daily News*, September 11 and 12, 1888).

[56] Barr, *Reconstruction to Reform*, p. 108; Texas Governors, *Governor's Messages*, p. 651.

[57] Robert C. Cotner, *James Stephen Hogg: A Biography*, p. 163. Kansas was the first state to enact such a law, having beaten Texas by some four weeks (Gammel, comp., *The Laws of Texas*, IX, 1169–70).

grants to various railroad companies, hoping that healthy competition between lines would keep rates low. Consolidation of most of the state's railroads in the early eighties reduced competition and permitted rate discrimination, rebates, and other inequitable practices.[58]

Manipulations by Jay Gould and other railroad tycoons in Texas soon brought both private and government opposition. The Constitution of 1876 had laid the groundwork for regulation, and Lawrence Sullivan Ross had helped prepare constitutional articles to protect Texas citizens from unfair railway practices. After other regulation was introduced by the constitutional convention, the Patrons of Husbandry, the Farmers' Alliance, the Greenbackers, and other citizens in the late 1870s demanded a regulatory commission.[59]

While serving in the legislature, Ross sponsored bills limiting railroad rates and fining violators. But although he acknowledged the need to regulate intrastate railroads, Ross did not believe that a regulatory commission would solve the state's problems. He also doubted the constitutional right for elected representatives to delegate some of their powers to an appointed committee. Nevertheless, he voted in favor of the commission bill, which failed to pass.[60]

When Ross first campaigned for governor he took a moderate stand on the railroad question, insisting that investments be safeguarded while the public received protection from arbitrary action by the railroads. At the same time, public outcry against rate discrimination and other abuses prodded the Democratic party in Texas to action. The 1886 party platform contained a lengthy article protesting the worst abuses, pledging its candidates to pass laws correcting them, and bringing the railroads under stricter control.[61]

Ross skirted the subject of railroads in his first inaugural address, leaving a fuller discussion of the problem and its possible cures until his first message to the Twentieth Legislature two days later. In this address Ross recognized the railroad problem, but told the legislators

[58] Barr, *Reconstruction to Reform*, p. 112.

[59] *Journal of the Constitutional Convention Begun and Held in Austin, September 6, 1875*, pp. 265, 751; *Waco Daily Examiner*, March 30, 1875; Seth Shepard McKay, *Making the Texas Constitution of 1876*, p. 114; Barr, *Reconstruction to Reform*, p. 113; Spratt, *The Road to Spindletop*, p. 211.

[60] *Journal of The Senate of Texas: Being a Special Session of the Seventeenth Legislature*, pp. 20–21, 24–25; *Austin Daily Statesman*, October 13, 1888.

[61] *Galveston Daily News*, February 25, 1886; Ernest William Winkler, ed., *Platforms of Political Parties in Texas, 1846–1916*, p. 239.

that such rapidly developing agencies, revolutionizing in their influence, must necessarily create friction when adapted to the public need. Reminding the legislators that the manifest intention of the framers of the Constitution of 1876 had been to "encourage competition and to discourage or forbid combinations among these public agencies," Ross then declared that mere competition had failed as a solution to the railway problem. Therefore, he suggested that the legislature should that session pass laws prohibiting pooling or combinations between railroads and discrimination by certain railroads against shippers and other railroads.[62]

At the same time he denied that fixing rates by law and establishing a railroad commission would give permanent relief. He believed, instead, that railroads should be forced into active competition with one another if they wanted to enjoy public patronage. The members listened and eventually passed legislation including the new governor's recommendations.[63]

Although Ross believed a railroad commission would not permanently end problems between Texas citizens and the state's railways, he was not averse to enforcing laws already on the books. During his first term his attorney general, James S. Hogg, forced the state's railroads to follow their charters, disbanded the monopolistic Texas Traffic Association, and recovered 1.3 million acres from two dilatory lines. In this way the Democratic party fulfilled most of the promises in its 1886 platform regarding railroad regulation.[64]

When the election of 1888 approached, the Democratic policymakers again expressed their approval of railroad regulation, recommending that the Twenty-first Legislature define all "illegal combinations in restraint of trade" and impose severe penalties upon those corporations guilty of such action.[65]

Ross included a section on railways when addressing his second legislature in 1889. He then reminded the members that the power to regulate did not include the power to destroy and that regulation, not destruction, of the state's railroads should be their goal. He did not

[62] Texas Governors, *Governor's Messages*, pp. 566, 592–95; Gammel, comp., *The Laws of Texas*, IX, 905–909, 914, 935–36.

[63] Texas Governors, *Governor's Messages*, pp. 566, 592–95; Gammel, comp., *The Laws of Texas*, IX, 905–909, 914, 935–36.

[64] Barr, *Reconstruction to Reform*, p. 116; Cotner, ed., *Addresses and State Papers*, pp. 13–14; Winkler, ed., *Platforms of Political Parties*, p. 239.

[65] Winkler, ed., *Platforms of Political Parties*, p. 267.

mention a railroad commission, soon to be a topic of great deliberation, but instead stated his hope that "an equitable adjustment" would bring the issue to a "fair, honest and final settlement."[66]

In the meantime, this body of legislators soon proved more hostile to railroads and more favorable to regulation by commission than the preceding one. When the house passed a bill that would have established a railroad commission, opponents in the senate resisted it as unconstitutional. Nevertheless, those supporting the commission proposed a constitutional amendment to create just such a body.[67]

The question of a railroad commission was crucial to the 1890 gubernatorial race, and the voters overwhelmingly approved ratification of the commission amendment. In an address to the Twenty-second Legislature evaluating his second term, Ross closed by discussing the constitutional amendment recently passed providing a railroad commission.

Ross warned that if arbitrary or illiberal legislation were passed, investments and businesses would suffer, which would harm the state's entire economy. Instead, he hoped the legislators would be able to provide a "judicious system of control, in conformity with the people's wishes," which would arbitrate fairly in disputes between the railroads and the people and would also set a freight rate that was fair to all.[68]

Interestingly enough, the executive's fears that the commission would fail to solve the railroad problems were valid. Despite proponents' claims that the empowered commission would soon right all the industry's wrongs, the agency proved ineffective in practice. It did help reduce rates and discrimination on interstate hauls, but it was unable to reduce to any extent rates charged within the state. Furthermore (and this is why Ross opposed it), the commission took power from elected representatives and gave it to an appointed board not as responsive to the wishes of the citizens.[69]

Because Ross did not want to exceed his executive power or unduly influence the legislative branch in order to bring about reform, he has been considered an arch-conservative by some modern historians.

[66] Texas Governors, *Governor's Messages*, pp. 643–45.

[67] Spratt, *The Road to Spindletop*, pp. 213–14.

[68] Ibid., p. 214; Texas Governors, *Governor's Messages*, pp. 696–98. This was a change of viewpoint from his stand of four years before (see *Governor's Messages*, pp. 592–95).

[69] Texas Governors, *Governor's Messages*, pp. 594–95; Barr, *Reconstruction to Reform*, pp. 122–23.

However, the governor's progressive conservatism commended him to the general electorate of his time; in the eyes of contemporaries, there was much to praise about Ross. They spoke highly of his integrity, culture, and courage, and noted that his administration was remarkably free from friction and criticism. He had kept the peace, extended general goodwill, and promoted government thrift. Immigration and investment capital had poured into the Lone Star State, stimulating the economy into increasing prosperity. "You have done well," praised one newspaper. "Queenly Texas is proud of you and your record." [70]

Posterity has been more critical in its consideration of Ross's effectiveness as governor. To one historian, Ross was a leading conservative with limited vision for reform; to another, he represented the political and social beliefs of the past. Gubernatorial analyst Fred Gantt, Jr., considered Ross to be a "Man of the People," like most American governors. According to Gantt, he was not a strong leader or a reformer, but neither was he a figurehead, grafter, or showman. [71]

This analysis was not altogether applicable to Ross. Like his contemporaries, posterity has recognized his "common sense, patriotism, and inflexible honesty." Paul Bolton, evaluating the Ross administration, cited the low taxes, frontier peace, and progressive legislation of the Ross era. More than that, Bolton went to the heart of Ross's conservatism. "He believed strongly in free enterprise and thought that governmental paternalism would lead to the end of personal liberty and the decay of Democratic institutions." [72]

On balance, although conservative in spending state moneys, in maintaining law and order, and in protecting the Texas Confederate heritage, Ross was not a reactionary. Certainly he sympathized with the plight of indigent and disabled Confederate veterans and worked for the support of the state Confederate home. A law mandating racial segregation in passenger cars on Texas railroads was passed during his administration, but the governor's own relationship with the black community of the time was cordial. [73]

[70] Norman G. Kittrell, *Some Governors Who Have Been and Other Public Men of Texas*, p. 97; L. E. Daniell, comp., *Personnel of the Texas State Government With Sketches of Distinguished Texans . . .* , p. 17; *Austin Daily Statesman*, January 20, 1891.

[71] Cotner, *James Stephen Hogg*, pp. 106, 161; Lewis W. Newton, *Texas Yesterday and Today*, p. 271; Gantt, *The Chief Executive in Texas*, pp. 45–46.

[72] *Dictionary of American Biography*, s.v. "Ross, Lawrence Sullivan"; "L. (Sul) Ross," in Paul Bolton, *Governors of Texas*.

[73] Gammel, comp., *The Laws of Texas*, IX, 948–49, 1160–61; Texas Governors,

As governor, Ross was interested in the industrialization and modernization of Texas. Forward looking, he accurately predicted the political trends of this century. Although he lacked the political expertise to push programs through the legislature, he saw many of his suggestions, a number of them progressive, made into law.[74] A transitional governor in an era of change and development, he symbolized the best of the era that was ending and foreshadowed much of the future.

Governor's Messages, pp. 674–75; *Austin Daily Statesman*, February 8, 1887. Jim Crow laws were also passed when the reformer Hogg was in office (see Gammel, comp., *The Laws of Texas*, X, 46–47).

[74] Ross also began an official celebration of Arbor Day and recommended purchasing the collection of portraits of the state's governors painted by William A. Huddle (see Gammel, comp., *The Laws of Texas*, IX, 1106; and *Austin Daily Statesman*, December 4, 1888).

College President

RETIRING governors, like retiring presidents, must, unless they intend to leave public life completely, look about them for a position that is appealing but is not considered beneath the dignity of the office they have just quitted.[1] Such was the case when the time came for Lawrence Sullivan Ross to leave office in January, 1891. However, as before in Ross's life, the job sought the man. A need existed that he was asked to fill—the Agricultural and Mechanical College of Texas was in trouble and needed a president to resolve its problems.

Texas A&M College originated from an 1862 act of Congress donating 180,000 acres of public land for its benefit. However, since Texas as part of the Confederacy was then at war with the United States, the establishment of an agricultural and mechanical college in Texas had to wait until the normalization of public affairs in the late Reconstruction period. By a joint resolution, the Texas legislature in 1871 accepted the 1862 provision and passed its own act creating an institution to teach an agricultural, mechanical, military, and scientific curriculum. This act was supplemented by the Constitution of 1876, which made A&M a branch of the state university and provided for its maintenance and support by tax moneys. The institution opened its doors to students in the fall of 1876.[2]

Over the years the institution had grown and matured, increasing its enrollment and expanding its physical plant, while updating its curriculum and restructuring its academic organization. The late eighties,

[1] In Texas, the pattern has been for a departing governor to enter a profession or business. Of the twenty-four executives from Coke to Connally, only one, Samuel W. T. Lanham, retired completely (see Fred Gantt, Jr., *The Chief Executive in Texas: A Study in Gubernatorial Leadership*, pp. 66–67).
[2] Texas Legislature, House of Representatives, *House Journal*, 22nd Leg., reg. sess., 1891, p. 37.

under Louis Lowry McInnis as chairman of the faculty (the executive position then held instead of president), had been characterized by growth and maturity. But despite these outward manifestations of strength and harmony, all was not well on the College Station campus (adjacent to the town of Bryan). In the words of one historian of the period:

Notwithstanding these great advances in the technical aspects of the College—in its equipment, in the spirit of its teaching and in the facilities for research—the College had not yet come into that full and cordial popular esteem which was essential for the realization of its destiny. The public was still more or less critical of the changes in administrative policy, still somewhat skeptical of scientific agriculture and mechanic arts, especially of scientific agriculture as it was reported to be taught at the Agricultural and Mechanical College of Texas.[3]

Even more devastating to the institution's public image were the rumors that began to find their way off campus. Whispers of poor management, student discontent, professorial dissatisfaction, faculty factionalism, disciplinary problems, and campus scandals circulated until "serious trouble" was feared for the college.[4]

These whispers were voiced in the statements of those closely concerned with the affairs of the college. In early 1890 A. J. Rose, president of the board of directors, informed Chairman McInnis that he regretted the problems besetting the school. Lieutenant William S. Scott, commandant of cadets and instructor of military science and tactics, mentioned the "disgraceful squabbles" among faculty members and administrators.[5] Earlier, lack of harmony had begun to trouble the students, one of whom reported home on the situation.

Ma I am sorry to say that this school is going down faster than I ever saw. . . . I would not have said this but I heard two professors talking about it yesterday. They said in two more years that it would not be worth sending to.

---

[3] Henry C. Dethloff, *A Centennial History of Texas A&M University, 1876–1976*, I, 136, 146; Clarence Ousley, *History of the Agricultural and Mechanical College of Texas*, Bulletin of the Agricultural and Mechanical College of Texas, 4th series, vol. 6, no. 8, p. 58.

[4] *Galveston Daily News*, July 12, 1890. Dethloff, *Centennial History*, I, 146–47, cites "professional jealousy and factionalism" as well as "campus politics" as reasons for the difficulties.

[5] A. J. Rose to Louis L. McInnis, March 10, 1890, Louis Lowry McInnis Papers, Texas A&M University Archives, College Station, Texas (hereafter cited as McInnis Papers); William S. Scott to Rose, August 24, 1890, McInnis Papers.

They are not managing it rite but I think it will last long enough for me to graduate . . . that is I hope so.[6]

Another problem was the apparent lack of legislative confidence in the college. According to Dr. Mark Francis, for many years head of the veterinary school, legislators believed that nothing could be done for the institution and that any appropriations would simply be wasted. He recalled that requests for two badly needed buildings, one for the chemistry department and the other for veterinary medicine, were turned down during this period because of this lack of confidence.[7]

Events came to a head during the 1890 commencement, when it became apparent to the directors that a change was needed. "It was clearly seen," reported the *Galveston Daily News*, "that the educational departments were suffering from union with the executive or administrative. An administrative chief independent of the faculty was required."[8]

At the same time, as Henry C. Dethloff has pointed out, the board of directors recognized that the office of chief administrator of the college was no longer merely an academic post to be filled by an equal among peers; it was a position of prestige to be occupied by a person of some prominence. Therefore, the directors decided to re-institute the office of president and began to consider various prominent men as candidates.[9]

According to a *Dallas Morning News* article written several years later, the selection of a "strong executive officer to take charge of the college and restore order and public confidence" took some time. At last, on July 1, the board members unanimously agreed—they would offer the A&M presidency to then Governor Ross. Indeed, according to this article, the directors considered the situation so urgent that they appealed to Ross to resign his office and take immediate steps to save the college. Ross, however, refused to be hurried in making a decision. At last the board members responded that they would be willing to wait until Ross's term as governor expired. And there the matter

    [6] Lucius Holman to Mrs. P. G. Weeks, October 10, 1888, Lucius Holman Papers, Texas A&M University Archives, College Station, Texas.
    [7] Hubert Schmidt, *Eighty Years of Veterinary Medicine at the Agricultural and Mechanical College of Texas*, pp. 2–3.
    [8] *Galveston Daily News*, July 12, 1890.
    [9] Dethloff, *Centennial History*, I, 146; *Galveston Daily News*, July 12, 1890.

stood while the governor consulted his friends and considered his alternatives.[10]

Like the Roman patriot Cincinnatus retiring to his farm, he could have returned to his Brazos plantation, or to the "big cotton plantation" offered him earlier by his Mississippi friends and admirers. Ross also apparently received two other offers, both with salaries greater than the $3,500 per year offered by the directors of A&M. Furthermore, acceptance of a position at an educational institution was rare among former Texas governors. It was a difficult decision and one he took his time making.[11]

Meanwhile, events were transpiring to move him into the presidency. Someone, possibly a member of the board, leaked some information to the local press, and on July 3 the *Bryan Eagle* predicted that the people would be pleased by the board's choice of candidates for president and that the college would receive "a boost far ahead of the most sanguine expectations." Two days later the story broke in Austin as well as in Bryan. A capital city newspaper noted the highly complimentary nature of the offer made Ross, while in Bryan the citizenry turned out at a night meeting to enthusiastically approve the directors' action. "We regard the selection as a most happy one," read the resolutions prepared by the leaders of the crowd. "We earnestly hope that the directors will be successful in procuring his acceptance of the position, and the benefit of his valuable services to the institution."[12]

Other newspapers joined the refrain. Noting that the election of Ross to the presidency of A&M would give satisfaction throughout the state, the *Galveston Daily News* editorialized that Ross's "fatherly and patriotic impulses," as well as his "firm executive hand," would greatly benefit the college.[13]

[10] *Dallas Morning News*, March 25, 1892; Minutes of the Board of Directors, Texas A&M University, College Station, Texas (hereafter cited as Minutes, Board of Directors), I, 92.

[11] *Austin Daily Statesman*, September 25, 1887; *Galveston Daily News*, March 31, 1892; Minutes, Board of Directors, I, 94. Of the twenty-three executives who served from the end of Reconstruction to the early 1960s, only two besides Ross made this step. One, a predecessor, Oran M. Roberts, taught law at the University of Texas; a successor, Pat M. Neff, later became president of Baylor University (Gantt, *Chief Executive in Texas*, pp. 66–67).

[12] *Bryan Eagle*, July 3, 1890; *Austin Daily Statesman*, July 6, 1890. A fuller text of the resolutions appears in the *Bryan Eagle*, July 10, 1890.

[13] *Galveston Daily News*, July 7, 1890. The *News* followed this editorial with another of similar tone on July 12.

Despite the public enthusiasm generated by news of the college's offer, the governor still refused to be hurried in his choice. Beyond the benefits to Ross and his family through acceptance of the position, there were definite disadvantages to be considered. He had already been away from his farming interests for four years, and they could not but suffer without the master's eye upon them. Also, he and Lizzie both had many relatives and friends in the Waco area, whom they had seen only at long intervals over the past four years. Acceptance of the A&M offer would mean settlement in Bryan and further separation from family. Still another drawback, which would surface during the heated gubernatorial campaign of 1892, was that most of the board members electing him were the governor's own appointees. It would therefore appear to a critical observer—and there were many as the political races got under way in 1892—that Ross had appointed a board that would provide him with a position once he left Austin.[14]

Taking these and other circumstances into consideration, Ross at last decided that his duty lay in College Station. As a Confederate general, he had been willing to accept service where needed, and this same sense of duty motivated him now. Still, it was August 8 before he formally accepted the office tendered him by the board of directors. In this lengthy letter Ross delineated his views on education, saying he had always believed that students' "minds, hands, and hearts should be trained in unison" and that this training should be applied to the intelligent selection of their lifework. At the same time he reiterated his belief in the inherent nobility of labor. Touching on the importance of agriculture and agricultural training, he observed that the young men of Texas could acquire at A&M "a knowledge that will prepare them to achieve the highest and best results in any station, through the reliable factors—education, industry and a proper moral instruction by the application of plain moral precepts to every act of life." In this development, he added, military training was crucial. He closed by hoping that the institution would become the "pride of the State."[15]

Once the appointment was secure, the *Austin Daily Statesman* editorialized: "It is seldom, very seldom, the governor of a great State relinquishes the possession of power to become the director of an educational institution. . . . But at Bryan Gen. Ross will be the right man in

[14] *Austin Daily Statesman*, September 14, 1889; Dethloff, *Centennial History*, I, 152–53; *Dallas Morning News*, March 25, 1892.
[15] *Austin Daily Statesman*, August 9, 1890.

the right place. . . . A military man himself . . . he will be a most appropriate appendage to the military feature of the Bryan institution." [16]

The habit of military command aside, Lawrence Sullivan Ross was an excellent choice for the position of college president. Besides the tremendous prestige and administrative skills he would bring to the institution, he had long been a successful farmer. Finally, he had a life-long interest in education and a deep understanding of the problems inherent in educating young men, gained from his own difficulties in obtaining an education years before and from his own sons.

The board of directors, pleased by their choice and by the public's approval, set about smoothing the pathway for the incoming president, even before Ross's acceptance was made public. Having abolished the position of chairman of the faculty, they did not rehire former chairman Louis L. McInnis as professor of mathematics. There were many voluntary resignations among faculty and staff, and others were asked to resign. In this way, noted one observer, the board eliminated the factions on both sides and gave the new president the opportunity to hire and not fire employees. Nevertheless, this action planted the seeds of ill will, personal enmity, and public criticism that would later bear fruit. [17]

In the meantime, other changes were transforming the College Station campus. Arrangements were made to electrify the college buildings, while other improvements were discussed. Hoping for greater appropriations now that a friend of the college was in the executive office, the board also submitted a request for $128,000 for new buildings and improvements. [18]

At the same time subtler changes were happening elsewhere, changes that would have lasting effects on the future development of the school. Suddenly it became desirable to send a son to A&M. Norman G. Kittrell, upon asking a drummer, or salesman, from East Texas for news, was told that many fathers were preparing to send their sons to A&M that fall. "I believe every man that was a soldier under Gover-

---

[16] Ibid.

[17] *Fourteenth Annual Catalogue of the Agricultural and Mechanical College of Texas*, pp. 13–14; *Sixteenth Annual Catalogue of the Agricultural and Mechanical College of Texas*, pp. 6–7; Samuel E. Asbury to Dr. S. W. Geiser, November 4, 1946, quoted in David Brooks Cofer, *Second Five Administrators of Texas A. & M. College, 1890–1905*, pp. 44–46. For a more detailed study of the controversy surrounding the board's actions, see Dethloff, *Centennial History*, I, 146–53.

[18] *Report of the Agricultural and Mechanical College of Texas*, 1891, p. 8; Dethloff, *Centennial History*, I, 158–60.

nor Ross is going to send his son to school under him," continued the
salesman, adding that these men trusted Ross because they had followed him during four years of war.[19]

The drummer's prediction apparently came true: when the 1890–
91 session opened that fall, 500 students attempted to enroll. Eventually 316 were accepted, although this increase meant that the facilities constructed for 250 students would be strained to bursting. Even
then, latecomers were being turned away daily. Noting that A&M's enrollment was the largest in ten years, the *Bryan Eagle* observed that
the "present outlook is the most encouraging since the existence of the
institution."[20]

Anticipation was therefore great when former Governor Ross and
his family arrived from Austin the day after Hogg's inaugural ball.
However, as far as Lizzie and the children were concerned, anticipation far exceeded reality when they entered the president's home to
examine their new surroundings for the first time. "Everything looked
cheerless," Ross recalled. "The house had been long vacated, was
damp, and the rain coming in steady fall. No beds, no comfort in any
respect." Reaction among the first family of the college was immediate.
Harvey returned to Austin while Florine, the eldest daughter, "fled
outright" to visit friends. Frank and Neville along with their father
were "the only old soldiers who were willing to accept the situation
and make the most of it," until things could be remedied.[21]

This was, however, the low point of the president's reception.
Soon the house was indeed a home, with carpets down and "everything fixed up in good style," and Ross's acceptance by students and
faculty was indeed warm. By the time he formally took charge of the
college on February 2, he had come to feel that his presence was acceptable to all. On this occasion he spoke briefly to the young men and
was well received. Although he found the work "in the details somewhat annoying," it was not difficult, and he hoped he would soon have
things running smoothly. "I think I shall like it," he confided.[22]

Evidently this optimism was not without reason, for in a letter to

[19] Norman G. Kittrell, *Some Governors Who Have Been and Other Public Men of Texas*, p. 98.
[20] *Report of the Agricultural and Mechanical College*, 1891, p. 8; *Bryan Eagle*, October 2 and 16, 1890.
[21] *Austin Daily Statesman*, January 21, 1891; Ross to H. M. Holmes, February 2,
1891, Lawrence Sullivan Ross Papers, Texas A&M University Archives, College Station,
Texas (hereafter cited as Ross Papers, Texas A&M Archives).
[22] Ross to Holmes, February 2, 1891, Ross Papers, Texas A&M Archives.

the same correspondent dated eleven days later Ross reported that the cadets were his friends and that members of the board were "much pleased with the fact, that every thing wore a new aspect about the Institution—and all for the better." Already changes were happening, the first being in the new president's work. "The change was radical but not greater than I anticipated," Ross admitted. "I am settling down to a steady gate [*sic*]. No prancing or flourishes, but a complete acceptance of the situation, and a determination to make the most of it." Later he admitted that supervision of the institution turned his hair gray very quickly during these early days, but nevertheless he was satisfied with his position and the flow of events.[23]

Other changes were also transforming A&M. Expecting a surge in campus building programs, the president, R. H. Whitlock, F. E. Giesecke, A. J. Rose, and W. R. Cavitt formed a committee to locate future building sites. One of the first to be so located was the new president's residence, for which the board set aside the sum of $4,500.[24]

College fiscal affairs were also reorganized at this time. In February a "misapplication of funds" totaling $5,000 from McInnis's term necessitated calling in an expert accountant, whose investigations into college fiscal affairs soon showed that the institution account was overdrawn $6,435.55. At other times the account showed a surplus: this inequality of supply was the inevitable result of the way in which appropriated funds to support the college were obtained from the state legislature. To correct the situation, the accountant suggested closing the old set of books and opening a new one, using a simpler system of bookkeeping. At the same time President Ross would be designated treasurer by the college as he had been by the state legislature, thus eliminating the separate offices of treasurer and fiscal agent. Ross then posted a $20,000 personal bond "for the faithful performance of his duty."[25]

Although a few such necessary changes were made from the time Ross took office in early February until the spring term ended in June, most of the alterations involving persons and policies had to wait until Ross's first full academic year began in the fall of 1891.

---

[23] Ibid., February 13, 1891, Ross Papers, Texas A&M Archives; Ross to Holmes, August 9, 1891, Lawrence Sullivan Ross Papers, Texas State Archives, Austin, Texas (hereafter cited as Ross Papers, Texas State Archives).

[24] Minutes, Board of Directors, I, 99, 101.

[25] Ross to Holmes, February 13, 1891, Ross Papers, Texas A&M Archives; Minutes, Board of Directors, I, 107–108, 109, 116.

Students returning at that time, for example after a year's absence, would have recognized numerous changes and modifications.
First, the tall, soldierly figure of the new president could often be seen
at various times and places on campus. Second, the campus itself wore
a new aspect. A new three-story, forty-one room dormitory (later named
Ross Hall) had been built, and the president's home was under construction. The carpentry shop had expanded to fill the building it had
once shared with the machine and blacksmith shops, while the latter
two had moved to a building of their own nearby. An increase in enrollment—fifteen more students than in 1890 when the facilities were so
crowded—meant that even with the new hall, dormitory space was at
a premium. So desperate were the college authorities to find rooms for
everyone that Walter D. Adams and some of the other cadets found
themselves stowed away in the fourth floor of the main building.[26]

Increased enrollment meant many new faces among the students,
but there had also been changes among faculty and staff. By the time
the 1891–92 session opened, thirteen faculty and staff members from
the McInnis years had been dropped. Ten new members besides the
president had been added to the roster, while five of those remaining
had changed rank or had new assignments. Only thirteen positions remained the same.[27]

And if this upheaval among the college administration were not
enough to herald change, returning students found modifications in
policies and regulations governing student life. The most obvious was a
change in the school's admission and matriculation requirements. Under McInnis, the minimum age for entrance into the college course
had been sixteen. By fall, 1891, this had dropped to fifteen years, and
the method of matriculation had changed slightly. Instead of reporting
to the chairman of the faculty as before, prospective students now
waited upon President Ross, who used this interview to decide whether
the applicants should be admitted or readmitted. If the would-be students passed this appraisal they were sent, as in the past, to the various
professors for enrollment in their classes and to the commandant for
assignment to their cadet company and quarters.[28]

[26] *Sixteenth Annual Catalogue*, pp. 6–7, 37; *Report of the Agricultural and
Mechanical College of Texas*, 1893, p. 7; David Brooks Cofer, *Early History of Texas
A. and M. College through Letters and Papers*, p. 115; Charles William Crawford et al.,
One Hundred Years of Engineering at Texas A&M, 1876–1976, p. 27.

[27] *Fourteenth Annual Catalogue*, pp. 13–14; *Sixteenth Annual Catalogue*, pp. 6–7.

[28] *Fourteenth Annual Catalogue*, pp. 38–39; *Sixteenth Annual Catalogue*, p. 34;
Cofer, *Second Five Administrators*, p. 62.

Fees and expenses had also risen slightly during this time, from $140 for session fees in 1889–90 to $145 for 1891–92. The cost of books had also increased by $5, possibly because of changes in curricula. Finally, it was estimated that the "neat uniform" of gray cloth required of all cadets would cost about $18.[29]

At the same time the curricula had undergone various changes. The college still provided two main courses of study, the agricultural and the mechanical, which offered the student four possible degrees, the Bachelor of Scientific Agriculture or Scientific Horticulture, and the Bachelor of Mechanical Engineering or Civil Engineering. But now there were differences in the kinds of courses for the various classes and in the number of hours necessary to obtain a degree. Under Ross, hour requirements increased from 304 to 319.5 for the Bachelor of Scientific Agriculture degree and from 302 to 314 hours for the Bachelor of Scientific Horticulture. Corresponding increases were seen in the hour requirements for the degrees offered by the mechanical course.[30]

While increasing the number of hours required for the various degrees, the administration had also reorganized and updated the existing curricula, adding extra hours in English grammar, the sciences, mathematics, and history. Even today the curriculum for any of the four degrees is formidable. For example, an entering first-year student in 1891 would, during the fall term, take twenty-eight hours a week, including arithmetic; English grammar, composition, and declamation; a course on domestic animals; free-hand drawing and penmanship; infantry drill; and shop work in carpentry. In the winter and spring terms his courses of study would vary somewhat and would total twenty-six hours a week each term.[31]

Once that same student had decided on a field of specialization and began working toward a particular degree, the course load became heavier. The third-year or junior student working toward a degree in scientific agriculture was expected to carry a course load of 82 hours; a fourth-year or senior student aiming for the same degree, 83 hours in addition to writing a graduation thesis. For the Bachelor of Mechanical Engineering degree the junior's work load was even heavier, 84 hours,

[29] Minutes, Board of Directors, I, 79; *Fourteenth Annual Catalogue*, p. 39; *Sixteenth Annual Catalogue*, pp. 34–35.

[30] *Fourteenth Annual Catalogue*, pp. 28–31; *Sixteenth Annual Catalogue*, pp. 24–28.

[31] *Sixteenth Annual Catalogue*, pp. 24–25, 27–28.

while the senior was expected to complete 85.5 hours plus a thesis. The heaviest course load then was required of third- and fourth-year students in civil engineering. These young men completed 87 and 90 hours of work, respectively. Definitely the curriculum at A&M during Ross's first year was not to be taken lightly, or easily.[32]

Students glancing over the general regulations for their conduct would have found the rules essentially the same as before, although there was now an official prohibition of hazing. "If any student shall be guilty of hazing or of inciting others thereto, he shall be expelled and it shall be the duty of the President to place opposite his name in the Catalogue the words, 'expelled for hazing.'"[33]

Returning students also found a slight change in military organization and discipline. Appointment of the battalion's commissioned and noncommissioned officers was now to be made by the president, instead of the chairman of the faculty. As before, the appointment and rank of the cadets depended upon their handling of duty and responsibility, their conduct and class standing, and their skill as soldiers. General Ross's standards of excellence in this respect were undoubtedly high, since he had always stressed the importance of military training. Finally, the name of the Scott Volunteers, a company made up of the best-drilled cadets in the corps, had been changed during the summer of 1890 to the Ross Volunteers.[34]

Throughout this period of change, the new president and his family fared well despite some sickness on campus. Lizzie was now pleased with her home, and the children were settling in well. Although Ross confessed that directing the college had at first "made me turn gray very fast," he now found the work agreeable and pleasant, especially since he had "gradually gotten hold of the reins." Even more cheering was the "fine attendance from the best families of the state," who were sending their sons to A&M strictly on his account. At the same time, the state legislature had set aside more than $66,000 for the school over the next two years, $40,000 for support and maintenance, and more than $26,000 for improvements. This increase, coinciding with

[32] Ibid.

[33] Ibid., p. 40.

[34] *Fourteenth Annual Catalogue*, p. 45; *Sixteenth Annual Catalogue*, pp. 20, 39; David Brooks Cofer, ed., *Fragments of Early History of Texas A. & M. College*, pp. 23–26.

the federal government's increased support of the nation's Morrill colleges, meant the college would be able to grow.[35]

And grow it would, in the number of its students and faculty and in its physical facilities. But before the college could enjoy its greatest period of growth, it had to weather a storm of criticism then forming on the horizon, attacking the institution and the new president. The first thunderheads had appeared on the college horizon even before Ross formally took office in February, 1891. Apparently the weeding-out process accomplished before Ross arrived had created bitter resentment among several members of the faculty and staff, especially Thomas M. Scott, Louis L. McInnis, and William S. Scott. These men believed they had been forced out of their positions by individual or general animosity from the board of directors.

The first of these was Thomas M. Scott, business agent of the board, who resigned in February, 1890, supposedly to allow the chairman of the faculty greater power and latitude. Actually, explained Scott, the "God and morality part" of the board of directors listened to "slanderous talk" about him fomented by three faculty members bent on aggrandizement of their positions. When Scott charged the board with besmirching "a purer and better woman than any other at the college," he tendered his resignation.[36]

Next to come under fire was Louis L. McInnis. When the board of directors met on June 7, he was not reelected to his chair in mathematics, and the position he currently held as chairman of the faculty was abolished as of the first of July. The public explanation was that McInnis retired, although it appears he was removed to make way for the incoming president.[37]

According to a daughter, McInnis held his peace about his forced retirement and never manifested any resentment towards those responsible. However, a review of McInnis's correspondence over the next several years shows that he was a focal point for much discontent,

[35] Ross to Holmes, August 9, 1891, Ross Papers, Texas State Archives; H. P. N. Gammel, comp., *The Laws of Texas, 1822–1897*, X, 125–26; Texas Governors, Executive Series, *Governor's Messages, Coke to Ross (Inclusive) 1874–1891*, p. 670.

[36] Minutes, Board of Directors, I, 84; Dethloff, *Centennial History*, I, 148; Thomas M. Scott to Louis L. McInnis, November 9, 1890, McInnis Papers.

[37] Minutes of the Board of Directors, I, 88; Dethloff, *Centennial History*, I, 150, 153.

resentment, and even intrigue against the board and the new president. Over a number of months McInnis apparently wrote friends, acquaintances, former colleagues, alumni, and at least one state senator about his ouster.[38]

And far from being the passive sufferer, McInnis was willing at least to allow others to fight his battle for him. For ten months from July, 1890, to May, 1891, E. B. Cushing and other former students worked at getting up two petitions, the first recommending McInnis's management of the school and a later one asking that he be appointed to the A&M board of directors. The alumni also wrote similar letters to Governor Hogg and to members of the legislature. Eventually the request for a position on the board met stultifying opposition, because it was said McInnis's appointment would cause discord.[39]

At the same time, McInnis apparently considered taking his grievances to the state legislature, for his similarly ousted friend, Thomas Scott, warned him that little good could be accomplished. The board, Scott pointed out, had the power to appoint and remove whom they pleased in the interest of the college. Nevertheless, his correspondence with state senator Henry A. Finch suggests that he was still contemplating some such action. Finch regretted he had not been appointed to the committee scheduled to visit A&M so that he could help McInnis. Still, Finch had prompted the joint committee to investigate the situation at the college.[40]

Despite Finch's efforts, no investigation took place. Meanwhile, Ross's enemies continued to add to their arsenal of grievances. After an "Open Letter to the Board of Directors About Expenses" (at A&M) appeared in the *Galveston Daily News*, in which writer John H. Roberts compared Texas A&M unfavorably with Mississippi A&M, McInnis jotted down his own notes on the subject. These "Reasons Why A&M College of Texas is more expensive to its patrons than A&M of Miss." and "Why it is not a success in its Agricultural Dept." included the following:

[38] Dethloff, *Centennial History*, I, 151; Charles Puryear to Louis L. McInnis, June 30, 1890; E. B. Cushing to McInnis, July 12, 1890; R. B. Fulton to McInnis, July 14, 1890; Thomas M. Scott to McInnis, November 9, 1890; Henry A. Finch to McInnis, February 26, 1891, all in McInnis Papers.

[39] Cushing to McInnis, March 3, April 2, and May 4, 1891; Robert A. Rogers to Louis L. McInnis, April 4, 1891, both in McInnis Papers.

[40] Thomas M. Scott to McInnis, November 9, 1890; Finch to McInnis, February 26, 1891, both in McInnis Papers.

1st The A&M of Miss. has for its President a man who devotes his *whole* time to his duties. . . . He is not a retired politician enjoying a sinecure conferred by his own appointees. He is an educated man & an educator.

2nd The Board of Trustees of the A&M of Miss. are *gentlemen* of *education* & take great interest in the true welfare of the institution.

4th Miss. A&M College devotes special attention to agriculture and has a native as its professor, while in Texas the object is to make the Agl Dept a minimum & therefore the head is an importation whose greatest success is in spending money.

The list closed with a further observation that many other reasons "might be assigned in answer to Mr Roberts but they all are consequent on these before mentioned. If these evils are corrected the correction of the extravagant expenditure of money &c. will follow." [41]

McInnis's natural resentment of Ross as an outsider and his bitterness over his loss of prestige and position were shared by Lieutenant William S. Scott, previously instructor of military science and tactics. Scott was informed by the board in August, 1890, that the interests of the institution required a change in commandants and that the secretary of war would relieve him of his duties. Scott protested the action and threatened the board with a court of inquiry to look into the matter. Although Board President Rose assured Scott that the board members were satisfied with his performance at the college, the officer was not appeased. [42] In a letter written three months later Scott stated his hopes of seeing the "whole dirty work" of the board cleared up. He blamed his ills on Rose and on one of the faculty and concluded, "Well, the damned scoundrels may have occasion to repent their share in it yet." [43]

The most acrimonious of those who lost office because of or under Ross was Dr. J. D. Read, college physician and instructor of physiology. Read, who had been with the institution since 1882, was not reelected by the board when its members met in early June, 1891. Although the board minutes do not give the reason for this dismissal, it may have been because Read, a man of passionate likes and dislikes, long-held

[41]*Galveston Daily News*, September 1, 1892; undated, unsigned notes in McInnis's handwriting, McInnis Papers.

[42]A. J. Rose to William S. Scott, August 21 and 29, 1890; William S. Scott to Rose, August 24, 1890, both in McInnis Papers. Thomas M. Scott told McInnis that "Willie" was removed on the pretext he had sworn in the presence of cadets and hunted on Sunday (Thomas M. Scott to McInnis, November 9, 1890, McInnis Papers).

[43]William S. Scott to Louis L. McInnis, November 4, 1890, McInnis Papers.

grudges (particularly those resulting from the Civil War), and intoler-
ant attitudes towards those he considered in the wrong, was championing the cause of McInnis.[44] More than that, Read had an obsession
about "Northern Republicans" teaching at A&M. "Two of our Profs are
from Iowa—a state where an ex-Confederate is not allowed to vote,"
he complained. He believed that *"Southern men equally capable of
filling professorships* in our Southern institutions" could and should be
found.[45]

Read and his perspective on Northerners at A&M may have caused
M. A. Martin of Coleman to write McInnis on the subject in April,
1891. At that time, Martin asked for answers to a number of questions,
including the number of faculty members then at the college, their
state of birth, their political preference, under whose administration
they had been employed, and how long they had held their present
position. The reason for this inquiry, Martin explained, was that he
had been informed by a Mr. Read (a drug salesman and perhaps a rela-
tive of J. D. Read's) that nine of the faculty members were "imported
Yankee Republicans." If this was so, Martin declared, he intended let-
ting the people of Texas know about it. He requested this information
at McInnis's earliest convenience, since he was "anxious to know who
the men are that are instructing the youths of Texas."[46]

During the 1892 gubernatorial campaign, Read emerged as a bitter political enemy of Ross. As such he spread unflattering reports
about the operation of the college and gave inside information to Ross's
other political enemies, particularly Judge A. W. Terrell. Read still
hoped to obtain an investigation by the legislature, or, failing that,
have a plank included in that year's Democratic platform pledging the
party to an investigation into the affairs of the college.[47]

Besides the rumblings of ousted faculty and staff and of Ross's political enemies were those of irate parents and guardians. One, L. P.

[44] Minutes, Board of Directors, I, 111; J. D. Read to Louis L. McInnis, February 8,
1891, and April 2, 1892; Read to E. B. Cushing, April 11, 1891, both in McInnis Papers.
[45] Read to Cushing, April 11, 1891, McInnis Papers. He was still on the same subject two years later (see Read to McInnis, January 23, 1893, McInnis Papers). In 1895 the
A&M annual, *The Olio*, pp. 15–20, 35–48, noted that of the five board members, only
one was a Northerner. The faculty was even more heavily weighted toward the South:
twenty-three of the twenty-five faculty members were from below the Mason-Dixon
line.
[46] M. A. Martin to Louis L. McInnis, April 6, 1891, McInnis Papers.
[47] Read to McInnis, March 14 and April 2, 17, and 27, 1892, McInnis Papers.

Foley, was angry because "Joe," who he maintained was innocent of charges preferred by the commandant of cadets, was not reinstated by Ross after the president had considered his case. Foley threatened to take his grievance to the legislature, vowing, "I am not through with . . . that college yet. . . . If I can not get it before the legislature, I will surely get it into the newspapers."[48]

In the long run these were minor agitations. Nevertheless, they helped incite an attack on the college and its president during and following the election campaign of 1892.

In accepting the presidency of the Agricultural and Mechanical College, Lawrence Sullivan Ross found himself a step removed from the hurly-burly of state politics. It was not an unwelcome separation, for, as he once told his eldest daughter, "Your political friends can get you into more trouble than you can ever get out of."[49] Despite removal from the main political arena, he was still a personality to be considered in Texas politics. As early as June, 1891, parties dissatisfied with Hogg were sounding him to see if he would be interested in a third term as governor. He was not, nor was he interested in going to the U.S. Senate. Content with the progress being made at A&M, he confided that the prize of going to Washington did not appeal to him because he was "becoming too much in love with rest of body & mind to be sorely tempted by the applause of a fickle populace."[50]

It was a theme often repeated as the state's honeymoon with the Hogg administration faced the reality of day-to-day politics, but the result was the same: Sul Ross preferred to observe the political arena from a distance. With amusement he noted that his old friend and former campaign manager, George Clark, was "swinging around the circle stirring up the monkeys & having lots of fun," and added that Clark was "concocting a lot of devilment for the administration to chew over."[51]

By mid-February that election year Clark had decided to take the field against the redoubtable Hogg, and out of loyalty and friendship

[48] L. P. Foley to Louis L. McInnis, March 5, 1891, McInnis Papers.

[49] Ross to Holmes, February 13, 1891, Ross Papers, Texas A&M Archives. The quote is from Florine Ross Harrington to Myrtle Whiteside, June 24, 1938, cited in Whiteside, "The Life of Lawrence Sullivan Ross" (M.A. thesis, Barker Texas History Center, University of Texas at Austin, 1938), p. 110.

[50] Ross to Holmes, June 21, 1891, Ross Papers, Texas A&M Archives.

[51] Ibid., December 20, 1891, Ross Papers, Texas A&M Archives.

Ross announced that he, as an individual, favored Clark's candidacy. This admission was looked upon as nothing less than treason by the Hogg administration, which proceeded to the attack. In a speech made at Georgetown on March 19 in defense of the administration, Hogg supporter Judge A. W. Terrell observed: "Had this man [Hogg] pleased the corporations in his appointments he would not now be assailed. Had he consulted their emissaries and jockied with principle he could have served you four years without their abuse and then perhaps retired to some literary office conferred by his own appointees."[52]

Those present could not help but draw the conclusion that the judge was referring to former governors Roberts and Ross, who had both taken positions in state institutions of higher education. Such reference was extremely unpopular, but although Terrell later denied attacking Roberts, he offered no apologies or explanations about the matter to Ross or his friends.[53]

On March 27 Ross replied to Terrell, denouncing the unprovoked attack as politically motivated and, in return, questioning the judge's courage during the war of thirty years before. "Well, we had a time for a few days after my exchange with Terrell," he reported good-humoredly to his friend H. M. Holmes. "Lizzie heard from Austin that he would challenge me, and this I could see made her very uneasy." However, nothing in the line of a duel developed, and "even yet I am in receipt of letters almost daily thanking me for so artistically skinning him." So far, he added, he had won the fight, but what the outcome would be he did not know. If his predictions were verified, Clark did not have a chance. Then Ross reflected on what might be the result of his even minor support of Clark. "If Hogg gets in again he will probably decapitate me or make my position so unpleasant that I shall have to retire." But, he concluded, "the college has been greatly improved in my respect, and no one will be able to rob me of that credit."[54]

As Ross predicted, Clark, who ran against Hogg in a three-way split of the Democratic party, was not strong enough to win the elec-

---

[52] *Galveston Daily News*, February 14 and March 20, 1892. William C. Brann commented that Clark "rode into public office, not to say popularity, on the coat-tails of Sul Ross, and has never been able to get over it" (William Cowper Brann, *The Complete Works of Brann the Iconoclast*, II, 68).

[53] *Galveston Daily News*, March 22 and 31, 1892; *Dallas Morning News*, March 25, 1892.

[54] *Galveston Daily News*, March 31, 1892; Ross to Holmes, April 20, 1892, Ross Papers, Texas A&M Archives.

tion of 1892. Therefore, the president could only wait to see from which direction a new attack by his enemies would come.

It was not long in coming. Soon after the first of the year, the *Texas Farmer* berated what it called "classical dudery and military peacockery" at the Agricultural and Mechanical College, where young men acquired theoretical but not practical knowledge. Ross's large salary, the article claimed, had been practically wasted unless the "number of students his name commanded" could be "deemed a recompense." In the opinion of the writer, this recompense was more than offset by Ross's "open espousal of the cause of the greatest enemy of Texas agriculture and industry: an avowed corporation politician, in league with a negro boodler."[55]

This criticism by the *Texas Farmer*, added to political animosities from the past and the maneuverings of Ross's opponents connected with A&M, led to a hostile scrutiny of the college by the 1893 legislative visitation committee. The visitation itself was preceded by an open letter circulated in the legislature condemning the excessive expenses at A&M and "demanding that students should be provided with work at wages sufficient to pay their college expenses." This was a valid suggestion, but the move was seen as an underhanded attack on Sul Ross.[56]

The visitation committee, made up of three representatives and two senators, all Hogg men, made its scheduled swing, visiting the university at Austin, the Agricultural and Mechanical College, the Prairie View Normal School, the Sam Houston State Institute, and the medical branch of the university at Galveston. Ross said they came to College Station poisoned against the college and his management, but that when they left "they were so far converted that their report so far as I am concerned will give the Governor very little justification for a war upon me, which I am sure was contemplated."[57]

Even then, the report as laid before the legislature was extremely partisan in its method if not in its content. The *Dallas Morning News* summarized it as follows:

Among other things it states the office of the president of the college was created. Hazing has been suppressed. Excellent military discipline is main-

---

[55] *Texas Farmer*, January 28, 1893.
[56] *Galveston Daily News*, February 25, 1893.
[57] Texas Legislature, House of Representatives, *House Journal*, 23rd Leg., reg. sess., 1893, pp. 526–31; Ross to Holmes, no date, Ross Papers, Texas A&M Archives.

tained. The laundry work is condemned. Complaints of cooking are justified. The directors have created positions and made appointments which expose them to the charge of desiring to advance friends and relatives. Salaries have been frequently changed, always to increase them. The steward's salary . . . is excessive. The board of directors purchased cattle from its own members. The management's aim has been to divert the purpose of the college. . . . It has been converted into a military and a literary school, instead of an industrial school. Manual labor should be required of the students for pay and for instruction.[58]

Friends of the college were quick to point out the report's obvious weakness—that A&M was the only institution of the five to be singled out for detailed comment. Only five columns in the printed report were devoted to the committee's reports on the four other state schools, while six columns or three full pages were allotted to the Agricultural and Mechanical College. Also, the names and salaries of the presidents of the other institutions were not mentioned, nor were such matters as laundry or food services. Concluded the *Dallas Morning News*: "The agricultural and mechanical college is not above criticism . . . but neither is the university proper nor the medical or other branches. None of them is criticized in any respect whatever, while the Bryan institution—whose president voted against the favorite of the committee men—is attacked with an eagerness and zest suggestive of uncontrollable partisan frenzy."[59]

Three days later the same periodical fired a final salvo in the campaign. In this editorial the *News* suggested that what the people of Texas really wanted was "as much distance as possible between these institutions and mischief brewing politicians, who have no use for them except to degrade and work them as resources for political capital and as subjects of partisan agitation."[60]

J. D. Read's reaction was characteristic. Noting that most people considered the report a stab at the college, he repeated with satisfaction the comment of a former state senator who said he would "as soon give his son a pony, a six shooter, bottle of whiskey and deck of cards & start him out to get his education" as send him to the A&M College. According to A. A. Gulley, another friend and supporter of McInnis, it

[58]*Dallas Morning News*, March 5, 1893.

[59]*Galveston Daily News*, March 5, 1893; *House Journal*, 23rd Leg., pp. 526–31; *Dallas Morning News*, March 12, 1893.

[60]*Dallas Morning News*, March 15, 1893.

was too bad the committee "could not have set forth the facts more fully and recommended a general turning over of things."[61]

However, the public's faith in the college and its president was not abated by such criticism, for the 1893 fall enrollment was unexpectedly high. This agreeable surprise was "exceedingly gratifying" to the board, especially as this increase in enrollment came at a time of financial depression and closely followed the committee's harshly critical report.[62]

At the same time, this adverse opinion of the college brought about very few changes. Evidently Ross believed his position was strong enough after the furor surrounding the report subsided that he did not have to institute any major modifications of policies or practices. And the special emphasis on the military aspects of A&M student life was not altered, despite the committee's faultfinding.[63]

As the tumult of a changing administration, the election of 1892, and the legislative visitation of 1893 faded, A&M College found it had weathered the worst storm of the new president's administration. A period of serene but steady growth beckoned, promising respite from the turbulence of earlier days. The golden years of the Ross presidency still lay ahead.

[61] Read to McInnis, March 15, 1893; A. A. Gulley to Louis L. McInnis, March 18, 1893, both in McInnis Papers.

[62] Minutes, Board of Directors, I, 157.

[63] For a more detailed discussion of this period after the legislative visitation of 1893, see Dethloff, *Centennial History*, I, 164–66.

☆ 16 ☆

Last Years at A&M

WHEN the college session began in September, 1893, Texas A&M entered a period of quiet but continual growth. In the past lay the upheavals of other years, the storms of criticism about the new administration, the fears of political retaliation, and the questions of public support. Public opinion backed the college president in the furor just past, and the flow of prospective students into the institution that fall reached a new high. Before the flood could be stemmed, the administration had registered 343 young men.[1]

Each year more and more students wished to attend A&M. On the opening day of each session from fall, 1894, to 1898, President Ross announced through the daily press that the college could not accept any more students. Indeed, the crush to enter the institution had become so great that by his last year in office Ross formulated a new matriculation policy: from then on parents were requested to communicate first with the president before sending their sons to College Station.[2]

This steadily increasing enrollment meant that accommodations and classroom space could never quite keep up with the demand. In his 1894 report President Ross warned that although he did not believe

---

[1] *Report of the Agricultural and Mechanical College of Texas*, 1894, p. 5.

[2] Charles William Crawford et al., *One Hundred Years of Engineering at Texas A&M, 1876–1976*, p. 26; *Report of the Agricultural and Mechanical College of Texas*, 1896, p. 6; *Twenty-second Annual Catalogue Session 1897–98 Agricultural and . . . Mechanical College of Texas*, p. 29. Historian Clarence Ousley noted that "while the student attendance increased rapidly no small number of the entrants were immature and were lacking in purpose." This defect was later corrected, but at the time the increased enrollment "served admirably to enhance the College in popular esteem and to give it the prestige of numbers and confidence" (Ousley, *History of the Agricultural and Mechanical College of Texas*, Bulletin of the Agricultural and Mechanical College of Texas, 4th series, vol. 6, no. 8, p. 58).

the success of A&M should be determined by the number of students it enrolled, increased demand did indicate that ampler accommoda- tions must be provided. Otherwise, Ross observed, "the sons of Texas endowed with genius and seeking a practical education such as can be obtained nowhere else in the State, must be turned away to go beyond our borders." If the legislature insisted on prodigal spending of the public's money, "let it be in the interest of education; there is no cheaper defense to a community or commonwealth."[3]

Generally the legislators of Texas smiled upon the institution while Ross was president, appropriating extra tax dollars to build new facilities and to improve the old. From fall, 1891, to September, 1898, the college spent about $97,445 on improvements and on construction of new buildings. These included a new mess hall and a new dormitory, Ross Hall, a new frame infirmary; a new artesian well, a natatorium, and stand pipe and waterworks; four new frame residences for faculty; an electric light plant, an ice works, a laundry, and a cold storage room; and a slaughterhouse, a gymnasium, and a warehouse and artillery shed. Especially prominent were the natatorium, costing about $5,000 and including a swimming pool and bathing facilities for the students; a thirty-six patient infirmary, built for about $4,000 and featuring the first indoor toilets on campus; and the new mess hall, erected for $25,000 and seating 500 diners at a time.[4] Including the president's home, the ironworking and blacksmithing shop, and the brick sanitary closet begun in the summer of 1891, the amount spent for improve- ments soared to $109,545.[5]

This sum represented about one-fourth of the actual value of col- lege property in 1896. In May, 1891, the total value, including that of the agricultural experiment station, was about $365,614. By Decem- ber, 1894, it had increased to about $401,565; by September, 1896, to $424,406. This period was also increasingly prosperous for A&M. In July, 1893, and again in 1894, the college account showed a surplus of over $5,000 in the treasury at the end of the fiscal year. In 1894 the financial report credited President Ross's competent stewardship and

[3] *Report of the Agricultural and Mechanical College,* 1894, pp. 5, 9.

[4] Crawford et al., *One Hundred Years,* pp. 26–27. By throwing open rooms built at either end of the dining hall, another 150 students could be accommodated (*Bryan Eagle,* August 26, 1897).

[5] *Report of the Agricultural and Mechanical College of Texas,* 1891, p. 7; *Report of the Agricultural and Mechanical College of Texas,* 1899, p. 32.

praised his "deep solicitude for the general welfare of the institution."[6] This general prosperity also benefited the students, since the college was able to lower its expenses. "We have felt," explained Ross, "the full force of the duty resting upon us to keep the expenses of students as low as possible, in the interest of those for whose special benefit it was founded." It was, in his opinion, possible to educate a boy at A&M at a cost little above home expenses. Another factor was the program of student labor for pay, one of the few changes made after the 1893 legislative visitation.[7]

Expenditures of the various departments also increased while Ross was president. In 1891 the agricultural department owned equipment valued at about $8,736; the veterinary department, nearly $2,012; and civil engineering and physics, a total of $4,231. By September, 1898, spending for these departments had increased to almost twice the value of equipment held. Despite criticism that A&M had been transformed into a military and literary school, the evaluation of equipment for military science and the English department (which included history) was extremely low—less than $600 worth of military equipment, and well under $100 for English.[8]

But improvements on the A&M campus during the nineties were not confined to the college's physical plant. Early in 1892 Ross and W. R. Cavitt, a member of the board of directors, served as a committee to revise the college catalog, particularly those sections dealing with rules. Other changes followed: by 1898 a matriculating student was required to sign a pledge promising to obey the constituted authorities of the college and to support good order and discipline. He also had to certify that he owned no firearms or other deadly weapons.[9]

[6] Report of the Agricultural and Mechanical College, 1891, p. 8; Report of the Agricultural and Mechanical College, 1894, p. 18; Report of the Agricultural and Mechanical College, 1896, p. 24; Minutes of the Board of Directors, Texas A&M University, College Station, Texas (hereafter cited as Minutes, Board of Directors), I, 153, 168.

[7] Report of the Agricultural and Mechanical College, 1894, p. 7; Twenty-second Annual Catalogue, p. 29. Low cost of board was made possible by student consumption of dairy products, meat, vegetables, and fruit produced on campus (Report of the Agricultural and Mechanical College, 1894, pp. 7–8, 13).

[8] Report of the Agricultural and Mechanical College, 1891, p. 8; Report of the Agricultural and Mechanical College, 1899, pp. 32–33.

[9] Minutes, Board of Directors, I, 125; Twenty-second Annual Catalogue, p. 27. Texas' recent frontier past was evidenced by the additional provision that if a student did bring firearms or other deadly weapons to the college, they were to be deposited with the president (Twenty-second Annual Catalogue, p. 27).

Considering his experience with administration on several different levels, including that of the highest elected office in the state, it is not surprising that Ross made various changes during his years at College Station. First, he defined the college chain of command and provided for administrative succession when necessary. Next, he established a provision linking tenure of office for both president and professors with "good behavior and efficiency of service." At the same time, he decreed that faculty and administrators could not be dismissed without reasonable notice. Finally, Ross fixed a policy for attendance of faculty meetings by the president and the eleven department heads; in keeping with early fiscal reforms, a separate set of books and records was opened for the experimental farm.[10]

These administrative changes extended beyond the local campus. The Ross era, particularly between 1892 and 1896, was also a time of more cordial relations and greater cooperation between the Agricultural and Mechanical College and its arch-rival, the university in Austin.[11]

As important as Sul Ross's presidency was to the increased enrollment, physical growth, financial prosperity, and administrative development of the college, his most lasting impact was upon the students themselves and the traditions developed during his presidency. Among Ross's greatest achievements at A&M was his close relationship with the young men under his authority. Most students arrived on campus with respect and admiration for the president already instilled in them by their parents. Others, sent to the college by less ardent admirers of the former governor, soon found Ross's magnetic personality irresistible, for Ross had a way with young people that drew them to him and held their loyalty.[12]

At the same time, he personified a living hero out of the pages of recent Texas history. Students loved to hear him recount his adventures and repeated them in the pages of their annual, *The Olio*, published in 1895.[13]

[10] Minutes, Board of Directors, I, 125–26, 136, 143.

[11] Henry C. Dethloff, *A Centennial History of Texas A&M University, 1876–1976*, I, 162–63.

[12] David Brooks Cofer, *Second Five Administrators of Texas A. & M. College, 1890–1905*, p. 63; Ousley, *History*, p. 61; *Dallas Morning News*, January 4, 1898; Elizabeth Ross Clarke, "Life of Sul Ross," Ross Family Papers, Texas Collection, Baylor University, Waco, Texas (hereafter cited as Ross Family Papers, Baylor), p. 133.

[13] Cofer, *Second Five Administrators*, pp. 82–83; Dethloff, *Centennial History*, I, 167.

But despite their respect and admiration for Ross, the cadets best appreciated their president for his strength of character. Dignified of mien, calm of spirit, courteous of demeanor, Ross was accessible to his charges and tactful in dealing with their needs. Students later recalled his many kindnesses, extended unobtrusively, whether financial or personal. The president was slow to condemn but ready to encourage; those around him could not recall hearing Ross use profanity or seeing him visibly angry. He also showed limitless interest in college activities, participating in them himself when possible. He was the students' friend, and in return he considered the cadets his friends.[14]

The young men responded in kind to their president's character. Ross noted that at times he had some "petty annoyances," but with very few exceptions the boys conducted themselves "splendidly." Of course, his acquaintance with the parents of many of his students gave him a "sort of parental influence over the student body that rarely failed in curbing youthful impulse for mischief."[15]

And there is no doubt that a strong hand of discipline was required. It is clear from student reminiscences of the period that the cadets of A&M were brimful of mischief. Nevertheless, the president maintained a tight control over his students and their affairs. First, his policy of interviewing prospective students enabled Ross to cull potential troublemakers before he granted them entrance. Professor F. E. Giesecke, head of the department of drawing, recalled that the president rejected one applicant's request for admission because he determined during the course of the interview that the young man was a gambler.[16]

On the other hand, President Ross would go to great lengths to gain entrance for deserving students. At times he requested conditional entrance "when he thought that the circumstances and the character of the boy would warrant such an act," thus repaying the kindness he had received in Alabama years before. Once he determined that a particular young man belonged at A&M, Ross would cordially greet the newcomer in such a way that the boy knew he could always

[14] Cofer, Second Five Administrators, pp. 74, 82, 84–85; Ross to H. M. Holmes, February 13, 1891, Lawrence Sullivan Ross Papers, Texas A&M University Archives, College Station, Texas (hereafter cited as Ross Papers, Texas A&M Archives); Ousley, History, p. 61.

[15] Ross to Holmes, December 20, 1891, Ross Papers, Texas A&M Archives; Ousley, History, p. 61.

[16] Cofer, Second Five Administrators, pp. 38, 41, 61–62.

turn to his president as a friend if necessary. This in itself was exceedingly helpful to the nervous young men appearing for the first time on the College Station campus.[17]

Second, Ross exercised control through the monthly grade sheets prepared for each student. These the president read, signed, and annotated. Then, if a student's grades warranted it, a personal admonition was administered. One cadet, J. B. ("Josh") Sterns, reported that he was called into the president's office, only to find Ross studying a piece of paper with a large magnifying glass. Finally the president told Sterns he was just trying to see the boy's last month's grades. He then asked Josh what instructions his parents had given him before he arrived on campus. "I felt sure he was fixing to throw the derail under me," the young man recalled, and so he had to think fast. At last inspiration came: he told the president that his parents had told him to play football and baseball, to run and jump, box and wrestle, and then, if "he had any time left to study a little." Ross replied that Sterns was excused this time, but if it happened again, it would be no laughing matter.[18]

Many other unruly cadets also reaped the benefit of the president's long patience. Ross would bear with such students if he thought it possible to bring out their better qualities. Although Joseph E. Abrahams stayed too busy to get into much trouble, he recalled that when he did visit the president's office, Ross dealt with him calmly and with quiet dignity.[19]

Although he was prepared to deal with students individually, President Ross usually admonished the cadet corps as a whole during the morning chapel services. Then, using texts from Holy Writ and incidents gleaned from personal experiences through his long years of public service, he would instruct, exhort, encourage, and advise his listeners. According to one student, the cadets knew that when Ross arose in chapel they would hear something of more than ordinary interest; therefore, even the most restless of them settled down and listened intently. "We always expected a treat of kind words and we were never disappointed," he reported.[20]

[17] Ibid., pp. 84–85; *Battalion*, January, 1898, p. 15.

[18] Cofer, *Second Five Administrators*, p. 63; J. B. Sterns Reminiscences, Texas A&M University Archives, College Station, Texas.

[19] Cofer, *Second Five Administrators*, pp. 74, 85.

[20] *Battalion*, January, 1898, pp. 13, 16.

Student life at the Agricultural and Mechanical College was enriched in other ways during the Ross years. First, the military aspect at A&M was given foremost importance. Cadets and students were now synonymous: there was no longer any difference between the young men in each group. But although military training was stressed to the extent that the institution was accused of military peacockery, Ross considerably altered previous policies. By 1896 the cadet program had been refined to exclude unnecessary drills and instruction. The amount of guard duty expected of a cadet had been reduced by one-half, the practice of marching to and from class recitations had been abolished, and drill requirements had been drastically changed.[21]

Second, through changes in the military curriculum, the First or Senior Class began to receive instruction in artillery and signal drill and in target practice. During this period the college received from the U.S. government two breech-loading rifled field pieces and a supply of blank cartridges, as well as live small arms ammunition for target practice.[22]

But far more important for the cadets was the development of esprit de corps under Ross. It was at this time that the Ross Volunteers established many of the traditions for which the unit is famous today. Many times the Rosses, as the unit was known on campus, performed in their snow-white uniforms and helmets, skillfully exhibiting the manual of arms, the bayonet drill, and a spectacular "gun drill by music." They were seen at commencements, drill team competitions, and at United Confederate Veteran reunions, and in 1897 they participated with the other cadets in the San Jacinto celebration and battlefield dedication. At that performance the Rosses held the vast audience spellbound while they "executed in quick and double time" such precise movements that the severest military critic could find no fault with them. Thus the company "won a reputation that quickly spread throughout the state."[23]

[21] Dethloff, *Centennial History*, I, 167; *Report of the Agricultural and Mechanical College*, 1896, pp. 21–22.

[22] *Report of the Agricultural and Mechanical College*, 1896, p. 21.

[23] *Battalion*, June, 1896, p. 65, and June, 1897, pp. 8, 49; *Bryan Eagle*, April 22 and June 10, 1897; Minutes, Board of Directors, I, 174. After Ross's death, the unit's name was changed to honor succeeding presidents of A&M, first to Foster Guards and then to Houston Rifles. When Ross's son-in-law, Henry Hill Harrington, became president of the school in 1905, he asked that the select company of cadets permanently bear the name "Ross Volunteers" in honor of his illustrious predecessor (David Brooks Cofer, ed., *Fragments of Early History of Texas A. & M. College*, p. 27).

Other enrichments included nonmilitary extracurricular activities. The local branch of the Young Men's Christian Association arrived on campus in 1889 but experienced little growth until the Ross years, when it suddenly burgeoned. By 1893 the organization was flourishing to such a degree that it was able to cooperate with the college in building a gymnasium. Under the association's sponsorship athletic events were held, lectures presented, and social gatherings planned.[24]

In addition to the YMCA, other special interest clubs sprang up during this period. The Fat Man's Club, the Bowlegged Men's Club, and the Glee Club all drew their adherents, as did the College Dramatic Club and the Bicycle Club. There were also two literary societies on campus, the Calliopean and the Austin, which met weekly for practice in debate, declamation, and literary composition. Throughout the session the societies held public debates and presented speakers, and at the end of the academic year they jointly sponsored declamation and essay contests as well as debates, awarding prizes during commencement.[25]

Just before Ross came to A&M the two societies united in publishing the *College Journal*, a literary magazine that appeared each month until 1893. In the flowery prose of the time, the *Journal* reported college activities and the doings of its administration, faculty, staff, and students. In February, 1892, the *Journal* noted the completion of the president's new "mansion," describing it as a "thing of beauty both inside and outside," which added much to the "beauty and symmetry of the College campus."[26]

In 1893 the more newspaperlike *Battalion* began its long run, which has continued until the present. Although it retained the format of a literary magazine and was published cooperatively by the two literary societies, the *Battalion* at this time presented a more journalistic coverage of campus events, enlivened by photographs. The June, 1897, issue devoted considerable space to commencement, to the Ross Volunteers, and to Alpha Phi, the new former students' organization. At first published only monthly, the *Battalion* later developed into a

---

[24] *College Journal* 3 (February, 1891): 20, and 4 (February, 1893): 16.

[25] Dethloff, *Centennial History*, I, 173; *Battalion*, October, 1893, p. 4; *College Journal* 3 (March, 1892): 20; *Bryan Eagle*, June 13, 1895, and June 10 and October 7, 1897; *Sixteenth Annual Catalogue of the Agricultural and Mechanical College of Texas*, p. 42.

[26] *College Journal* 3 (October, 1891): 25, (November, 1891): 24, and (February, 1892): 20.

weekly and then a daily newspaper.[27] For a number of years the paper's masthead carried the words *Lawrence Sullivan Ross—Soldier, Statesman, Knightly Gentleman* as a tribute to Ross's influence on the college and its student publications.

In 1895 *The Olio*, the first college annual, appeared. Edited by volunteers selected from the entire school, the cloth-bound volume boasted numerous photographs and sketches of the buildings and grounds, comic sketches, editorials, articles, and poems. Also included were portraits of the president, faculty, and board of directors, as well as of most of the Corps of Cadets, with accompanying biographies when the importance of the subject demanded it.[28]

For those students with a taste for music, there was the "Band Orchestra" and the mandolin club. One cadet recalled that the college band began in 1895 with about thirteen students. Under the direction of George W. Gross, the musicians won a state reputation and later cooperated with the Corps of Cadets in their musical drills.[29]

On behalf of former students who were not alumni but who still wished to maintain ties with the Agricultural and Mechanical College, Alpha Phi, an association of former students, was founded. This was the creation of E. B. Cushing, who set out to organize the three thousand former students (as opposed to the three hundred alumni) into an assistance group to work for the upbuilding of the college. Eventually Alpha Phi assimilated the older groups, the Alumni Association and the Association of Ex-Cadets, ultimately developing into the modern Association of Former Students.[30]

The organized sports of baseball and football came to Texas A&M during the nineties.[31] Baseball was the earliest, appearing about the same time as the new president took office. Although baseball sparked considerable interest throughout this period, the real excitement in sports seems to have been generated by football. Apparently this newest competitive team sport first appeared at College Station in 1894.

[27] Vick Lindley, *The Battalion: Seventy Years of Student Publications at the A&M College of Texas*, pp. 1–7.

[28] *Bryan Eagle*, June 13, 1895; *The Olio: An Annual Published by the Corps of Cadets of the Agricultural and Mechanical College of Texas*, p. 32.

[29] *Battalion*, June, 1897, pp. 51–52; David Brooks Cofer, *Early History of Texas A. and M. College Through Letters and Papers*, p. 113.

[30] *Battalion*, October, 1896, p. 23, and June, 1897, p. 39; Dethloff, *Centennial History*, I, 170–71.

[31] Dethloff, *Centennial History*, I, 171.

On December 6, the *Bryan Eagle* covered a game between A&M and a Galveston team; the college team won by eight points. The *Eagle* reporter noted that the game was one of "feverish interest from beginning to end" and that it was "eagerly watched" by a throng of visitors from Bryan. Although he was not well enough acquainted with the game to give a correct report, the journalist added that a special correspondent from the *Galveston News* considered it the best game he had ever witnessed. The exceedingly rough-and-tumble character of the game in those days resulted in several injuries, which the reporter learned were slight for football.[32]

One innovation favored by Ross that would have enriched student life was coeducation. Women, usually the daughters of administrators, faculty, and staff, appeared on campus as sponsors for various college groups and events, but during the nineties there were usually few women on campus. Although President Ross favored coeducation, believing that the cadets "would be improved by the elevating influence of the good girls," this change of policy had to wait until the 1960s.[33]

Not only was the Ross era one of enriched student life on the A&M campus, but these years represented enrichment of the surrounding community as well. College commencements, for example, were elaborate three-day affairs. Attending the exercises were president, faculty, and staff; members of the board of directors; graduates, alumni, and former students; families of the students; and members of the legislature, various other prominent men of Texas, and friends and supporters of the college from all over the state.

The exercises of the first day began after breakfast on Sunday with guard mount by the cadets, followed by inspection of the dormitories by the commandant and his staff, members of the board, and visitors. After this inspection, everyone proceeded to the assembly hall for religious services, completed that evening by the annual YMCA address. On Monday came the inspection of the departments, when stock, apparatus, and appliances were on display, as well as an exhibition of student products. The rest of the second day was given to battalion review and infantry drill, a meeting of the alumni association, and a joint cele-

[32]*Bryan Eagle*, December 6, 1894.

[33]*Bryan Eagle*, April 1, 1897. After Ross's death, several faculty daughters attended classes with the cadets, but as courtesy students only (Austin Earle Burges, *A Local History of Texas A. & M. College, 1876–1916*, p. 15; Cofer, *Early History*, pp. 118–19).

bration by the two literary societies, featuring debates, addresses, music, essays, and declamations, with the awarding of prizes. Tuesday, commencement day proper, continued with services in the chapel, addresses, conferring of degrees, and announcement of honor students, succeeded in the afternoon by a sham battle, complete with the firing of the school's two rifled pieces. After a performance by the Ross Volunteers, the "grand graduation dress parade" of the cadets marked the end of military service for that year. Commencement celebrations culminated with a ball, or "hop," held in the mess hall Tuesday evening.[34]

Interaction between the college and the surrounding community extended beyond the once-a-year commencement exercises, however. Records show that in November, 1892, President Ross and another representative of the college attended the convention of American Agricultural and Mechanical Colleges. That same month, the college set aside fifteen hundred dollars for an exhibit at the World's Fair. Other college exhibits appeared at the State Fair of Texas, held in Dallas. In May, 1895, the corps traveled to Houston to take part in the United Confederate Veteran reunion. Two years later, the Texas Academy of Science met at A&M. In his welcoming address, President Ross emphasized the value of scientific education by detailing the many results of scientific discoveries. Even more important, at least to the future development of the Texas livestock industry, was the college experiment station's research on Texas cattle fever. In 1898, this resulted in a demonstration by Dr. Mark Francis of the veterinary department proving that cattle could be immunized against the malady.[35]

Similarly, these were years of personal enrichment for Sul Ross. Appointment to (and subsequent refusal of) a seat on the railroad commission proved anew the esteem in which the people of his state held him. His children were growing up, finding careers and mates, while he played an important role in the development of the Confederate veterans movement in Texas. Thus these were busy years, the harvest time of Ross's life.

During the nineties, Ross was frequently considered for a third

[34] *Bryan Eagle*, June 13, 1895, and June 10, 1897. An invitation from 1895 shows flags of the United States and Texas, military equipment, and in the center the Lone Star with "Texas" and the initials "AMC" intertwined (Ross Family Papers, Neville P. Clarke Collection, Bryan, Texas [hereafter cited as Ross Family Papers, Clarke Collection]).

[35] Minutes, Board of Directors, I, 131, 144–45, 165, 174, 192; *Bryan Eagle*, December 24, 1897; Ousley, *History*, pp. 108–10.

gubernatorial term. In the earliest months of the 1894 political campaign, Ross reported to his correspondent H. M. Holmes that newspaper people were beginning to mention his name in connection with a
third term—in fact, they were pointedly sending him marked copies of
their publications asking that he run again. Even the word-of-mouth
report was the same: the people of Texas wanted Sul Ross to return to
politics. This was an "utter & complete endorsement" of his administration, but despite such flattering inducements Ross preferred to
stay where he was.[36]

The election of 1894 ended without a Ross candidacy. However,
when Governor-elect Charles A. Culberson began making appointments for his new administration, he chose to appoint Lawrence Sullivan Ross, along with John H. Reagan and L. J. Storey, to the railroad
commission. Again duty called, but as in 1890 he pondered long before
making a decision.[37]

By late December it seemed certain that Ross would resign the
college presidency and accept the position on the railroad commission,
although he delayed making his decision until the meeting of the board
of directors on January 1. Meanwhile, a great public outcry opposing
the projected move began to be heard.[38] Letters and petitions began to
pour in begging Ross to stay in College Station. Among the others was
a particularly appealing one from the citizens of Bryan and Brazos
County, stressing the prosperity and harmony of the past four years
and praising his "beneficient influence," "daily example," and "great
popularity." Continued the petition: "We hold, furthermore, that the
educational interests of any State are paramount to all others, and that
these appeal to you in the strongest terms to remain where you are.
Should you leave the college at this most inopportune time we have
many reasons to feel the deepest anxiety for its future. We firmly believe, therefore that duty calls on you to remain in this most important
position."[39]

Almost overwhelmed by the outpouring of requests urging him to
remain in his present position, Ross agreed to stay on at the college.

[36] Ross to Holmes, February 23, 1894, Ross Papers, Texas A&M Archives.
[37] *Bryan Eagle*, December 20, 1894, and January 3, 1895.
[38] Newspaper clippings, December 28 and 29, 1894, name of paper unknown,
from Louis Lowry McInnis Papers, Texas A&M University Archives, College Station,
Texas (hereafter cited as McInnis Papers).
[39] Clipping, December 28, 1894, in McInnis Papers.

He had no idea, he said, that such an estimate was placed upon his services as president; he added that as governor of Texas he had never felt more highly honored than he did as president of the A&M College.[40]

Ross enjoyed other honors, all within the family circle, during this time. Of the Ross children, Lawrence, Jr., was already out on his own when the family moved to College Station, but the younger children were still at home. Harvey, the next eldest son, spent several years trying to find suitable employment. He finally settled down to clerking in an uncle's store in Waco while supervising the family plantation on the Brazos. Florine, the eldest daughter, married A&M professor Henry Hill Harrington in 1892 and presented the president with his first grandchild, a boy, in 1893. Frank, probably the most brilliant of the children, entered A&M at fifteen, graduated with honors, and became a physician. The youngest daughter, Elizabeth ("Bessie"), attended Waco Female College and then H. Sophie Newcomb Memorial College in New Orleans, while Neville, the baby of the family, was a cadet when his father died.[41]

While his family was growing up around him, Ross took an active interest in the development and growth of the Texas Division of the United Confederate Veterans. In 1893 he became the division's first commander, and he was reelected the next year despite his protestations. It was an office he continued to hold for several years; for one term, he was commander-in-chief of the entire United Confederate Veteran organization. Before his death four Confederate veteran camps—those at Bonham, Denton, Henrietta, and New Boston—had been named in his honor, and the L. S. Ross Chapter of the Daughters of the Confederacy had been founded at Bryan.[42]

[40] *Bryan Eagle*, January 3, 1895. In appreciation of his decision to stay, the faculty and staff presented the president with a gold-headed cane (*Eagle*, January 17, 1895).

[41] Ross to H. M. Holmes, December 30, 1893, Lawrence Sullivan Ross Papers, Texas State Archives, Austin, Texas; Ross to Holmes, March 10, 1891, July 22 and November 5, 1892, February 23 and August 27, 1894, and June 13, 1895, all in Ross Papers, Texas A&M Archives; Frank Ross to L. S. Ross, November 15, 1895, and Branott V. B. Difons to Mrs. L. S. Ross, September 8, 1896, both in Ross Family Papers, Clarke Collection; *Houston Post*, June 2, 1960.

[42] *Minutes of the Third Annual Meeting and Reunion of the United Confederate Veterans of the Division of Texas, Held in the City of Waco, Texas, April 5th, 6th and 7th, 1894*, pp. 14–15; Clement A. Evans, ed., *Confederate Military History: A Library of Confederate States History, in Twelve Volumes, Written by Distinguished Men of the South*, XI, 635; *Waco Times-Herald*, January 4, 1898; Minutes, Board of Directors, I, 174; *Confederate Veteran* 7 (July, 1897): 382–83; *Bryan Eagle*, April 22, 1897.

Despite the president's busy schedule, Ross still found opportunity from time to time for the recreation he loved best. One of the legacies of his frontier upbringing was that he loved to hunt; another, that he could never sleep well inside. Therefore one of his favorite forms of recreation was a camp-out hunting and fishing trip. While governor he had indulged in a yearly hunting trip, usually in Liberty County. After he became president of A&M, he would sometimes slip off for a few days of fishing and hunting with his sons or friends.[43] One summer early in his tenure at A&M, Ross was on a hunt; when the neighboring citizens learned he was there, they "flocked around until we had at dinner one day 25 men." Fortunately, Ross found a bee tree laden with honey that the men cut down, and the honey, along with venison, gave Sul enough to feed his guests. "I think they would gladly vote for me to renew the trip at my earliest convenience," he commented good-humoredly.[44]

During the Christmas vacation of 1897–98, despite a record-breaking ten days of cold rain, the president, his son Neville, and several friends went out deer hunting in the Navasota River bottoms. All went well until Ross overexerted himself in the chase and then broke his fast with underdone biscuit and partially cooked sausage. The result was acute indigestion followed by a severe chill.[45]

Not wishing to spoil the sport for the others, Ross insisted that the rest of the party remain in the field while he went home alone in his buckboard. Arriving at College Station Thursday evening, December 30, he complained of continued indigestion and received medical treatment. On Friday and Saturday he was very restless but was somewhat improved Sunday, the second of January. However, about 5:00 P.M. on Sunday he suffered an "acute congestion of the stomach and bowels," and his condition, which until then had not been considered serious, became so alarming that his family was notified.[46] Although the patient

[43] Norman G. Kittrell, *Some Governors Who Have Been and Other Public Men of Texas*, p. 98; Clarke, "Life of Sul Ross," Ross Family Papers, Baylor, p. 131; *Austin Daily Statesman*, November 10, 1887, November 13 and 20, 1888, and January 14, 1890; Ross to Holmes, July 22, 1892, and August 27, 1894, Ross Papers, Texas A&M Archives; *Bryan Eagle*, August 1, 1895.

[44] Ross to Holmes, July 22, 1892, Ross Papers, Texas A&M Archives.

[45] *Bryan* (Daily) *Eagle*, December 26, 1897; Robert Eberspacher to David B. Cofer, August 17, 1954, Ross Papers, Texas A&M Archives; *Dallas Morning News*, January 5, 1898.

[46] Eberspacher to Cofer, August 17, 1954, Ross Papers, Texas A&M Archives; *San Antonio Semi-Weekly Express*, January 7, 1898.

rallied somewhat Monday morning, by that afternoon there was no longer any doubt that Ross was on his deathbed. Retaining consciousness until about an hour before his death, he bade farewell to Lizzie, to his sister Mrs. Tom Padgitt, and to his children present and died peacefully at 6:35 P.M.[47] He was fifty-nine years and three months old, and he had been president of the A&M College one month short of seven years.

While state and Southland mourned, the remains of the beloved president were escorted back to Waco by the entire student population of A&M. Once in Waco, others—Confederate veterans in faded gray uniforms—made up his honor guard. Others whose lives had been somehow touched by Sul Ross crowded into Waco for the semimilitary funeral, and thousands attended the interment in Oakwood Cemetery.[48] All Texas seemed to join in expressions of grief over the unexpected loss—a loss that was to be felt even more in the days to come.

[47] *Waco Times-Herald*, January 4, 1898; *Dallas Morning News*, January 5, 1898. The exact cause of Ross's death is not known. In years past it was attributed to a number of vague causes, including chill, indigestion, and congestion, and to his old Wichita village wounds, which apparently bothered him throughout his life (*Waco Times-Herald*, January 4, 1898). Roger N. Conger et al., in *Rangers of Texas*, p. 130, maintain Ross was accidentally poisoned by the camp cook, but this theory has been largely discounted by Ross's descendants (interview with Elizabeth Ross Clarke [Ross's granddaughter], Waco, Texas, March 30, 1972; interview with Elizabeth Williams Estes [Ross's grandniece], April 22, 1975). The matter is further confused by the absence of a death certificate (Flora L. Sheppard, deputy county clerk, Brazos County, Bryan, Texas, July 23, 1973, personal communication). Evidence indicates, however, that the cause of death was probably a coronary heart attack, which can be brought on by physical exertion in cold, windy weather; digestion of a particularly indigestible meal; and emotional stress such as the excitement of the hunt. This affliction strikes suddenly, with no previous warning (see Howard B. Sprague, M.D., "The Heart and Circulatory System," *Better Homes and Gardens Family Medical Guide*, ed. Donald B. Cooley [New York: Meredith Press, 1964, 1966], pp. 87–90).

[48] A Ross daughter said five thousand (Clarke, "Life of Sul Ross," Ross Family Papers, Baylor, pp. 134–35; *San Antonio Daily Express*, January 5, 1898; *San Antonio Semi-Weekly Express*, January 7, 1898). For a detailed description of the funeral, see "Sul Ross Is Laid in His Grave," *Dallas Morning News*, January 6, 1898.

The Legacy of a Life

IN the days, weeks, and months after his death, those who had known Lawrence Sullivan Ross expressed what his life had meant to them. Comrades of ranger fights, veterans of the Civil War, statesman friends of governmental days, and the faculty, alumni, and students of A&M College poured forth praise. His courage, honesty, and public spirit were extolled, and he was compared to George Washington and Robert E. Lee as a Southern ideal.[1]

Other memorials took more lasting form. Less than a week after Ross's death, the former cadets of A&M were planning a suitable monument. Funds poured in, but the memorial was not actually begun until the state appropriated ten thousand dollars toward the project in 1917. The ten-foot bronze statue, a creation of Pompeo Coppini, was unveiled on May 4, 1919, with appropriate ceremonies. Since then the statue, which now stands in front of the Academic Building on the Texas A&M campus, has become a focal point of campus life.[2]

Considering Ross's concern for higher education, it is fitting that the same Thirty-fifth Legislature in 1917 established another memorial—Sul Ross Normal College, now Sul Ross State University, at Al-

---

[1] George Bruce Halstead, *Washington, the Ideal of the South: Resurgent in Lee and Ross. Address before the Charles Broadway Rouss Camp of Sons of Confederate Veterans, February 21, 1899*, 20 pp.

[2] *Galveston Daily News*, January 10, 1898; Norman G. Kittrell, *Address Delivered at the Unveiling of the Monument of Gen. Lawrence Sullivan Ross, Ex-Governor of Texas and Ex-President of the Agricultural and Mechanical College, at College Station, Friday, May 4th, 1919*, 16 pp.; Pompeo Coppini, *From Dawn to Sunset*, pp. 228–42; George Sessions Perry, *The Story of Texas A. and M.*, pp. 74–75; *Waco News-Tribune*, October 30, 1969. Coppini was to have done an equestrian statue of Ross for a Waco memorial group, but for a number of reasons the project was never completed (Coppini, *From Dawn to Sunset*, pp. 122–23).

pine. The college opened its doors in June, 1920, and has been operating ever since.[3]

Considering the varied offices of public trust filled by Ross—soldier, statesman, educator—it is difficult to decide where his greatest influence lay. Certainly his military career, both as a ranger and as a Confederate officer, was conspicuous, and his service in the constitutional convention, legislature, and governor's office was beneficial to his state. But contemporaries and posterity alike have agreed that the presidency of Texas A&M College was Ross's crowning achievement and his most valuable contribution to Texas society of his time.[4]

Under his leadership the college reached new heights of growth and development. His presence won the institution needed prestige and appropriations, while his administration smoothed many problems and tensions. At the same time Ross's own well-known military background, combined with his belief in a strong military element in American society, gave the school the patriotic military traditions it holds to the present. The number of students grew, new buildings went up all over the campus, and public faith in the institution returned.

His influence at A&M has lasted until the present: year after year, freshmen scrub and polish the Ross statue as a part of their introduction to life on the A&M campus, while the Ross Volunteers march in parades and other public functions, thus keeping Ross's name in the public memory. Since 1955 A&M students have sung "Soldier, Statesman, Knightly Gentleman," by Philip B. Goode and Sara Jane Goode, a humorous fight song extolling the virtues of Aggies, or Texas A&M students, in the Ross tradition.[5] And it was the strong patriotic military tradition of the school that helped keep the campus quiet during the student unrest of the sixties.[6]

At a distance Sul Ross seems a soldier-statesman-educator in the molds of George Washington and Robert E. Lee, always responsive to duty. Seen closer up, however, Ross's character fragments into a complexity of mosaiclike pieces, many of them complementary or even con-

---

[3] Cecil Eugene Evans, *The Story of Texas Schools*, pp. 295–96.

[4] *Battalion*, January, 1898, p. 11; David Brooks Cofer, *Second Five Administrators of Texas A. & M. College, 1890–1905*, p. 90.

[5] Don Heath, "The Aggie Corps," *San Antonio Light*, April 6, 1969; *Waco News-Tribune*, October 30, 1969; copy in Lawrence Sullivan Ross Papers, Texas A&M University Archives, College Station, Texas.

[6] Heath, "The Aggie Corps."

tradictory. Fearless in the face of physical danger, he was timid of ridicule. Hotheaded as a youth, he early learned self-control. Adventuresome and never abandoning the danger and freedom of the frontier, he loved his wife, family, and fireside and suffered when away from them. Harsh in dealing with enemies who had overstepped the bounds of what he considered civilized warfare, Ross valued spiritual and cultural ideals. He quoted Byron and Shakespeare while struggling at times with the basics of English grammar. Raised to the highest elected office in Texas, he remained a model of modesty and simplicity. A Jeffersonian Democrat believing in a minimum of government, he favored certain innovations in state services. A zealous Confederate in his young manhood, in his last years he tamed the A&M College cadets and instilled into coming generations a tradition of patriotism to the re-United States. Born in Iowa Territory, he served his adopted state with greater devotion than many of her native sons; his influence in Texas long exceeded his lifetime.

Of all the thousands of words spoken and written in tribute to Ross, the meaning of his life was perhaps best summarized in an editorial that appeared in the *Dallas Morning News* the morning after his death.

It has been the lot of few men to be of such great service to Texas as Sul Ross. . . . Throughout his life he has been closely connected with the public welfare and . . . discharged every duty imposed upon him with diligence, ability, honesty and patriotism. . . . He was not a brilliant chieftain in the field, nor was he masterful in the art of politics, but, better than either, he was a well-balanced, well-rounded man from whatever standpoint one might estimate him. In his public relations he exhibited sterling common sense, lofty patriotism, inflexible honesty and withal a character so exalted that he commanded at all times not only the confidence but the affection of the people. . . . He leaves a name that will be honored as long as chivalry, devotion to duty and spotless integrity are standards of our civilization and an example which ought to be an inspiration to all young men of Texas who aspire to careers of public usefulness and honorable renown.[7]

In the Oakwood Cemetery of Waco, Texas, there stands a sturdy gravestone. A double spray of leaves, reminiscent of the twin gold-wreathed collar ornaments of a Confederate general officer, adorns the upper corners. Otherwise the stone is as modest and unassuming as the man it represents. On the marker the words *Lawrence Sullivan*

---

[7] *Dallas Morning News*, January 4, 1898.

Ross. Sept. 27, 1838. Jan. 3, 1898 stand out in bold relief. There are no references to the red men he had slain, to the bluecoats he had battled, to the outlaws he had brought to justice. His productive years as senator, governor, and college president are not recalled to the public memory. Only the name and pertinent dates meet the eye, but they are enough. For all informed Texans, the name of Lawrence Sullivan Ross is his fame.

Bibliography

ARCHIVAL COLLECTIONS

Arlington, Texas. Private collection of Dr. and Mrs. Malcolm D. McLean.
    L. H. Graves Diary, original owned by Kathryn Stoner O'Connor.
    Kathryn Stoner O'Connor Collection. Victor M. Rose Papers.
Arlington, Texas. University of Texas at Arlington. Robertson Colony Collection.
    T. S. Sutherland Papers.
Austin, Texas. Texas State Archives.
    Adjutant General Papers.
    Election Returns. Secretary of state.
    Governor's Papers. Correspondence, executive documents, executive
    record books, and letters. Sam Houston, Edward Clark, and Lawrence
    Sullivan Ross.
    Register of State and County Officers. Department of State.
    Texas Indian Affairs Papers, 1854–60.
Austin, Texas. Barker Texas History Center.
    James H. Baker Diary.
    W. C. Cochran Reminiscences.
    Benjamin Franklin Gholson Recollections.
    Captain Willis Lang Diary.
    Victor M. Rose Papers.
    Lawrence Sullivan Ross Letters.
    Lawrence Sullivan Ross Vertical File. Barker Texas History Center Library.
Bryan, Texas. Private collection of Dr. and Mrs. Neville P. Clarke.
    Ross Family Bible.
    Ross Family Papers.
College Station, Texas. Private collection of Mrs. Paul Mason.
    Ross Family Papers.
    Ross Family Scrapbook.
College Station, Texas. Texas A&M University.
    Minutes of the Board of Directors.
College Station, Texas. Texas A&M University Archives.
    Lucius Holman Papers.
    Louis Lowry McInnis Papers.
    Lawrence Sullivan Ross Papers.
    J. B. Sterns Reminiscences.

Lorena, Texas. Private collection of Elizabeth Williams Estes.
  Gibson-Denison-Ross-Williams Family Scrapbook.
  Ross Family Papers.
New Haven, Connecticut. Yale University Library.
  Edward M. House Collection.
Waco, Texas. Baylor University. Texas Collection.
  George Barnard Papers.
  Ross Family Papers.
Waco, Texas. McLennan County Courthouse.
  Deed Records.
  District Court Minutes.
  Marriage Records.
Washington, D.C. Library of Congress.
  Grover Cleveland Papers.
Washington, D.C. National Archives. Civil Archives Division, Department of State.
  Amnesty Oaths.
Washington, D.C. National Archives. General Services Administration.
  Lawrence Sullivan Ross Military Service Record.
  Lawrence Sullivan Ross Staff Officers File, National Archives, RG 109, General and Staff Officers' Papers, file of L. S. Ross.
  Unpublished Muster Rolls. Sixth Texas Cavalry.

THESES

Bonner, Michael Edd. "The Confederate Military Career of L. S. Ross." M.A. thesis, Texas Christian University, 1969.
Dillard, Raymond L. "A History of the Ross Family, Including Its Most Distinguished Member, Lawrence Sullivan Ross." M.A. thesis, Baylor University, 1931.
Stuart, Ben C. "The Texas Indian Fighters and Frontier Rangers." M.A. thesis, Barker Texas History Center, University of Texas at Austin, 1916.
Webb, Juanita. "The Administration of Governor L. S. Ross, 1887–1891." M.A. thesis, Barker Texas History Center, University of Texas at Austin, 1935.
Whiteside, Myrtle. "The Life of Lawrence Sullivan Ross." M.A. thesis, Barker Texas History Center, University of Texas at Austin, 1938.

PUBLIC DOCUMENTS

Day, James M., ed. and comp. *House Journal of the Ninth Legislature Regular Session of the State of Texas, November 4, 1861–January 14, 1862.* Austin: Texas State Library, 1964.
———. *Senate and House Journals of the Tenth Legislature First Called Session of the State of Texas, May 9, 1864–May 28, 1864.* Austin: Texas State Library, 1965.
———. *Senate Journal of the Tenth Legislature Regular Session of the State of Texas, November 3, 1863–December 16, 1863.* Austin: Texas State Library, 1964.

Journal of the Constitutional Convention Begun and Held in Austin, September 6, 1875. Galveston: Galveston News Co., 1875.

Journals of the Congress of the Confederate States of America, 1861–1865. 7 vols. Washington, D.C.: Government Printing Office, 1904–1905.

McLennan County, Texas, Cemetery Records. Vols. 1–2. Waco: Central Texas Genealogical Society, 1965 and 1972, respectively.

McLennan County, Texas, Marriage Records, 1850–1870. Waco: Central Texas Genealogical Society, n.d.

Texas Governors. Executive Series. *Governor's Messages. Coke to Ross (Inclusive) 1874–1891.* Austin: A. C. Baldwin & Sons, Printers and Binders, 1916.

Texas Legislature, House of Representatives. *House Journals,* 17th Leg.–23rd Leg., 1881–93.

———, Senate. *Senate Journals,* 17th Leg. 1881, 1882. Dallas: A. H. Belo Corp., State Printers, 1881.

U.S. Bureau of the Census. Unpublished returns. "Seventh Census of the United States, 1850: Population Schedule, Milam County, Texas."

———. Unpublished returns. "Eighth Census, 1860: Free Inhabitants and Slave Population Schedules, McLennan County, Texas."

U.S. Congress, House. *House Executive Documents.* 35th Cong., 2d sess., 1859.

———. *House Executive Documents.* H. Doc. 31. 39th Cong., 2d sess., 1866.

U.S. Department of Agriculture. Bureau of Animal Industry Special Bulletin. *Proceedings of an Interstate Convention of Cattlemen, Held at Fort Worth, Texas, Tuesday, Wednesday, and Thursday, March 11, 12, and 13, 1890.* Washington, D.C.: Government Printing Office, 1890.

———. Department of the Interior. *Annual Reports of the Commissioner of Indian Affairs,* 1855–59.

———. Supreme Court. *Record, Supreme Court, United States, United States v. Texas in Equity.* Washington, D.C.: Judd and Detweiler, Printers, June, 1894.

———. War Department. *The War of the Rebellion: A Compilation of the Official Records of the Union and Confederate Armies.* 128 vols. Washington, D.C.: Government Printing Office, 1880–1901.

Winfrey, Dorman H., ed. *Texas Indian Papers, 1846–1859.* Austin: Texas State Library, 1960.

PERIODICALS

In many cases, newspaper titles varied frequently from year to year.

Austin Daily Democratic Statesman, 1874–76.

Austin Daily Statesman, 1878–98.

Austin Southern Intelligencer, 1856–61.

Austin State Gazette, 1858–61.

Battalion, 1893–98, 1964–70.

Birmingham (Ala.) *News-Age Herald,* December 29, 1940.

Bryan Eagle, 1890–98.
Clarksville (Tex.) *Standard*, 1858–61.
College Journal, 1890–93.
Confederate Veteran, 1891–98.
Corpus Christi Caller, 1886.
Dallas Daily News, 1886.
Dallas Herald, 1857–65.
Dallas Home and State, May 4, 1887.
Dallas Morning News, 1886–98, May 23, 1965.
El Paso Times, August 13 and 28, 1886.
Fort Worth Daily Democrat, June 7, 1878.
Fort Worth Gazette, February 6, 1889.
Fort Worth Star Telegram, July 4, 1953.
Galveston Daily News, 1876–98.
Galveston News, November 28, 1875.
Graham (Tex.) *News*, October 10, 1971.
Harper's Weekly, 1858–65.
Henderson (Tex.) *Times*, 1888.
Houston Chronicle, February 17, 1929.
Houston Daily Post, 1886–98.
Houston Post, June 2, 1960.
Houston Telegraph, November 30, 1875.
Houston Tri-Weekly Telegram, 1858–65.
Marshall (Tex.) *Republican*, 1861–65.
Memphis Commercial Appeal, September 16, 1934.
Meridian (Miss.) *Daily Clarion*, January 28, 1865.
Mobile Advertiser and Register, 1861–65.
Mobile Register and Advertiser, 1861–65.
Nashville Christian Advocate, 1854–60.
New York Herald, May 25, 1890.
New York Times, 1858–65, 1890.
San Antonio Daily Express, January 5, 1898, and November 22, 1908.
San Antonio Express. August 2, 1892.
San Antonio Light, June 27, 1968, and April 6, 1969.
San Antonio Semi-Weekly Express, January 7, 1898.
(Waco) *Southwest*, January 16, 1861.
(Austin) *State Gazette*, November 25, 1875.
Texas Farmer, 1892–98.
Waco Daily Examiner, 1874–87.
Waco News-Tribune, May 7, 1957, October 30, 1969.
Waco Times-Herald, 1898, 1905.
Waco Tribune, 1898.
Waco Tribune-Herald, October 30, 1949, September 22, 1957, July 10, 1960.
Waco Weekly Examiner and Patron, 1875.
Washington Post, 1890.
(Weatherford, Tex.) *White Man*, September 13, 1860.

PERSONAL CORRESPONDENCE

Arehart, C. M., registrar, Florence State University, Florence, Alabama, December 9, 1968.

Carefoot, Carol J., archivist, Texas State Library, Austin, Texas, February 13, 1975.

Estes, Elizabeth Williams, June 26, 1979.

Guillot, Robert M., president, Florence State University, Florence, Alabama, August 15, 1973.

Johnson, Gordon, Sheriffs' Association of Texas, February 26, 1980.

Kretschmann, James F., supervisory park historian, Vicksburg Military Park, Vicksburg, Mississippi, December 19, 1968.

Parker, Elmer O., for Gary D. Ryan, assistant director, Old Military Records, National Archives, Washington, D.C., December 24, 1968.

Sheppard, Flora L., deputy county clerk, Brazos County, Bryan, Texas, July 23, 1973.

INTERVIEWS

All interviews were conducted by author.

Clarke, Elizabeth Ross. Waco, Texas, March 30, 1972.

Clarke, Dr. and Mrs. Neville P. Bryan, Texas, various dates.

Dethloff, Henry C. College Station, Texas, August 27, 1973.

Estes, Elizabeth Williams. Lorena, Texas, April 22, 1975.

BOOKS

Abel, Annie Heloise. *The American Indian as Participant in the Civil War.* Cleveland: Arthur H. Clark Co., 1915.

———. *The American Indian as Slaveholder and Secessionist: An Omitted Chapter in the Diplomatic History of the Southern Confederacy.* Cleveland: Arthur H. Clark Co., 1915.

Allen, Albert H., ed. *Arkansas Imprints, 1821–1876.* New York: R. R. Bowker Co., 1947.

The American Heritage Picture History of the Civil War. New York: American Heritage Publishing Co., 1960.

Ashcraft, Allan C. *Texas in the Civil War: A Résumé History.* Austin: Texas Civil War Centennial Commission, 1962.

Athearn, Robert G., ed. *Soldier in the West: The Civil War Letters of Alfred Lacy Hough.* Philadelphia: University of Pennsylvania Press, 1957.

Barkley, Mary Starr. *History of Travis County and Austin.* Waco: Texian Press, 1963.

Barr, Alwyn. *Reconstruction to Reform: Texas Politics, 1876–1906.* Austin: University of Texas Press, 1971.

Barron, Samuel B. *The Lone Star Defenders: A Chronicle of the Third Texas Cavalry, Ross' Brigade.* 1908. Reprint. Waco: W. M. Morrison, 1964.

Barry, James Buckner. *A Texas Ranger and Frontiersman: The Days of Buck*

Barry in Texas, 1845–1906. Edited by James K. Greer. Dallas: Southwest Press, 1932.

Berlandier, Jean Louis. *The Indians of Texas in 1830.* Edited by John C. Ewers and translated by Patricia Reading Leclercq. Washington, D.C.: Smithsonian Institution Press, 1969.

Bettersworth, John K., ed. *Mississippi in the Confederacy as They Saw It.* 2 vols. Baton Rouge: Louisiana State University Press, 1961.

Boatner, Mark Mayo III. *The Civil War Dictionary.* New York: David McKay Co., 1959.

Bolton, Paul. *Governors of Texas.* Corpus Christi: Caller-Times Pub. Co., 1947.

Boyd, Minnie Clare. *Alabama in the Fifties: A Social Study.* 1931. Reprint. New York: AMS Press, 1966.

Brann, William Cowper. *The Complete Works of Brann the Iconoclast.* 12 vols. New York: Brann Publishers, 1898–1919.

Brooks, Elizabeth. *Prominent Women of Texas.* Akron, Ohio: Warner Co., 1896.

Brown, John Henry. *Indian Wars and Pioneers of Texas.* Austin: L. E. Daniell Co., n.d.

Burges, Austin Earle. *A Local History of Texas A. & M. College, 1876–1916.* College Station, Tex., 1915.

Burleson, Georgia J. *The Life and Writings of Rufus C. Burleson, D.D., LL.D.* N.p., 1901.

Cartwright, Frederick F., and Michael D. Biddiss. *Disease and History.* New York: Thomas Y. Crowell Co., 1972.

Castel, Albert. *General Sterling Price and the Civil War in the West.* Baton Rouge: Louisiana State University Press, 1968.

Clark, George. *A Glance Backward or Some Events in the Past History of My Life.* Houston: Rein & Sons, [1914].

Cockrell, Monroe F., ed. *The Lost Account of the Battle of Corinth and Court-Martial of General Van Dorn.* Jackson, Tenn.: McCowart-Mercer Press, 1955.

Cofer, David Brooks, ed. *Early History of Texas A. and M. College Through Letters and Papers.* College Station, Tex.: Association of Former Students, 1952.

―――. *Fragments of Early History of Texas A. & M. College.* College Station, Tex.: Association of Former Students, 1953.

―――. *Second Five Administrators of Texas A. & M. College, 1890–1905.* College Station, Tex.: Association of Former Students, 1954.

Coggins, Jack. *Arms and Equipment of the Civil War.* Garden City, N.Y.: Doubleday & Co., 1962.

Conger, Roger N. *Pictorial History of Waco.* Waco: Texian Press, 1964.

Conger, Roger N. et al. *Rangers of Texas.* Waco: Texian Press, 1969.

Coombes, Zachariah Ellis. *The Diary of a Frontiersman, 1858–1859.* Edited by Barbara Neal Ledbetter. Newcastle, Tex., 1962.

Coppini, Pompeo. *From Dawn to Sunset.* San Antonio: Naylor Co., 1949.

Cotner, Robert C. *James Stephen Hogg: A Biography.* Austin: University of Texas Press, 1959.

————, ed. *Addresses and State Papers of James Stephen Hogg.* Austin: University of Texas Press, 1951.

————. *The Texas State Capitol.* Austin and New York: Pemberton Press, 1968.

Coulter, Ellis Merton. *College Life in the Old South.* Athens: University of Georgia Press, 1928.

Cox, Jacob D. *Atlanta.* Campaigns of the Civil War Series, no. 9. New York: Charles Scribner's Sons, 1882.

Crane, William C. *Life and Select Literary Remains of Sam Houston of Texas.* 1884. Reprint. Freeport, N.Y.: Books for Libraries Press, 1972.

Crawford, Charles William et al. *One Hundred Years of Engineering at Texas A&M, 1876–1976.* N.p., 1976.

Crouch, Carrie Johnson. *A History of Young County, Texas.* Austin: Texas State Historical Association, 1956.

Cumming, Kate. *Kate: The Journal of a Confederate Nurse.* Edited by Richard Barksdale Harwell. Baton Rouge: Louisiana State University Press, 1959.

Daniell, L. E., comp. *Personnel of the Texas State Government With Sketches of Distinguished Texans . . .* Austin: L. E. Daniell Co., 1889.

DeShields, James T. *Cynthia Ann Parker: The Story of Her Capture.* 1886. Reprint. San Antonio: Naylor Co., 1934.

————. *They Sat in High Place: The Presidents and Governors of Texas.* San Antonio: Naylor Co., 1940.

Dethloff, Henry C. *A Centennial History of Texas A&M University, 1876–1976.* 2 vols. College Station: Texas A&M University Press, 1975.

Dick, Everett. *The Dixie Frontier: A Social History of the Southern Frontier from the First Transmontane Beginnings to the Civil War.* New York: Capricorn Books, 1964.

Dictionary of American Biography, 1928 ed. S.v. "Ross, John," "Ross, Lawrence Sullivan."

Dorris, Jonathan Truman. *Pardon and Amnesty Under Lincoln and Johnson: The Restoration of the Confederates to Their Rights and Privileges, 1861–1898.* Chapel Hill: University of North Carolina Press, 1953.

Dyer, John P. *From Shiloh to San Juan: The Life of "Fightin' Joe" Wheeler.* Baton Rouge: Louisiana State University Press, 1961.

————. *The Gallant Hood.* Indianapolis and New York: Bobbs-Merrill Co., 1950.

Eaton, Clement. *The Growth of Southern Civilization, 1790–1860.* New York: Harper & Row (Torchbook), 1963.

Eby, Frederick, comp. *Education in Texas Source Materials.* University of Texas Bulletin no. 1824, Education Series no. 2. Austin: University of Texas, 1918.

Elkins, John M. *Indian Fighting on the Texas Frontier.* Amarillo, Tex.: Russel and Cockrell, 1935.

Evans, Cecil Eugene. *The Story of Texas Schools.* Austin: Steck Co., 1955.

Evans, Clement A., ed. *Confederate Military History: A Library of Confederate States History, in Twelve Volumes, Written by Distinguished Men of the South.* 12 vols. Atlanta: Confederate Publishing Co., 1899.

Farrell, Mary D., and Elizabeth Silverthorne. *First Ladies of Texas: The First One Hundred Years, 1836–1936.* Belton, Tex.: Stillhouse Hollow Pub., 1976.

Ferguson, Walter Keene. *Geology and Politics in Frontier Texas, 1845–1909.* Austin and London: University of Texas Press, 1969.

Fifth Annual Catalogue of the Trustees, Professors and Students of Baylor University. Galveston: Civilian Book and Job Office, 1857.

Ford, John S. *Rip Ford's Texas.* Edited by Stephen B. Oates. Austin: University of Texas Press, 1963.

Fourteenth Annual Catalogue of the Agricultural and Mechanical College of Texas. Austin: State Printing Office, 1890.

Fourth Annual Catalogue of the Trustees, Professors and Students of Baylor University. Galveston: Civilian Book and Job Office, 1856.

Fox, William F. *Regimental Losses in the American Civil War, 1861–1865.* 1889. Reprint. Morningside Book Shop, 1974.

Frantz, Joe B. *The Driskill Hotel.* Austin: Encino Press, 1973.

Freeman, Douglas Southall. *Robert E. Lee: A Biography.* 4 vols. New York: Charles Scribner's Sons, 1934–36.

French, Samuel G. *Two Wars: An Autobiography of General Samuel G. French.* Nashville: Confederate Veteran, 1901.

Friend, Llerena. *Sam Houston: The Great Designer.* Austin: University of Texas Press, 1954.

Gammel, H. P. N., comp. *The Laws of Texas, 1822–1897.* 10 vols. Austin: Gammel Publishing Co., 1898.

Gantt, Fred, Jr. *The Chief Executive in Texas: A Study in Gubernatorial Leadership.* Austin: University of Texas Press, 1964.

Georgia Historical Commission. *Georgia Civil War Historical Markers.* The Commission, 1964.

Graves, John. *Goodbye to a River.* New York: Alfred A. Knopf, 1960.

Haley, J. Evetts. *Charles Goodnight: Cowman and Plainsman.* Norman: University of Oklahoma Press, 1949.

Halsted, George Bruce. *Washington, the Ideal of the South: Resurgent in Lee and Ross. Address before the Charles Broadway Rouss Camp of Sons of Confederate Veterans, February 21, 1899.* Austin: Ben C. Jones & Co., 1899.

Hartje, Robert J. *Van Dorn: The Life and Times of a Confederate General.* Nashville: Vanderbilt University Press, 1967.

Hay, Thomas Robson. *Hood's Tennessee Campaign.* New York: Neale Co., 1929.

Hayes, Rutherford B. *Diary and Letters of Rutherford Buchard Hayes, Nineteenth President of the United States.* Edited by Charles R. Williams. 5 vols. Columbus: Ohio State Archaeological and Historical Society, 1922.

Henderson, Harry Mc.C. *Texas in the Confederacy.* San Antonio: Naylor Co., 1955.

Henry, Robert Selph. *"First With the Most" Forrest.* Indianapolis: Bobbs-Merrill Co., 1944.

Hicks, Edwin P. *Belle Starr and Her Pearl.* Little Rock: Pioneer Press, 1963.

Hogan, William Ransom. *The Texas Republic: A Social and Economic History.* Austin: University of Texas Press (paperback), 1969.

Hood, John Bell. *Advance and Retreat—Personal Experiences in the United States and Confederate States Armies.* New Orleans: G. P. T. Beauregard, 1880.

Hubbard, John Milton. *Notes of a Private.* St. Louis: Nixon-Jones Printing Co., 1913.

Hyer, Julien. *The Land of Beginning Again: The Romance of the Brazos.* Atlanta: Tupper & Love, 1952.

Jackson, Grace. *Cynthia Ann Parker.* San Antonio: Naylor Co., 1959.

Jackson, Pearl Cashell. *Texas Governors' Wives.* Austin: E. L. Steck, 1915.

Johnson, Adam Rankin. *The Partisan Rangers of the Confederate States Army.* Edited by William J. Davis. Louisville: George G. Fetter Co., 1904.

Johnson, Robert Underwood, and Clarence Clough Buel, eds. *Battles and Leaders of the Civil War.* 4 vols. 1887. Reprint. New York: Thomas Yoseloff, 1956.

Kelley, Dayton, ed. *The Handbook of Waco and McLennan County.* Waco: Texian Press, 1972.

Kerr, Homer L., ed. *Fighting with Ross's Texas Cavalry Brigade, C.S.A.* Hillsboro, Tex.: Hill Junior College Press, 1974.

Key, William. *The Battle of Atlanta and the Georgia Campaign.* New York: Twayne Publishers, 1958.

King, Edward, and J. Wells Champney. *Texas: 1874. An Eyewitness Account of Conditions in Post-Reconstruction Texas.* Edited by Robert S. Gray. Houston: Cordovan Press, 1974.

Kittrell, Norman G. *Address Delivered at the Unveiling of the Monument of Gen Lawrence Sullivan Ross Ex-Governor of Texas and Ex-President of the Agricultural and Mechanical College at College Station Friday, May 4th, 1919.* N.p., n.d.

————. *Some Governors Who Have Been and Other Public Men of Texas.* Houston: Dealy-Adey-Elgin Co., 1921.

Lale, Max S., and Key, Hobart, Jr., eds. *The Civil War Letters of David R. Garrett Detailing the Adventures of the 6th Texas Cavalry, 1861–1865.* Marshall, Tex.: Port Caddo Press, [1963].

Lazenby, Marion Elias. *History of Methodism in Alabama and West Florida: Being an Account of the Amazing March of Methodism through Alabama and West Florida.* Methodist Publishing House, 1960.

Lindley, Vick. *The Battalion: Seventy Years of Student Publications at the A&M College of Texas.* College Station: Student Activities Office, 1948.

Long, E. B. *The Civil War Day by Day: An Almanac, 1861–1865.* Garden City, N.Y.: Doubleday & Co., 1971.

McKay, Seth Shepard. *Making the Texas Constitution of 1876*. Philadelphia: University of Pennsylvania Press, 1924.

——. *Seven Decades of the Texas Constitution of 1876*. Lubbock: Texas Technological College Press, 1942.

——, ed. *Debates in the Texas Constitutional Convention of 1875*. Austin: University of Texas Press, 1930.

Marcy, Randolph B. *Thirty Years of Army Life on the Border*. New York: Harper & Bros., 1866.

Maury, Dabney H. *Recollections of a Virginian in the Mexican, Indian, and Civil Wars*. 3rd ed. New York: Charles Scribner's Sons, 1894.

Mayhall, Mildred. *Indian Wars of Texas*. Waco: Texian Press, 1965.

Miller, Francis T., ed. *The Photographic History of the Civil War*. 10 vols. New York and London: Thomas Yoseloff, 1957.

Minutes of the Third Annual Meeting and Reunion of the United Confederate Veterans of the Division of Texas, Held in the City of Waco, Texas, April 5th, 6th and 7th, 1894. Bryan, Tex.: Eagle Press, 1894.

Neighbours, Kenneth F. *Indian Exodus: Texan Indian Affairs, 1835–1859*. Quanah, Tex.: Nortex Press, 1973.

Newcomb, William W., Jr. *The Indians of Texas, from Prehistoric to Modern Times*. Austin: University of Texas Press, 1961.

Newton, Lewis W. *Texas Yesterday and Today*. Dallas: Turner Co., 1949.

Nordyke, Lewis. *Cattle Empire*. New York: William Morrow & Co., 1949.

Nunn, William C. *Texas Under the Carpetbaggers*. Austin: University of Texas Press, 1962.

——, ed. *Ten Texans in Gray*. Hillsboro, Tex.: Hill Junior College Press, 1968.

Nye, Wilbur S. *Carbine and Lance: The Story of Old Fort Sill*. Norman: University of Oklahoma Press, 1937.

The Olio: An Annual Published by the Corps of Cadets of the Agricultural and Mechanical College of Texas. Columbus, Ohio: Terry Engraving Co., 1895.

Olmsted, Frederick Law. *A Journey Through Texas: Or a Saddle-Trip on the Southwestern Frontier*. New York: Dix, Edwards and Co., 1857.

Ousley, Clarence. *History of the Agricultural and Mechanical College of Texas*. Bulletin of the Agricultural and Mechanical College of Texas, 4th series, vol. 6, no. 8. College Station, 1935.

Perry, George Sessions. *The Story of Texas A. and M.* New York: McGraw-Hill, 1951.

Personne [pseud.]. *Marginalia: Or, Gleanings from an Army Note-Book*. Columbia, S.C.: F. G. De Fontaine & Co., 1864.

Philpott, William B., ed. *The Sponsor Souvenir Album and History of the UCV Reunion, 1895*. Houston: Sponsor Souvenir Co., 1895.

Pike, James. *Scout and Ranger: Being the Personal Adventures of James Pike of the Texas Rangers in 1859–60*. 1865. Reprint. New York: Da Capo Press, 1972.

Polk, Stella Gibson. *Mason and Mason County: A History*. Austin: Pemberton Press, 1966.

Preece, Harold. *Lone Star Man: Ira Aten, Last of the Old Texas Rangers*. New York: Hastings House, 1961.

Price, George F. *Across the Continent with the Fifth Cavalry*. New York: Antiquarian Press, 1959.

Ragland, Hobart D. *The History of Rush Springs*. Rush Springs, Okla.: Gazette Printing Co., 1952.

Raines, C. W., ed. *Six Decades in Texas or Memoirs of Francis Richard Lubbock*. Austin: Ben C. Jones and Co., 1900.

Ramsdell, Charles William. *Reconstruction in Texas*. Austin: University of Texas Press (paperback), 1970.

Rankin, Melinda. *Texas in 1850*. 1850. Reprint. Waco: Texian Press, 1966.

Rascoe, Burton. *Belle Starr: "The Bandit Queen."* New York: Random House, 1941.

Report of the Agricultural and Mechanical College of Texas. Austin: Henry Hutchings, State Printer, 1891; Ben C. Jones & Co., State Printers, 1893, 1894, 1896; Von Boeckmann, Moore & Schutze, State Contractors, 1899.

Richardson, Rupert Norval. *Colonel Edward M. House: The Texas Years, 1858–1912*. Abilene, Tex.: Abilene Printing & Stationery Co., 1964.

————. *The Comanche Barrier to South Plains Settlement*. Glendale, Calif.: A. H. Clark, 1933.

————. *The Frontier of Northwest Texas, 1846 to 1876: Advance and Defense by the Pioneer Settlers of the Cross Timbers and Prairies*. Glendale, Calif.: A. H. Clark, 1963.

Rose, Victor M. *Ross' Texas Brigade: Being a Narrative of Events Connected with Its Service in the Late War Between the States*. 1881. Reprint. Kennesaw, Ga.: Continental Book Co., 1960.

Ross, Lawrence Sullivan. *Education of the Colored Race*. N.p., n.d.

Schmidt, Hubert. *Eighty Years of Veterinary Medicine at the Agricultural and Mechanical College of Texas*. College Station, Tex.: College Archives, 1958.

Sherman, William Tecumseh. *Memoirs of General W. T. Sherman, Written by Himself*. 3rd ed. (2 vols. in 1). Bloomington: Indiana University Press, 1971.

Shuffler, R. Henderson. *Son, Remember . . .* College Station, Tex.: A&M Press, 1951.

Sixteenth Annual Catalogue of the Agricultural and Mechanical College of Texas. Austin: Henry Hutchings, State Printer, 1892.

Sleeper, John, and J. C. Hutchins, comps. *Waco and McLennan County, Texas: Containing a City Directory of Waco, Historical Sketches of the City and County; Biographical Sketches and Notices of a Few Prominent Citizens*. 1876. Reprint. Waco: Texian Press, 1966.

Smith, Arthur Douglas Howden. *Mr. House of Texas*. New York: Funk & Wagnalls Co., 1940.

————. *The Real Colonel House*. New York: George H. Doran Co., 1918.

Sonnichsen, Charles Leland. *I'll Die Before I Run: The Story of the Great Feuds of Texas*. New York: Harper & Bros., 1951.

Sowell, Anderson J. *History of Fort Bend County*. Houston: W. H. Coyle & Co., 1904.

Sparks, A. W. *The War Between the States as I Saw It. Reminiscences Historical and Personal*. Tyler, Tex.: Lee Burnett, Printers, 1901.

Spratt, John Stricklin. *The Road to Spindletop: Economic Change in Texas, 1875–1901*. Dallas: Southern Methodist University Press, 1955.

Texas Almanac and State Industrial Guide, 1978–1979. Dallas: A. H. Belo Corp., 1978.

Thoburn, Joseph B., and Muriel H. Wright, *Oklahoma: A History of the State and Its People*. 4 vols. New York: Lewis Pub. Co., 1929.

Tilghmann, Zoe A. *Quanah, the Eagle of the Comanches*. Oklahoma City: Harlow Pub. Co., 1938.

Tolbert, Frank X. *An Informal History of Texas: From Cabeza de Vaca to Temple Houston*. New York: Harper & Bros., 1961.

Trantham, Henry. *1845–1920 the Diamond Jubilee: A Record of the Seventy-fifth Anniversary of the Founding of Baylor University*. Waco: Baylor University Press, 1921.

Twenty-second Annual Catalogue Session 1897–98 Agricultural and . . . Mechanical College of Texas. Austin: Ben C. Jones & Co., State Printers, 1898.

Wallace, Ernest, and E. Adamson Hoebel. *The Comanches: Lords of the South Plains*. Norman: University of Oklahoma Press, 1952.

Warner, Ezra J. *Generals in Gray: Lives of the Confederate Commanders*. Baton Rouge: Louisiana State University Press, 1959.

Weaver, Richard M. *The Southern Tradition at Bay: A History of Postbellum Thought*. Edited by George Gore and M. E. Bradford. New Rochelle, N.Y.: Arlington House, 1968.

Webb, Walter Prescott. *The Texas Rangers: A Century of Frontier Defense*. 2d ed. Austin: University of Texas Press, 1965.

Welch, June Rayfield. *The Texas Governor*. Dallas: G. L. A. Press, 1977.

West, Granville C. *McCook's Raid in the Rear of Atlanta and Hood's Army*. Washington, D.C.: Military Order of the Loyal Legion of the United States, 1898.

White, Michael A. *The History of Baylor University, 1845–1861*. Waco: Texian Press, 1968.

Wilbarger, J. W. *Indian Depredations in Texas*. Austin: Hutchings Printing House, 1889.

Wilkes, William O. *History of the Waco Medical Association with Reminiscences and Irrelevant Comments*. Waco: Hill Printing & Stationery Co., 1931.

Williams, Amelia W., and Eugene C. Barker, eds. *The Writings of Sam Houston*. 8 vols. Austin: University of Texas Press, 1938–43.

Winkler, Ernest William, ed. *Platforms of Political Parties in Texas, 1846–1916.* Austin: State Publishing Co., 1916.
Wooten, Dudley G., ed. *A Comprehensive History of Texas, 1685–1897.* 2 vols. Dallas: W. G. Scarff, 1898.
Wright, Marcus J. *General Officers of the Confederate Army.* New York: Neale Pub. Co., 1911.
———. *Texas in the War, 1861–1865.* Edited by Harold B. Simpson. Hillsboro, Tex.: Hill Junior College Press, 1965.
Wyeth, John A. *That Devil Forrest.* New York: Harper & Bros., 1959.
Yearns, Wilfred Buck. *The Confederate Congress.* Athens: University of Georgia Press, 1960.

ARTICLES

Antony, Augusta H. "Lawrence Sullivan Ross, Soldier and Statesman." *Texas Magazine* 6 (September, 1912): 429–31.
Billingsley, William Clyde, ed. "'Such Is War': The Confederate Memoirs of Newton Asbury Keen," pts. 1–4. *Texas Military History* 6 and 7 (Winter, 1967–Fall, 1968): 239–53, 44–70, 103–19, and 176–94, respectively.
Bragg, Jefferson Davis. "Baylor University, 1851–1861." *Southwestern Historical Quarterly* 49 (July, 1945): 51–65.
Brown, D. Alexander. "Pea Ridge." *Civil War Times Illustrated* 6 (October, 1967): 4–11, 46–48.
Callaway, W. A. "Hard Service with Ross's Brigade." *Confederate Veteran* 28 (September, 1920): 328–29.
———. "Hard Times with Ross's Cavalry." *Confederate Veteran* 28 (December, 1920): 447–48.
———. "Incidents of Service." *Confederate Veteran* 28 (October, 1920): 372.
Conger, Roger N. "The Tomás de la Vega Eleven-League Grant on the Brazos." *Southwestern Historical Quarterly* 61 (January, 1958): 371–82.
Connally, E. L. "Capture of Cynthia Ann Parker." *Texana* 2 (Spring, 1964): 74–77.
Crimmins, M. L. "First Sergeant John W. Spangler, Co. H., Second United States Cavalry." *West Texas Historial Association Yearbook* 26 (October, 1950): 68–76.
Cuthbertson, Gilbert. "The Jaybird-Woodpecker War." *Texana* 10, no. 4 (1972): 297–309.
Duty, Tony E. "The Home Front—McLennan County in the Civil War." *Texana* 12, no. 3 (1974): 197–238.
Franks, Kenny A. "Operations Against Opothleyhola, 1861." *Military History of Texas and the Southwest* 1, no. 3 (1972): 187–96.
Gard, Wayne. "The Fence-Cutters." *Southwestern Historical Quarterly* 51 (July, 1947): 1–15.
Gibson, A. M. "Confederates on the Great Plains: The Pike Mission to Wichita Agency." *Great Plains Journal* 4 (1964): 7–16.
Gougler, Doyle. "Sul Ross: Indian Fighter, Governor of Texas and Builder of

Texas A&M in Its Golden Age." *Cattleman* 50 (August, 1963): 39, 64, 67.

"Hood's Nashville Campaign." *Civil War Times Illustrated* 3 (December, 1964): 3–50.

Jarman, Robert A. "A Mississippian at Nashville." Edited by Richard M. McMurry. *Civil War Times Illustrated* 12 (May, 1973): 8–15.

"The Killing of Chief Peta Nouona." *Frontier Times* 4 (December, 1926): 42–43.

Langton, Rosalind. "Life of Colonel R. T. Milner." *Southwestern Historical Quarterly* 44 (April, 1941): 407–51.

McMurry, Richard M. "'The Hell Hole': New Hope Church." *Civil War Times Illustrated* 11 (February, 1973): 32–43.

Ramsdell, Charles W., Jr., ed. "Memories of a Texas Land Commissioner, W. C. Walsh." *Southwestern Historical Quarterly* 44 (April, 1941): 481–97.

Richardson, Rupert N., ed. "The Death of Nocona and the Recovery of Cynthia Ann Parker." *Southwestern Historical Quarterly* 46 (July, 1942): 15–21.

Rowell, John W. "McCook's Raid." *Civil War Times Illustrated* 13 (July, 1974): 4.

Scott, Joe M. "Crossing the Mississippi in 1864." *Confederate Veteran* 29 (February, 1921): 64–65.

Sunderland, Glenn W. "The Battle of Corinth." *Civil War Times Illustrated* 6 (April, 1967): 28–37.

Wellman, Paul I. "Cynthia Ann Parker." *Chronicles of Oklahoma* 12 (June, 1934): 163–71.

Willett, Robert J., Jr. "The First Battle of Franklin." *Civil War Times Illustrated* 7 (February, 1969): 16–23.

Williams, Robert H. "The Case for Peta Nocona." *Texana* 10, no. 1 (1972): 55–72.

Index

Panola County, 181
Parker, Cynthia Ann, 28n.20, 54–56, 57, 58
Parker, Isaac, 57
Parker, Quanah, 55n.27, 56, 58
Parker County, 44, 49
Parker's Fort, 57
Paschal, I. A., 117
Patrons of Husbandry. *See* Grangers
Pea Ridge, Arkansas, 72, 73, 74
Pea Ridge campaign, 73–76
Pearl River, 99
Pease, Elisha M., 117
Pease River, 25, 52, 56
Pemberton, John C., 91
Penateka Comanches, 23
Phifer, Charles W., 32, 80; at Corinth, 84–87
Pickett, E. B., 132, 138
Pike, Albert, 66, 67n.16, 73
Pinson, R. A., 92, 94
Placido (Tonkawa chief), 24n.7, 25
Pockmark, Jim (Caddo chief), 24n.7
Polk, Leonidas, 102, 107
poll tax, 134, 146
Pontotoc, Mississippi, 92
Powder Springs, Georgia, 103
Prairie View Normal School, 146, 215
Price, Sterling, 70–72, 73–75, 80, 81–87
Prince, William, 4
Prohibitionists, 152–53, 155, 157, 164–65, 169
Pryor, Charles, 32
Pulaski, Tennessee, 109

Queen's Hill, Mississippi, 97

Racoon Creek, Georgia, 103
railroad commission, 175–76, 194, 195, 228–29
railroad regulation, 191–95
Rainey, Anson, 143
Rally Hill, Tennessee, 109
Read, J. D., 211, 212, 216
Reagan, John H., 24n.8, 33n.33, 117n.5, 229
Reconstruction, 115–23, 124, 125, 130, 161
Red River, 25, 26, 43, 66, 173
Reed, Jim, 127–28

regular troops (of Texas), 24 and n.8, 25–31, 36; and Ross, 50–53, 55, 56
remnant tribes, 23, 36, 64, 65. *See also* Brazos Reservation Indians
Republican Party, 142, 169; in constitutional convention, 131–32, 134, 137
Republic of Texas, 5, 6
Reservation War, 36–37, 41, 51n.13
Rice, Septimus P., 19
Richardson, Robert V., 100–101
Richmond, Texas, 171, 172, 173
Roberts, John H., 210, 211
Roberts, Oran M., 146n.23, 168, 201n.11, 214
Robertson, Elijah Sterling Clack, 134, 139n
Robertson, Felix H., 15
Robertson County, 128
Roddey, Philip D., 92
Rogers, William P., 86
Rome, Georgia, 103
Rose, A. J., 199, 205, 211
Rose, Victor M., 141n.3; as editor, 140, 142, 149; and Ross candidacy, 140, 141, 148
Rosecrans, William S., 82–83, 84, 89, 92
Ross, Ann (sister), 14n.3
Ross, Catherine Fulkerson (Mrs. Shapley Ross) (mother), 3, 5, 8, 9, 15, 22, 32, 122, 156, 157; value to Texas, 12n.26
Ross, Elizabeth (Bessie) (daughter), 118n.8, 230
Ross, Elizabeth Tinsley. *See* Ross, Lizzie Tinsley (Mrs. Sul Ross) (wife)
Ross, Florine (Mrs. Henry Hill Harrington) (daughter), 118n.8, 204, 230
Ross, Frank (son), 118n.8, 147, 204, 230
Ross, Harvey (son), 9n.15, 26n.16, 31n.28, 118n.8, 204, 230
Ross, James Tinsley (son), 118n.8
Ross, Kate. *See* Padgitt, Kate Ross (Mrs. Tom Padgitt) (sister)
Ross, Lawrence (grandfather), 3, 4
Ross, Lawrence Sullivan (Sul): as brigadier general, 87, 89, 91, 94, 97, 99; character of, 9–10, 13, 16–17, 19–20, 21, 70–71, 148, 234–35; children of, 93 and n.55, 118 and n.8, 122, 143, 146, 156, 208, 228, 230; Civil War campaigns of, 73–76, 81–87, 91, 92,